# Computer Exercises
## for Paralegals in
## WordPerfect, Lotus 1-2-3, dBase,
## LEXIS, and WESTLAW

# Computer Exercises for Paralegals in WordPerfect, Lotus 1-2-3, dBase, LEXIS, and WESTLAW

## Kristen L. Battaile
**University of San Diego**

**Little, Brown and Company**
Boston  New York  Toronto  London

Library of Congress Catalog No. 93-78851
ISBN 0-316-08375-5

EB-M

*Published simultaneously in Canada*
*by Little, Brown and Company (Canada) Limited*

**Printed in the United States of America**

# Contents

# Preface

This workbook is written as a reference and instructional tool for the paralegal student and the practicing legal professional. It contains instructions and practice exercises for WordPerfect® for DOS, WordPerfect® for Windows, Lotus® 1-2-3® for DOS, dBase III Plus®, dBase IV®, LEXIS®, and WESTLAW®.

My intent in creating the workbook has been to provide the reader with the fundamentals of each software program, while including some advanced and little known features for the more experienced user. Each chapter contains exercises and examples of how the program is used in the legal field. For example, in the WordPerfect chapters, there are examples of how to create columns for deposition summaries and how to use the pleading macro or pleading style and columns to create a pleading caption on ruled and numbered pleading paper. The chapters have been written so that the reader may follow along on the computer but are also extensively illustrated to help the reader understand the concepts when not at the computer. Each chapter also includes a detailed table of contents and an index for quick access to specific information.

Due to the variety of computer systems and software used in the training of paralegals, and used by the practicing legal professional, I have tried to include the most popular software packages used in paralegal schools and law offices. The versions of the programs referenced in the chapters are the most current versions as of the date of writing of the workbook. As new versions are released, the fundamentals of the programs tend to remain the same, and the workbook instructions will continue to be effective.

I hope that this workbook will provide the reader with a fundamental understanding of these software programs and with the ability to immediately apply the knowledge to work in a legal career.

*Kristen L. Battaile*

May 1993

# Acknowledgments

I am grateful to the companies whose products I have included in this workbook for their generous permission to reprint information about and examples of their products:

**Auto-Cite®** is a registered trademark of Lawyers Cooperative Publishing.

**dBase III Plus®** and **dBase IV®** are registered trademarks of Borland International, Inc.

**LEXIS®** and **NEXIS®** are registered trademarks of Mead Data Central, Inc.

**Lotus®** and **1-2-3®** are registered trademarks of Lotus Development Corporation.

**Microsoft®** is a registered trademark of Microsoft Corporation. **Windows™** is a trademark of Microsoft Corporation.

**Shepard's®** and **Shepard's PreView®** are registered trademarks of McGraw-Hill, Inc.

**WESTLAW®** is a registered trademark of West Publishing Company.

**WordPerfect®** is a registered trademark of WordPerfect Corporation.


Figures 1.1-1.30, WordPerfect v.5.1, copyright © WordPerfect Corporation 1989. Reprinted with permission from WordPerfect Corporation.

Figures 2.1-2.45, WordPerfect v.5.2 for Windows, copyright © 1992 WordPerfect Corporation. All rights reserved. Reprinted with permission from WordPerfect Corporation.

Figures 3.1-3.34 (screen shots), copyright © 1993 Lotus Development Corporation. Used with permission of Lotus Development Corporation.

Figures 4.1-4.28, dBase III Plus is a product of Borland International, Inc. The screen prints from this program are used with the permission of Borland International, Inc.

Figures 5.1-5.41, dBase IV is a product of Borland International, Inc. The screen prints from this program are used with the permission of Borland International, Inc.

Figure 6.1-6.27, reprinted with permission of Mead Data Central, Inc., provider of the LEXIS/NEXIS© services.

Figure 6.16 (screen contents), copyright © 1993 McGraw-Hill, Inc.

# Computer Exercises
# for Paralegals in
# WordPerfect, Lotus 1-2-3, dBase,
# LEXIS, and WESTLAW

# CHAPTER 1

# WORDPERFECT® FOR DOS

# *Chapter Preface*

WordPerfect® is the word processing software used by the majority of law offices. Its popularity is due to its wide range of features and its user support. This chapter will acquaint you with WordPerfect and some of these features. The exercises at the end of the chapter will instruct you in how to perform several law office-related word processing functions. The commands used in this chapter are based upon WordPerfect version 5.1 for DOS. However, the majority of these commands will work with versions 5.0 and later.

# Section One—The Basics

## A. ENTERING WORDPERFECT

To enter WordPerfect type:     **WP [Enter]**

<u>OR</u> select the WordPerfect option from a menu screen.

Upon entering the program, you will see the WordPerfect screen as shown in Figure 1.1.

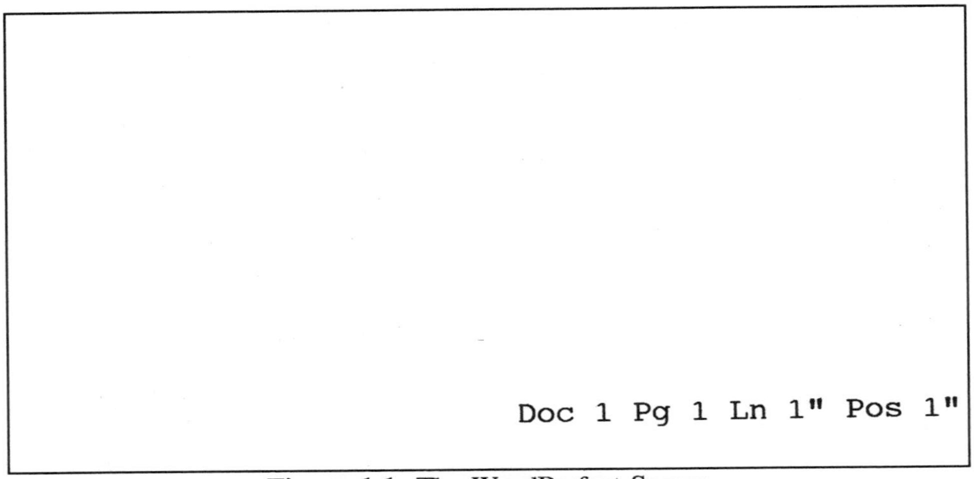

```
                                        Doc 1 Pg 1 Ln 1" Pos 1"
```

**Figure 1.1**  The WordPerfect Screen

## B. THE WORDPERFECT ENVIRONMENT

### 1.  The Status Line

When you enter WordPerfect for DOS, you will find a blank screen with a Status Line in the lower right-hand corner. The Status Line displays the document number (you may be in two at once), the page number and the line, and position of the cursor in inches or another measurement. If the document currently on the screen has been saved, the location (path) and name of the document will be displayed in the lower left-hand corner of the screen as shown in Figure 1.2.

```
         SUPERIOR COURT OF THE STATE OF CALIFORNIA

           IN AND FOR THE COUNTY OF SAN DIEGO

THE ABC CORPORATION, a California  )    Case No. 100111
Corporation,                       )
                                   )
                                   )    ANSWER OF DEFENDANT JOE
              Plaintiff,           )    SMITH
                                   )
        vs.                        )
                                   )
JOE SMITH, and DOES 1 through 50,  )
                                   )
            Defendants.            )
_____)

        Comes now Defendant JOE SMITH who responds to the Complaint on

file herein as follows:
C:\WORK\SMITH.ANS
                                        Doc 1 Pg 1 Ln 6" Pos 3.3"
```

**Figure 1.2**  The document name and the status line appear
at the bottom of the WordPerfect screen


## 2.  Executing Commands

In WordPerfect for DOS, commands are accessed with the function keys or the pull-down menus (versions 5.1 and later). In this chapter, a command will be referenced by its function key, or key combination. The function keys are simply a more efficient way to access commands than by using the pull-down menu selections. In WordPerfect for Windows, the pull-down menus are more sophisticated and are a practical alternative to the function keys.

The function keys used to perform a command will be enclosed in brackets. For example, the function key for underlining will be referred to as [F8]. The key combination for centering will be referred to as [Shift]+[F6]. The plus symbol (+) indicates that the [Shift] key is to be held down while pressing [F6]. When a function key or key combination evokes further menu choices, the menu items to be selected will follow the function keystrokes and be separated by commas. For example, to change from single spacing to double spacing you select the Format function with **[Shift]+[F8]**. You then must select item **1** from a menu for **Line**, and then item **6** from another menu for **Line Spacing**. Then you type a **2** to change to double spacing. This all would be referred to as:

**[Shift]+[F8], 1, 6, 2**

Many times when you are finished with commands, you are left at a menu screen. To return to your document, either press the **[Enter]** key until you return to the document screen, or press the Exit key **[F7]**.

When a command is shown separated by commas, such as [Home], [Up Arrow], you will press the **[Home]** key and release it, and then press the **[Up Arrow]** key. WordPerfect will remember that you have pressed the first key.

### 3. Units of Measure

The line and position measurements within the Status Line are usually set in inches. The inch measurement is based upon the actual measurements from the borders of the paper in your printer. This allows you to measure where you would like text placed upon a page and then to move the cursor to that measurement to begin typing.

The other units of measure available in WordPerfect are:

- **centimeters**
- **points**
- **1200ths of an inch**
- **WordPerfect version 4.2 units**

The units of measure can be changed in the Setup, Environment menu:  **[Shift]+[F1], 3, 8**.

### 4. The Function Keys

The function keys are the keys at the top or left-hand side of the keyboard labeled F1 through F10 or F12. WordPerfect utilizes all of these function keys. The keys F1 through F10 each have four separate functions. The F11 and F12 keys each have one function which are repeats of the often used functions found on the F3 and F4 keys.

The F1 through F10 keys perform one function when pressed by themselves, and others when the [Alt], [Shift] or [Ctrl] keys are held while pressing them. The [Alt], [Shift], and [Ctrl] keys do not perform any task when they are pressed alone.

It is important that when you press a function key, you depress the key and immediately release it. Holding down a function key will cause it to repeat the function. The only keys which should be held down are the [Alt], [Shift], and [Ctrl] keys.

Below is a list of each of the function keys and their corresponding WordPerfect applications.

| FUNCTION KEY | [CTRL]+ | [ALT]+ | [SHIFT]+ | ALONE |
|---|---|---|---|---|
| F1 | Shell | Thesaurus | Setup | Cancel |
| F2 | Spell | Replace | Backward Search | Forward Search |
| F3 | Screen | Reveal Codes | Switch | Help |
| F4 | Move | Block | Left, Right Indent | Left Indent |
| F5 | Text In/Out | Mark Text | Date/Outline | List Files |
| F6 | Tab Align | Flush Right | Center | Bold |
| F7 | Footnote | Columns/Table | Print | Exit |
| F8 | Font | Style | Format | Underline |
| F9 | Merge/Sort | Graphics | Merge Codes | End Field |
| F10 | Macro Define | Macro | Retrieve | Save |
| F11 | Reveal Codes | | | |
| F12 | Block | | | |

> *If your function keys F1 and F3 do not seem to be functioning in the manner consistent with the above commands, the Keyboard Layout may have been set up for **Alternate**. The Alternate setup changes the [Esc] key to Cancel, the F1 key to Help, and the F3 key to the function of the [Esc] key. To change back to the **Enhanced** keyboard that corresponds to the above command structure, access the Setup menu, select Keyboard Layout, highlight "Enhanced" and press 1:*
>
> **Shift+F1, 5, Enhanced, 1**

*WordPerfect for DOS*

7

## 5. The Pull-Down Menus

WordPerfect version 5.1 for DOS added pull-down menus that can be accessed with a mouse or the keyboard. These menus offer another way to perform the commands found on the function keys.

The pull-down menus can be displayed by pressing the mouse's right button or by pressing **[Alt]+[=]**. The mouse's right button, and **[Alt]+[=]**, will also turn the menus off. The WordPerfect screen display may be set up so that the pull-down menus are displayed at the top of the screen at all times. This is done with the Setup function, **[Shift]+[F1], 2, 4, 8**. The pull-down menu options are shown in Figure 1.3.

```
File Edit Search Layout Mark Tools Font Graphics Help          (Press F3 for Help)



                 SUPERIOR COURT OF THE STATE OF CALIFORNIA

                   IN AND FOR THE COUNTY OF SAN DIEGO

THE ABC CORPORATION, a California  )      Case No. 100111
Corporation,                       )
                                   )      ANSWER OF DEFENDANT JOE
                Plaintiff,         )      SMITH
                                   )
        vs.                        )
                                   )
JOE SMITH, and DOES 1 through 50,  )
                                   )
                Defendants.        )
_____)

     Comes now Defendant JOE SMITH who responds to the Complaint on

file herein as follows:
C:\WORK\SMITH.ANS                         Doc 1 Pg 1 Ln 6" Pos 3.3"
```

**Figure 1.3** The Pull-Down Menus

To select an option from the pull-down menus using the mouse, press the right mouse button and move the mouse pointer to the top of the screen where the menus appear. The mouse pointer is a small highlighted square that appears when you move the mouse. Move the mouse pointer to a menu option and press the left mouse button to open the menu. An item within the menu is selected by moving the mouse pointer to the option and pressing the left mouse button. A selection is canceled by pressing the right mouse button.

Using the keyboard, menus may be selected by pressing **[Alt]+[=]** and then using the **[Arrow]** keys to move between, and pull down, the menus. An option is selected by highlighting it and pressing the **[Enter]** key, or by pressing the highlighted letter corresponding to the option. The menus can be closed by pressing the right mouse button, pressing **[Alt]+[=]**, or pressing the **[Esc]** or **[F1]** key. The File menu is shown in Figure 1.4.

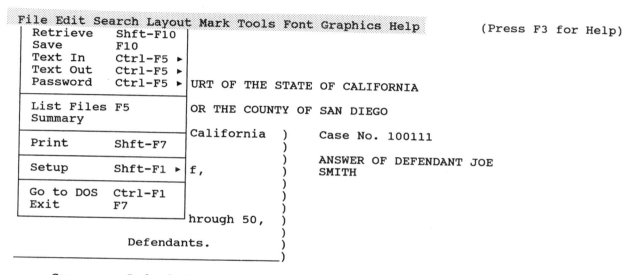

Figure 1.4  The File Menu

An arrow to the right of a menu option indicates that there is a submenu to the option. Figure 1.5 displays the submenu of the menu selection: **File, Password**.

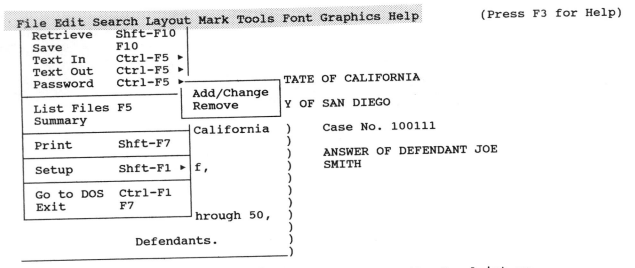

```
File Edit Search Layout Mark Tools Font Graphics Help
Retrieve    Shft-F10
Save        F10
Text In     Ctrl-F5  ►
Text Out    Ctrl-F5  ►
Password    Ctrl-F5  ►         TATE OF CALIFORNIA
                    Add/Change
List Files F5       Remove     Y OF SAN DIEGO
Summary
                    California  )    Case No. 100111
Print       Shft-F7             )
                                )    ANSWER OF DEFENDANT JOE
Setup       Shft-F1  ► f,       )    SMITH
                                )
Go to DOS   Ctrl-F1             )
Exit        F7                  )
                     hrough 50, )
                                )
            Defendants.         )
                                )
```

    Comes now Defendant JOE SMITH who responds to the Complaint on

file herein as follows:                    Doc 1 Pg 1 Ln 6" Pos 1.1"
C:\WORK\SMITH.ANS

**Figure 1.5**  The File, Password Submenu

## 6.  WordPerfect Help

WordPerfect has one of the best Help facilities available in a word processor. The [F3] key accesses WordPerfect's Help menu (the [F1] key in the Alternate keyboard).

While in Help, you can receive help for a particular key or key combination, or you may locate the function keys necessary to perform an action in the Help index. An explanation of an individual key or a key combination is available by pressing the key or keys while in the Help facility. For example, the **[F2]** key, when pressed while in the Help facility, brings up the message shown in Figure 1.6.

```
Search

     Searches forward (F2) or backward (Shift-F2) through your text for a
     specific combination of characters and/or codes.  After entering the
     search text, press Search again to start the search.  If the text is
     found, the cursor will be positioned just after (to the right of) it.
     Lowercase letters in the search text match both lowercase and uppercase.
     Uppercase letters match only uppercase.

     Extended Search
     Pressing Home before pressing Search extends the search into headers,
     footers, footnotes, endnotes, graphics box captions, and text boxes.  To
     continue the extended search, press Home, Search.




Selection: 0                                      (Press ENTER to exit Help)
```

**Figure 1.6** WordPerfect's Help for the [F2] Key

To see an index of WordPerfect features, and their corresponding key combinations, you can press any letter of the alphabet while in the Help facility. For example, if you cannot remember how to change to double spacing, press the letter "S" for "spacing" while in the Help facility. Further pages of the "S" index can be seen by continuing to press the [S] key. "Spacing Lines" is found on the second screen of the "S" index as shown in Figure 1.7. The WordPerfect key for the command, as well as the actual keystrokes necessary to perform the command, are displayed.

To leave the Help facility, press the **[Space Bar]** or the **[Enter]** key. Further help can be obtained in a WordPerfect manual or by calling WordPerfect's user support (800) telephone number. This number is listed in your WordPerfect manual.

```
Features [S] (continued)              WordPerfect Key      Keystrokes

Set Tabs                              Format               Shft-F8,1,8
Settings, Initial (Default)           Setup                Shft-F1,4
Setup                                 Setup                Shft-F1
Shadow Print                          Font                 Ctrl-F8,2,6
Sheet Feeder                          Print                Shft-F7,s,3,3
Sheet Feeder Help                     Print                Shft-F7,s,6,Shft-F3
Shell, Go To                          Shell                Ctrl-F1,1
Short Form                            Mark Text            Alt-F5,4
Short Form, Table of Authorities      Mark Text            Alt-F5,4
Short/Long Filename Display           List                 F5,Enter,5
Side-by-side Columns Display          Setup                Shft-F1,2,6,7
Size Attribute Ratios                 Setup                Shft-F1,4,8,6
Size of Print (Attributes)            Font                 Ctrl-F8,1
Small Capitalized Print               Font                 Ctrl-F8,2,7
Small Print                           Font                 Ctrl-F8,1,4
Soft Hyphen                           Soft Hyphen          Ctrl,-
Sort                                  Merge/Sort           Ctrl-F9,2
Space, Hard                           Space Bar            Home,Space
Spacing Justification Limits          Format               Shft-F8,4,6,4
Spacing Lines                         Format               Shft-F8,1,6
More... Press s to continue.

Selection: 0                                        (Press ENTER to exit Help)
```

**Figure 1.7** Help for a particular feature can be found in the Help index
by pressing a letter corresponding to the feature

## 7. Cursor Movement

The **cursor** is the flashing underline or box that appears on the screen. The cursor shows where characters will be entered as you type them on the keyboard. To practice moving the cursor, type a few lines of text onto the WordPerfect screen.

To move the cursor you may use the **[Arrow]** keys on your keyboard, or the same keys on the numeric keypad (be sure that [Num Lock] is off). The cursor may be moved to any position in your document, except to a position where you have not yet entered any text, spaces, or returns.

In addition to the [Arrow] keys, the following keystrokes may be used to move the cursor.

| KEYSTROKES | ACTION |
|---|---|
| [End]  or<br>[Home], [Right Arrow] | To move to the end of a line. |
| [Home], [Left Arrow] | To move to the beginning of a line. |
| [Ctrl], [Right or Left Arrow] | To move one word to the left or right. |
| [Home], [Up Arrow] | To move to the top of the screen. |
| [Home], [Down Arrow] | To move to the bottom of the screen. |
| [Home], [Home], [Up Arrow] | To move to the top of the document. |
| [Home], [Home], [Down Arrow] | To move to the bottom of the document. |
| [Home], [Home], [Home], [Up Arrow] | To move to the top of the document in front of all codes. |
| [Page Up] | To move up one page. |
| [Page Down] | To move down one page. |
| [Ctrl]+[Home] | The Go To key combination. To move to a specific page. You will be prompted for a page number. |

## 8. Insert Versus Typeover

There are two typing modes in WordPerfect, Insert and Typeover. When you enter WordPerfect, the program is in the Insert mode.

In the Insert mode, text that already exists will be pushed to the right as you enter new text. In the Typeover mode, text that is typed will overwrite existing text and spaces.

To "toggle" between Insert and Typeover, press the [Insert] key. When you are in the Typeover mode, the word "Typeover" will appear in the lower left corner of your screen.

## 9. Switching Between Documents

WordPerfect allows you to work on two separate documents in the program at the same time. You switch between the two documents by pressing **[Shift]+[F3]**.

When you first enter WordPerfect, you are in Document 1. You can tell which document you are in by checking the Status Line at the bottom of the screen. You can retrieve a document into Document 1 at this point, or begin drafting a new document. When you move to Document 2, with [Shift]+[F3], you may retrieve, or begin drafting, another document. The benefit of having two documents in WordPerfect at the same time is that text can be moved or copied from one document to the other. This feature is useful when you are taking text from an old document to draft a new document. You can be drafting the new document in Document 1, and retrieve the old document into Document 2. Then, text from Document 2 can be copied into Document 1 where it is needed.

## C. EDITING A DOCUMENT

### 1. Deletions

When editing a document, deletions of a character or a group of characters will need to be made. WordPerfect offers a variety of ways to delete text. The two primary keys that perform deletions are [Delete] and [Backspace],

| KEYSTROKES | ACTION |
|---|---|
| **[Delete]** | Deletes the character directly above the cursor. |
| **[Backspace]** | Deletes the character immediately to the left of the cursor. |

To delete more than one character at a time, the **[Delete]** and **[Backspace]** keys may be held down, or the following key combinations may be used.

| KEYSTROKES | ACTION |
| --- | --- |
| [Ctrl]+[Backspace] | Deletes the word currently containing the cursor, or the word to the immediate left of the cursor. |
| [Ctrl]+[End] | Deletes all characters from the cursor to the end of the current line. |
| [Ctrl]+[Page Down] | Deletes all text to the bottom of the current page. |

## 2. Blocking Text

Blocking text is the marking of text prior to performing some action upon the text. Blocking text is a function of **[Alt]+[F4]** or the **[F12]** key. The cursor is moved to the beginning of the text to be blocked, and Block is selected using either function key option. A blinking **Block on** will appear in the lower left-hand corner of the screen. Moving the cursor with the [arrow] keys will highlight the text to be blocked. When the desired text is highlighted, actions such as moving, copying, deleting, saving, and printing may be performed upon the block.

When highlighting text, the highlighting may be moved with any of the keys you normally use to move the cursor. You may also press any character on the keyboard to move the highlight to the next occurrence of that character within the document. For example, pressing a period will move the highlight block to the end of the sentence. Pressing the **[Enter]** key will move it to the end of a paragraph.

> *Occasionally you will need to perform more than one action upon a block, such as bolding and underlining a <u>word or phrase</u>. To do this, you would block the text once and perform the bold or underline. The same text can then be blocked again by turning on the block function and pressing **[Ctrl]+[Home]** twice. The remaining action, bold or underline, may then be performed.*

## 3. Deleting a Block

If you wish to delete a block of text, turn on the Block feature with **[Alt]+[F4]** or **[F12]**, highlight the text, and press the **[Delete]** key. As a safety feature, WordPerfect will ask you in the lower left-hand corner of the screen if you really wish to delete the block. Select **Y** or **N**.

## 4. Retrieving Deleted Text (Undelete)

WordPerfect saves you if you have deleted text that you wanted to keep.

The [F1] (Cancel) key will restore any of your three previous deletions. Move the cursor to where you want the text to return and press [F1]. The text last deleted from the document will appear at the cursor, and the following options will be displayed at the bottom of the screen:

Undelete: 1 Restore; 2 Previous Deletion: 0

Select 1 if the displayed deletion is the one you wish to restore. Select 2 to display the other two previous deletions. Continuing to press 2 will toggle between the three deletions. When the desired deletion is displayed, select 1 to restore it.

## 5. Canceling a Command

The [F1] (Cancel) key can also be used to cancel a command or back out of a menu or screen. For example, if you have turned on the Block command inadvertently, pressing the [F1] key will Cancel the Block command.

## 6. Centering

Centering a word or phrase can be accomplished in a number of ways.

a. *Before Typing Text*

Document titles and pleading headings often need to appear in the center of the printed page. To center text which you will be typing, press [Shift]+[F6]. This command places the cursor in the center of the screen. Type the text and press the [Enter] key.

b. *After Typing Text*

If the text to be centered has been typed at the left margin, move the cursor to the beginning of the text and press [Shift]+[F6]. Use the [Down Arrow] key to move down to the next line, or press the [End] key to move to the end of the line and press [Enter].

c. *Setting Center Justification*

If you have more than one line that needs to be centered, you may select center justification, **[Shift]+[F8], 1, 3, 2**. You will need to press **[F7]** or the **[Enter]** key twice to return to the WordPerfect screen. All text that you type at this point will be centered. Try turning on the center justification at the left margin and type the text below.

**ARTICLES OF INCORPORATION**
**OF**
**XYZ CORPORATION**

To return to full justification, select **[Shift]+[F8], 1, 3, 4**.

> *Full justification will result in a document with the text aligned against the left and right margins. Left justification will align the text against the left margin and leave the right margin ragged. Right justification will align the text against the right margin and leave the left margin ragged.*

d. *Blocking and Centering*

Another way of center justifying more then one line is to type the lines at the left margin, and then block the lines and press **[Shift]+[F6]**. Try typing the text below, and then block and center the text. WordPerfect will ask you if you wish to center justify; answer yes.

**ARTICLES OF INCORPORATION**
**OF**
**XYZ CORPORATION**

WordPerfect will return you to your selected justification after centering the text.

## 7. Bold Type

Occasionally, you will want a word, or sequence of words, to stand out in **bold type**. For example, points and authorities can appear more authoritative when the heading for each point stands out from the rest of the text as shown below.

**B.**
**DEFENDANT HAS THE BURDEN OF**
**SHOWING THAT THE COUNTY IN WHICH**
**THE ACTION IS BROUGHT IS IMPROPER**

It is the Defendant's burden to offer sufficient facts to show to this Court that San Diego County is not the proper court to hear the case. <u>Massae v. Superior Court</u> (1981) 118 Cal. App. 3d 527, 530, 173 Cal. Rptr. 527.

Bolding can be performed while the text is being entered, or later by blocking the text and selecting the Bold command.

a. *Before Typing Text*

To type in bold print, press **[F6]** prior to typing the text to be bolded. With many monitors, you will see the position measurement in the Status Line become brighter when you press **[F6]**. When you have finished typing the text that is to be bolded, press **[F6]** again.

b. *After Typing Text*

If you have already typed the text you desire to be bolded, **Block** the text, and then press **[F6]**.

## 8. Underlining

Underlining is used to <u>emphasize</u> a character, word, or block of text. As you can see in the point and authorities example, case names are usually underlined (or italicized). Underlining is performed in the same manner as bolding. Note that if you are using a color monitor, underlining may appear as a highlight. The printed copy will contain the underlines.

a. *Before Typing Text*

To underline a word or passage, press **[F8]**, type the text, and then press the **[F8]** key again.

b. *After Typing Text*

If what you wish to be underlined has already been typed, **Block** the text and then press **[F8]**.

## PRACTICE EXERCISE

Using some of the commands covered thus far, let us take a portion of an old complaint and conform it to a set of facts for a new case.

The preliminary paragraphs of the old complaint are shown below. These are the paragraphs that can be used to establish the venue for a complaint. Type these paragraphs into WordPerfect. (You do not need to start with a blank screen to perform this exercise.)

**Plaintiff JOHN PORT alleges:**

**1. Plaintiff, JOHN PORT, is, and at all times herein mentioned was, a resident of San Diego County, California.**

**2. Plaintiff is informed and believes, and on that basis alleges, that Defendant, MARK SAMPSON, is, and at all times herein mentioned was, an individual residing in San Diego County, California, within the North County Judicial District.**

Now, using some of the WordPerfect commands that we learned above, we will revise these opening paragraphs to conform to the new facts. The new facts are that Plaintiff, Joe Smith, is suing ABCD Corporation, a California Corporation. The new plaintiff and defendant reside within the same jurisdiction as the old parties.

a) Begin the revision by moving the cursor to the beginning of the first mention of "JOHN PORT." Using the **[Delete]** key, delete the entire name. Then, type the name of our new plaintiff "JOE SMITH" in this space.

b) Next, move to the "J" at the second "JOHN PORT" and use **[Ctrl]+[Backspace]** to remove both words. Then, type in: "JOE SMITH."

c) Now, move to paragraph 2 of the complaint and remove the name of the old defendant with **[Ctrl]+[Backspace]**. Replace the name with: "ABCD CORPORATION."

d) The capacity of this defendant needs to be changed to reflect its status as a corporation. Move to the "a" at the beginning of "an individual" and turn the Block feature on with **[Alt]+[F4]** or **[F12]** so that we may perform a Block Delete. Extend the block highlight to the end of the sentence with the arrow keys or by pressing the period **[.]** key. Then, press the **[Delete]** key and respond with a **Y** for yes.

    e)   Now, type in the following: "a corporation organized pursuant to the laws of the State of California, having its principal office in San Diego County, California, within the North County Judicial District."

Your new paragraphs should look as follows:

**Plaintiff JOE SMITH alleges:**

    **1.   Plaintiff, JOE SMITH, is, and at all times herein mentioned was, a resident of San Diego County, California.**
    **2.   Plaintiff is informed and believes, and on that basis alleges, that Defendant, ABCD CORPORATION, is, and at all times herein mentioned was, a corporation organized pursuant to the laws of the State of California, having its principal office in San Diego County, California, within the North County Judicial District.**

## D. SAVING AND RETRIEVING FILES

To save a document, you must store it on some type of secondary storage device (magnetic disk, tape, etc.), and give it a name. To retrieve a document, you must identify where it is stored and the name of the document. Remember, as you are typing a document in WordPerfect, the document is temporarily stored in RAM. If your computer is turned off, a power outage occurs, or the computer or network suddenly crashes, your RAM and your document are erased.

There are two methods for saving documents in WordPerfect for DOS, **Save and Continue** and **Save and Exit.**

There are also two methods for retrieving documents, **Retrieve** and **List Files**. These methods will be discussed below.

### 1.  Save and Continue

The [F10] Key allows you to save a document and continue working. I recommend that Save and Continue be used often while drafting a document. That way, if there is a loss of power to the computer, you will only lose the text that has not yet been saved. WordPerfect's Automatic Backup feature will also save your document in the event of a loss of power to the computer. However, it should not be relied on so much that you disregard the [F10] key.

*If your document has never been saved*, the following message will appear when the **[F10]** key is pressed.

**Document to be saved:**

At this point, you enter the drive and directory where you would like the file to be stored, and give the file a name. In WordPerfect the document name can be one to eight characters with an optional period and one- to three-character extension. An example of an appellate brief being stored in the \Smith directory of the C: drive is shown below.

**Document to be saved:C:\SMITH\APPELLAT.BRF**

If you would like to practice saving your current document, at the "Document to be saved:" prompt, specify where you would like the document to be saved (A:, B:, C:), and give your file a name. You may also simply type in a name for your file without a drive letter. The document will be saved to the default drive and directory designated in the **Setup Menu, [Shift]+[F1], 6, 7**, or to the location of the WordPerfect program files. It is not a good practice to type in a file name without specifying a drive and directory. Many times the files will become commingled with the WordPerfect program files and cause disk organization problems.

After typing the document name, pressing the **[Enter]** key saves the document. The document path and name will be displayed in the lower left-hand corner of the screen.

*If the document has previously been saved*, pressing the **[F10]** key will display the following message.

**Document to be saved:C:\SMITH\APPELLAT.BRF**

Pressing the **[Enter]** key to confirm the document name will bring up the next message:

**Replace C:\SMITH\APPELLAT.BRF?** No (Yes)

Pressing the **[Y]** key will replace the stored version of your document with the current document on the screen. It is important that you respond "Yes" here if you wish to save your document. However, if this is a new document that you are saving for the first time, receiving the "Replace" message means that you already have another document with this name. If this is the case, respond "No" and repeat the process giving your document a different name.

## 2.  Save and Exit

The [F7] key allows you to Save your document and exit to a blank WordPerfect screen or exit the program entirely. The messages that you receive are similar to the Save and Continue messages.

When **[F7]** is pressed, a message asking if you wish to save the document appears in the lower left-hand corner of the screen:

**Save document?** Yes (No)

Pressing the **[Enter]** key, or the **[Y]** key, will answer yes to this question.

You will then be prompted with the same messages as with Save and Continue. After responding to these messages, a message asking if you wish to exit WordPerfect will appear:

**Exit WP?** No (Yes)

Responding with the **[Enter]** key, or the **[N]** key, will give you a blank WordPerfect screen to begin a new document. Responding with the **[Y]** key will exit the program. Pressing the **[F1]** (Cancel) key will return you to your current document. If you are following along with this Workbook, respond "No" to this prompt so that you may continue working in the program.

### 3. Retrieve

The [Shift]+[F10] key combination allows you to retrieve a document by name. It is important that you have a blank WordPerfect screen before you retrieve a document, unless you intend to retrieve the document into the one in which you are currently working.

The [Shift]+[F10] command will prompt you for the location and name of the document as shown below.

**Document to be retrieved:**

At this point you will type the drive, directory, and file name of the document and press **[Enter]**. For example:

**Document to be retrieved:C:\SMITH\APPELLAT.BRF**

### 4. List Files

The [F5] key gives you a list of the files located within a specific directory. When this feature is selected, the current default directory (the pre-set storage location) is displayed in the lower left-hand corner of the screen as shown in Figure 1.8.

```
Dir C:\WP51\*.*                                    (Type = to change default Dir)
```

**Figure 1.8** Pressing [F5], List Files, displays the directory of the files
to be listed and allows you to change the directory

If this is the location of the files you wish to see, you may press the **[Enter]** key here. You may also type a different location, such as **"C:\SMITH."** Pressing the **[Enter]** key will list the files.

If you intend to be working primarily within the SMITH directory, you may wish to change it to the default directory while you are working in this session of WordPerfect. After you have pressed [F5], pressing the [=] key will let you change the default directory. Typing "C:\Smith" and pressing the [Enter] key twice will change the default directory and take you to the list of the files as shown in Figure 1.9.

```
01-14-92  01:32p              Directory C:\SMITH\*.*
Document size:       0  Free:  5,380,096 Used:      12,821    Files:        6

.    Current    <Dir>                   ..    Parent    <Dir>
APPELLAT.BRF      327  01-14-92 01:32p   DEPO    .OTL   2,263  08-09-91 05:21a
INVOICE .DBF      262  11-22-91 07:54p   INVOICE .DBT   2,560  11-22-91 07:54p
INVOICE .MDX    4,096  11-22-91 07:54p   NETWORTH.WK1   3,313  05-07-91 06:10p
```

```
1 Retrieve; 2 Delete; 3 Move/Rename; 4 Print; 5 Short/Long Display;
6 Look; 7 Other Directory; 8 Copy; 9 Find; N Name Search: 6
```

**Figure 1.9**  The List Files Screen

In the List Files screen, you may retrieve a file, or perform some other action upon it, by highlighting the file name with the [Arrow] keys and selecting the number of an action shown at the bottom of the screen.

You may look at a file before you retrieve it by highlighting the file name and pressing the [Enter] key or the number 6. When you are looking at a document in this manner, the format may be different than when it is actually retrieved into the WordPerfect screen. You may return to List Files from looking at a document by pressing the [Enter] key or the [Space Bar].

You may perform actions on several files simultaneously by marking the desired file names with an asterisk ([*]). You may mark individual files by highlighting the file names and pressing the [*] key. You may mark all of the files by pressing [Home], [*]. The marks may be removed by highlighting individual file names and again pressing the [*] key, or by pressing [Home], [*].

If you accidentally return to the WordPerfect screen from List Files before you have completed your selections, you may resume where you left off in List Files by pressing the [F5] key twice.

The options available in the List Files screen are explained below.

| | | |
|---|---|---|
| **1 Retrieve** | | Retrieves the highlighted document into the WordPerfect screen. |
| **2 Delete** | | Deletes the highlighted document. |
| **3 Move/Rename** | | Renames the highlighted document (if you wish) and/or moves the file to a new location. |
| **4 Print** | | Prints the highlighted document without your having to retrieve it into WordPerfect. |
| **5 Short/Long Display** | | Allows you to switch between short and long document names, if you have elected to use long document names. |
| **6 Look** | | Lets you look at the highlighted document prior to retrieving. You may not alter the document in Look. |
| **7 Other Directory** | | Lets you change within List Files to another directory. |
| **8 Copy** | | Lets you copy the highlighted document to another location. |
| **9 Find** | | Lets you search the files in the current directory for a specific file name or words or phrases present within the body of a document. This is a valuable feature when you cannot remember what you have named a file. |
| **N Name Search** | | Highlights the file name which most closely resembles the characters that you enter. |

You may leave the List Files screen by pressing the **[Space Bar]**, **[F7]**, or the **[F1]** (Cancel) key.

> *If you would like to permanently change the default directory so that all files will be stored in a certain location unless otherwise specified, you may do this in the* **Setup Menu** *under* **Location of Files**, *[Shift]+[F1], 6, 7.*

## E. MOVING AND COPYING TEXT

When editing a document, it is often necessary to move or copy text from one position to another. Moving text removes it from its old location and places it in a new location that you select. Copying leaves the original text in place and copies that text to a new location. To move or copy text, you can Block it and then select the Move or Copy command. If you are moving or copying a *sentence*, *paragraph*, or *page*, you can go directly to the command without blocking.

### 1. Blocking and Moving or Copying

The steps for Blocking and Moving or Copying text are essentially the same.

a) Turn the **Block** on with **[Alt]+[F4]** or the **[F12]** key, and highlight the text to be moved or copied.

b) While the **Block on** is flashing in the lower left-hand corner of the screen, select **[Ctrl]+[F4]**. The following options are displayed at the bottom of the screen.

> **Move: 1** Block; **2** Tabular Column; **3** Rectangle: **0**

Even though the options begin with the word "Move," this command is also used for copying.

c) Select **1** for **Block**, because we are moving or copying a block of text. The following options are then displayed.

> **1** Move; **2** Copy; **3** Delete; **4** Append: **0**

d) Select **1** for **Move**, or **2** for **Copy**. The following instruction is then displayed.

> Move cursor; press **Enter** to retrieve.

e) Move the cursor to where you want the text to be moved or copied, and press the **[Enter]** key.

### 2. Moving or Copying a Sentence, Paragraph, or Page

WordPerfect saves you the trouble of having to block the text when you are moving or copying a sentence, paragraph or page. Once again, the steps for moving and copying are essentially the same.

a) Place the cursor within the sentence, paragraph, or page you wish to move or copy.

b) Press **[Ctrl]+[F4]**. The following options will be displayed.

> **Move: 1 Sentence; 2 Paragraph; 3 Page; 4 Retrieve: 0**

Even though the options begin with the word "Move," this command is also used for copying.

c) Select the number corresponding to what you wish to move or copy. The following options are then displayed.

> **1 Move; 2 Copy; 3 Delete; 4 Append: 0**

d) Select **1** for **Move**, or **2** for **Copy**. The following instruction is then displayed.

> **Move cursor; press Enter to retrieve.**

e) Move the cursor to where you want the text to be moved or copied and press the **[Enter]** key.

---

*Canceling a Move command.* *You will have a problem if you cancel a Move command while you are moving the cursor to the new location. Pressing the [F1] (Cancel) key at this point cancels the Move but, since the first part of the move sequence removes the text from the old location, the text is gone. You may retrieve the text by placing the cursor at its original location and using [Ctrl]+[F4], selecting 4 for Retrieve and then 1 for Block: [Ctrl]+[F4], 4, 1.*

---

## 3. Quick Cut and Paste

There is a special feature that will allow you to perform a quick move on a block of text. Block the text you want to move and press **[Backspace],[Y]** to cut it from the document. Move your cursor to the new location and paste the text in by pressing **[F1], [1]**. You may paste the same text in other locations by repeating the **[F1], [1]** keystrokes. This command deletes the blocked text and then performs a restore in the new location.

# F. Other WordPerfect Features

## 1. Margins and Line Spacing

Margins, line spacing, and a number of other page and document settings are adjusted in the Format screen shown in Figure 1.10. The Format screen is accessed with **[Shift]+[F8]**.

```
Format

    1 - Line
                Hyphenation                 Line Spacing
                Justification               Margins Left/Right
                Line Height                 Tab Set
                Line Numbering              Widow/Orphan Protection

    2 - Page
                Center Page (top to bottom) Page Numbering
                Force Odd/Even Page         Paper Size/Type/Labels
                Headers and Footers         Suppress
                Margins Top/Bottom

    3 - Document
                Display Pitch               Redline Method
                Initial Codes/Font          Summary

    4 - Other
                Advance                     Printer Functions
                Conditional End of Page     Underline Spaces/Tabs
                Decimal Characters          Border Options
                Language                    End Centering/Alignment
                Overstrike
Selection: 0
```

**Figure 1.10**  The Format Screen

Left and right margins are adjusted under selection **1-Line**. Top and bottom margins are adjusted under selection **2-Page**. Line spacing is adjusted under selection **1-Line**. You may select single, double, or any other increment of spacing, whether it be 1.25 or 6 lines.

## 2. Tabs and Indenting

The [Tab] key and the [F4] key serve the functions of tab and indent, respectively. The spacing for tabbing and indenting is set in the Format screen by selecting **Line** and then **Tab Set: [Shift]+[F8], 1, 8**. Normally the tabs are pre-set to occur every five spaces on the screen.

To change the tabs, access Tab Set with **[Shift]+[F8], 1, 8**. The Tab Set bar is shown in Figure 1.11.

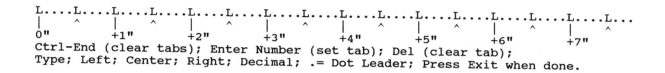

```
L....L....L....L....L....L....L....L....L....L....L....L....L....L....L...
|    ^    |    ^    |    ^    |    ^    |    ^    |    ^    |    ^    |    ^
0"       +1"       +2"       +3"       +4"       +5"       +6"       +7"
Ctrl-End (clear tabs); Enter Number (set tab); Del (clear tab);
Type; Left; Center; Right; Decimal; .= Dot Leader; Press Exit when done.
```

**Figure 1.11** The Tab Set Screen

The current tab settings are indicated by Ls. Unwanted tabs may be deleted by moving the cursor to them and pressing the **[Delete]** key. All the current tab settings may be deleted by moving the cursor to the leftmost tab stop and pressing **[Ctrl]+[End]**. To set new tabs, move to where you want the tab, with the **[Arrow]** keys or the **[Space Bar]**, and press the **[Tab]** key. You may also type a position number and press **[Enter]** to have a tab placed at an exact location. For example, if you need a tab at exactly 3.25 inches, type **3.25** and press **[Enter]**. If you want the first tab to begin at one inch and then have tabs every inch after that, you would type **1,1** and press **[Enter]**. You leave the tab screen by pressing the **[F7]** key. Pressing **[F7]** again will return you to the document.

Within your document, you may tab with the **[Tab]** key, or indent with the **[F4]** key. The **[Tab]** key indents the first line of the text to a tab stop. After the first line, the text will word wrap back to the left margin like the text in this paragraph.

The **[F4]** Indent key indents the entire paragraph to the tab stop. The text will word wrap to the tab stop until the **[Enter]** key is pressed at the end of the paragraph.

The **[Shift]+[F4]** key combination indents both the right and left margins to a tab stop. The text will word wrap within the indent until the **[Enter]** key is pressed at the end of a paragraph.

The **[F4], [Shift]+[Tab]** key combination leaves the first line of the paragraph at the left margin, and subsequent text word wraps to the tab stop until the **[Enter]** key is pressed at the end of the paragraph.

The tab and indent features are used frequently when typing long quotations from code sections or case reporters. An example of [Shift]+[F4] and the [Tab] key are shown below.

**Rule 373 states in pertinent part:**

> **In ruling on the motion the court shall consider all matters relevant to a proper determination of the motion, including the court's file in the case and the affidavits and declarations and supporting data**

submitted by the parties and, where applicable, . . . the diligence of the parties in pursuing discovery or other pretrial proceedings, . . . the nature of any extensions of time or other delay attributable to either party, . . . whether the interests of justice are best served by dismissal or trial of the case; and any other fact or circumstance relevant to a fair determination of the issue.

The interests of justice would best be served by a trial on the merits in this action. Therefore, plaintiff herein should be allowed to proceed to trial.

### 3. Reveal Codes

WordPerfect hides its formatting codes to allow you to work with a clean screen. To view the formatting codes, you need to access the **Reveal Codes** feature within **[Alt]+[F3]** or **[F11]**. When accessed, Reveal Codes divides the screen, displaying the normal text at the top, and the text with codes at the bottom as shown in Figure 1.12.

Revealing codes is useful when you wish to delete a **bold**, <u>underline</u>, tab or other code which has been inserted into a document. It is also useful when your document suddenly

begins to do something
that you did not intend
it to do.

```
     Revealing codes is useful when you wish to delete a bold,
underline,     tab or other code which has been inserted into a
document.   It is also useful when your document suddenly
               begins to do
               something that
               you did not
               intend it to
               do.


                                   Doc 2 Pg 1 Ln 1.17" Pos 1"
{   ▲    ▲    ▲    ▲    ▲    ▲    ▲    ▲    ▲    ▲    ▲    ▲    }   ▲
[HRt]
[Tab]Revealing codes is useful when you wish to delete a [BOLD]bold[bold],[SRt]
[UND]underline[und],[Tab]tab or other code which has been inserted into a[SRt]
document.   It is also useful when your document suddenly[HRt]
[L/R Mar:2.5",4.5"]begins to do[SRt]
something that[SRt]
you did not[SRt]
intend it to[SRt]
do.[HRt]
[HRt]

Press Reveal Codes to restore screen
```

**Figure 1.12** The hidden codes of a document revealed with Reveal Codes

The Reveal Codes feature, shown in Figure 1.12, displays the actual codes present within the text. You can see that a bolded word is preceded by an uppercase **[BOLD]**, and followed by a lowercase **[bold]**. This indicates where the bold begins and where it ends. An underlined word is indicated in the same manner with **[UND]** and **[und]** codes. Where the **[Enter]** key has been pressed is indicated by a hard return (**[Hrt]**). A word wrap is indicated by a soft return (**[Srt]**). The margin problem with this text begins with a margin code (**[L/R Mar:2.5",4.5"]**) that has inadvertently made its way into the text.

Using the **[Arrow]** keys to move the cursor in the upper half of the screen also moves a highlight bar in the lower half of the screen. To remove any of the codes, move the highlight bar to the code and press the **[Delete]** key. With a bold or underline, deleting either the uppercase or lowercase code will remove both codes.

Reveal Codes is turned off by again pressing either **[Alt]+[F3]** or **[F11]**.

## 4. Page Breaks

When you reach the bottom of a page in your document, a single hashed line will appear across the screen as shown in Figure 1.13. This single hashed line is called a soft page break. WordPerfect automatically ends a page with a soft page break according to the preset page length of your document.

```
     WHEREAS, the Directors of the Corporation desire to hold

monthly regular meetings in addition to the annual meeting of the

Board;

     NOW, THEREFORE BE IT RESOLVED, that the Board of Directors of

the corporation shall hold regular meetings on the first Monday of

each month at 1:00 p.m.;

     FURTHER RESOLVED, that Article III, Section 8, of the Bylaws

of the corporation is hereby amended to reflect these changes in

the dates of the meetings of the Board of Directors.  The Secretary

of the corporation is hereby directed to make a notation of this
-------------------------------------------------------------------------
change in the Bylaws of the corporation.


C:\WORK\XYZCORP.MIN                        Doc 1 Pg 2 Ln 1.33" Pos 1"
```

**Figure 1.13** A single hashed line appears where WordPerfect automatically ends a page

When you wish to end a page in a place other than where the soft page break occurs, you can use a "**hard page break.**" In the example shown in Figure 1.13 above, a hard page break could be used to make the current page stop after the second paragraph. To create a hard page break, the cursor is placed where you want the new page to begin and **[Ctrl]+[Enter]** is pressed. A double hashed line indicates the location of a hard page break as shown in Figure 1.14.

```
     WHEREAS, the Directors of the Corporation desire to hold

monthly regular meetings in addition to the annual meeting of the

Board;

     NOW, THEREFORE BE IT RESOLVED, that the Board of Directors of

the corporation shall hold regular meetings on the first Monday of

each month at 1:00 p.m.;


===============================================================================
     FURTHER RESOLVED, that Article III, Section 8, of the Bylaws

of the corporation is hereby amended to reflect these changes in

the dates of the meetings of the Board of Directors.  The Secretary

of the corporation is hereby directed to make a notation of this

change in the Bylaws of the corporation.
C:\WORK\XYZCORP.MIN                            Doc 1 Pg 2 Ln 1" Pos 1"
```

**Figure 1.14** A hard page break is indicated by a double hashed line

A hard page break is indicated by a **[HPg]** code in Reveal Codes. A soft page break is indicated by a **[SPg]** code.

## 5. Text Appearances and Sizes

In addition to bolding and underlining, text may be <u>double underlined</u>, *italicized*, outlined, shadowed, SMALL CAPPED, redlined, or ~~striken out~~, using different text appearances. Text Appearance is selected with **[Ctrl]+[F8], 2**. The type of appearance is then selected. To turn off the appearance and return to normal typing, press the **[Right Arrow]** key to move outside of the code, or use **[Ctrl]+[F8], 3**. If the text has already been typed, it can be blocked prior to using **[Ctrl]+[F8], 2**.

*WordPerfect for DOS*

Text may also be printed in different sizes. The sizes, <sup>superscript</sup>, <sub>subscript</sub>, fine, small, large, very large, and extra large, may be selected with **[Ctrl]+[F8], 1**. To turn off the size and return to normal typing, press the **[Right Arrow]** key to move outside of the code, or use **[Ctrl]+[F8], 3**. If the text has already been typed, it can be blocked prior to using **[Ctrl]+[F8], 1**.

## 6. Changing Fonts

Fonts are the typeface of a document. The initial font of your document, called the "Base Font," is listed in the Format Menu, **[Shift]+[F8], 3, 3.** You may change the Initial Font at this menu. Subsequent font changes in your document may be made in the Base Font screen, using **[Ctrl]+[F8], 4.** At the font screen, highlight the desired font and press 1 to select the font. If your printer prints scalable fonts, you will be prompted for a point size. After making a selection, you will be returned to the WordPerfect screen and further type will be printed in the new font. The type does not change on the screen.

You may notice that your screen margins will change as you change fonts. This is due to the changing size of the type. A code indicating where the new font begins can be seen in Reveal Codes.

## 7. The Date Feature

WordPerfect provides a way to incorporate the date from your computer's internal clock into documents. The Date feature, **[Shift]+[F5]**, allows you to place the current date or a **date code** within a document. Selecting **1** inserts the current date; selecting **2** inserts a date code. Both options place the current date within a document. The date code, however, will place the current date into the document each time the document is retrieved into WordPerfect. The date code option is used primarily with form documents and form letters.

## 8. Spell Checking

Checking the spelling within a document is one of the great features of a word processor. The Spell Check feature will read each word within a document and compare it to the words within its dictionary. When it finds a word that does not match, the spell checker will stop and give alternative spellings, and/or allow you to edit your spelling.

*It is important* that you do a Save and Continue, **[F10]**, prior to spell checking your document. The Spell Check feature has been known to freeze computers, requiring that the computer be restarted, thus erasing the RAM where the document was stored.

WordPerfect's Spell Check feature is accessed with **[Ctrl]+[F2]**. When you press **[Ctrl]+[F2]**, the main options are:

**1** to check the **Word** containing the cursor.

**2** to check the current **Page**.

**3** to check the entire **Document**.

When Spell Check finds a word it does not recognize, the list of alternative spellings is supplied on the bottom half of the screen as shown in Figure 1.15. You may select one of these spellings by typing its corresponding letter. If the word is not misspelled, select one of the options at the bottom of the screen to skip the word and continue.

```
    WHEREAS, the Directors of the Corporation desire to hold

monthly regular meetings in adition to the annual meeting of the

Board;

    NOW, THEREFORE BE IT RESOLVED, that the Board of Directors of

                                    Doc 1 Pg 1 Ln 7" Pos 3.8"
{   ▲    ▲    ▲    ▲    ▲    ▲    ▲    ▲    ▲    ▲    ▲    }   ▲    ▲

    A. addition          B. aditio           C. aditios
    D. audition          E. adaption         F. adhesion
    G. adoption          H. edition          I. ideation




Not Found: 1 Skip Once; 2 Skip; 3 Add; 4 Edit; 5 Look Up; 6 Ignore Numbers: 0
```

**Figure 1.15** The Spell Check Feature

If a word is found by Spell Check to be misspelled, but the proper spelling is not provided, press **4** to Edit the word, and then press **[F7]** to continue the spell checking.

### 9. The Thesaurus

WordPerfect contains a thesaurus to assist you in drafting your documents. A thesaurus supplies synonyms for a variety of words. To use the thesaurus feature, place the cursor within a word and press **[Alt]+[F1]**. The thesaurus for the word *desire* is shown in Figure 1.16.

```
        WHEREAS, the Directors of the Corporation  desire  to hold

monthly regular meetings in addition to the annual meeting of the
┌desire=(v)═══════════════╤desire-(n)════════════════╤
│   1 A •ache             │  5    •ambition          │     •reject
│     B •aspire           │       •aspiration        │
│     C •long             │       •longing           │  9  •dislike
│     D •wish             │       •want               │     •aversion
│     E •yearn            │       •yearning          │     •generosity
│                         │                          │
│   2 F •covet            │  6    •appetite          │
│     G •crave            │       •craving           │
│     H •need             │       •lust              │
│     I •want             │       •obsession         │
│                         │       •passion           │
│   3 J •choose           │                          │
│     K •prefer           │  7     avarice           │
│                         │       •greed             │
│   4 L •ask              │                          │
│     M •request          │ desire-(ant)──────────── │
│     N •urge             │  8    •spurn             │
└─────────────────────────┴──────────────────────────┘
1 Replace Word; 2 View Doc; 3 Look Up Word; 4 Clear Column: 0
```

**Figure 1.16**  WordPerfect's Thesaurus for the word *desire*

Further synonyms may be seen for the words within the synonym list by pressing the letter corresponding to the word. For example, in Figure 1.16, pressing the letter **D** displays the synonyms for the word *wish* in the second column as shown in Figure 1.17.

```
        WHEREAS, the Directors of the Corporation  desire  to hold

monthly regular meetings in addition to the annual meeting of the
┌desire=(v)═══════════════╤wish=(n)══════════════════╤
│   1   •ache             │  1 A •desire             │     •long
│       •aspire           │    B •hope               │     •want
│       •long             │    C •longing            │     •yearn
│       •wish             │                          │
│       •yearn            │  2 D •dream              │ wish-(ant)────────────
│                         │    E •fancy              │  6    •aversion
│   2   •covet            │    F •whim               │       •fulfillment
│       •crave            │                          │
│       •need             │  3 G •ambition           │  7    •obtain
│       •want             │    H •aspiration         │
│                         │    I •objective          │
│   3   •choose           │                          │
│       •prefer           │  4 J  behest             │
│                         │    K •command            │
│   4   •ask              │    L •request            │
│       •request          │                          │
│       •urge             │ wish-(v)──────────────── │
│                         │  5 M •hope               │
└─────────────────────────┴──────────────────────────┘
1 Replace Word; 2 View Doc; 3 Look Up Word; 4 Clear Column: 0
```

**Figure 1.17**  Synonyms for the word *wish*.

The letters identifying the selections may be moved from one column to another with the **[Arrow]** keys. You may select a word from the synonyms by selecting **1** for Replace Word and typing the letter corresponding to the new word.

## 10. Searching

WordPerfect contains a Search feature that can search for a word or group of characters or WordPerfect code within your document. You may search forward or backward in a document, or replace a word, phrase, or code with another word, phrase, or code.

### a. *Forward Searching*

The [F2] key searches forward in a document. Pressing the **[F2]** key prompts for the word or characters for which you are searching. The word or characters within a search are called the "search term." After entering the search term, press the **[F2]** key again to begin the search. The search will stop at the first instance of the search term. The search can be continued by again pressing the **[F2]** key. Using lowercase letters in the search term will match both lowercase and uppercase text. Using uppercase letters will only match uppercase text.

### b. *Backward Searching*

If you wish to search backwards towards the top of the document, use **[Shift]+[F2]**. The prompts will be the same as with forward searching.

> *When editing a large document, I find it helpful to mark where I have left off in my editing with three asterisks, "\*\*\*." The next time I enter the document to work on the editing, I simply run a search for "\*\*\*."*

### c. *Search and Replace*

When you wish to replace a word, phrase, or code with another word, phrase or code, use the Search and Replace feature, **[Alt]+[F2]**. For example, you have typed a 25-page legal memorandum and find that you have spelled the Plaintiff's name, "Kerrigan," as "Carrigan" throughout the document. The Search and Replace feature can fix this error very quickly. Pressing **[Alt]+[F2]** accesses Search and Replace and asks if you wish the search to stop every time it finds the name in order to confirm the replacement. For this search, we would respond **N**. You are then prompted for the search term. In this case it would be "Carrigan." After typing "Carrigan," you press **[F2]** and are prompted to enter the replace term. The replace term in this example is "Kerrigan." Pressing **[F2]** again begins the Search and Replace.

# G. Printing

To receive a hard copy of a document, you must send it to a printer. As a safety measure, use the **[F10]** Save and Continue feature prior to printing your document. Occasionally, a printer problem will freeze your computer.

The **[Shift]+[F7]** key combination accesses WordPerfect's Print menu as shown in Figure 1.18.

```
Print

     1 - Full Document
     2 - Page
     3 - Document on Disk
     4 - Control Printer
     5 - Multiple Pages
     6 - View Document
     7 - Initialize Printer


Options

     S - Select Printer                    HP DeskJet 500
     B - Binding Offset                    0"
     N - Number of Copies                  1
     U - Multiple Copies Generated by      WordPerfect
     G - Graphics Quality                  Medium
     T - Text Quality                      High




Selection: 0
```

**Figure 1.18** The WordPerfect Print Menu

The options available in the print menu are explained below.

**1**   Prints the entire document.

**2**   Prints the current page containing the cursor.

**3**   Prints a document from a disk.

**4**   Gives you the Control Printer menu where you can cancel and control print jobs.

**5**   Allows you to print selected pages from the document. For example, 5-10 or 1,3,5-10.

**6** Allows you to view how your document will look printed. This is a very helpful feature when you are using graphics and fonts.

**7** Sends fonts you have designated to be present at the beginning of the print job to the printer.

**S** Lets you select the type of printer you are using.

**B** Allows for space for binding the pages of the document if this is required.

**N** Lets you print more than one copy of the document. The number selected remains during your work session until you change it back to one.

**U** If your printer has the ability to print more than one copy of the current print job on its own, this option can be used to have the printer handle the printing of copies. This will print documents faster.

**G** Determines the quality of the graphics when printed.

**T** Determines the quality of the text when printed.

## H. EXITING WORDPERFECT

Exiting WordPerfect is accomplished with **[F7] Save and Exit**. As was covered in Section D, when you press the **[F7]** key, WordPerfect will display the prompts for saving a document. Respond to these prompts, and then respond **Y** for yes when asked if you wish to exit WordPerfect. Responding **N** for no will give you a blank WordPerfect screen.

## *Section Two—Advanced WordPerfect Features*

## A. BULLETS AND SPECIAL CHARACTERS

There are many special characters, not available on the keyboard, that can be accessed from WordPerfect using the compose key, **[Ctrl]+[V]**, or the **[Alt]** key and the number key pad. These keys allow you to use characters found in WordPerfect's character sets. These character sets are shown in the WordPerfect manual, and can also be found in the CHARACTER.DOC file in the WordPerfect program files. To use the compose key, you press **[Ctrl]+[V]** and then type the number of the character set followed by a comma and the number of the character. For example, to create a section symbol, §, use the compose key and type **4,6** (character set 4, character number 6):

    **[Ctrl]+[V] 4,6**

You can also create a section symbol using the **[Alt]** key and the numbers on the number key pad as follows:

**[Alt]+21**

Releasing the **[Alt]** key inserts the character into your document. This method will not work with the numbers on the alphanumeric portion of the keyboard.

Bullets and some common characters used in legal documents are shown below with their compose key keystrokes and **[Alt]** keystrokes (where available). You will see that there are some alternatives to naming the character set and the character number with some characters using the compose key. For example, the registered trademark symbol, ®, can be created with: **[Ctrl]+[V], OR**

| Symbol | [Ctrl]+[V] | [Alt]+ |
|--------|------------|--------|
| § | 4,6 | 21 |
| ® | 4,22 <br> or  OR | |
| © | 4,23 <br> or  OC | |
| ™ | 4,41 <br> or  TM | |
| SM | 4,42 <br> or  SM | |
| ○ | 4,37 | |
| ● | 4,44 | |
| ○ | 4,1 | 9 |
| • | 4,0 <br> or  ** | 7 |
| · | 4,3 | |

> *When you create some characters, a box will appear on the screen in place of the character. The character can be seen in the Print menu by viewing the document, or in the printed copy of the document.*

*WordPerfect for DOS*

*39*

# B. MACROS

A **Macro** allows you to program a single keystroke combination to record several keystrokes. There are two ways to identify macros: with the **[Alt]** key and a letter of the alphabet, or with a word.

A common macro is one that switches to double-spaced type, something you will do quite frequently when drafting legal documents. The WordPerfect keystrokes necessary to switch from single spacing to double spacing are:

**[Shift]+[F8], 1, 6, 2, [Enter], [F7]**

You can create a macro that, when you strike a single key combination (e.g., [Alt]+[D]), performs all of these keystrokes for you.

## 1. Creating a Macro

Creating a macro in WordPerfect involves the following steps:

a) Press **[Ctrl]+[F10]**.

b) Define the macro with either a word or by holding down the **[Alt]** key and selecting any letter from A to Z. **[Alt]+[any letter]** is the most common way to store a macro.

> *If WordPerfect says the macro already exists, cancel the command with the [F1] key. Begin again with Step 1 and try [Alt] plus another letter.*

c) Enter a brief description of the macro for reference purposes and press **[Enter]**. The words **Macro Def** will begin flashing in the lower left-hand corner of the screen. This is to inform you that every key you press at this point will be recorded within the macro.

d) Input the keystrokes you wish to use.

> *[Ctrl]+[Page Up] gives you added features to include within your macro such as "pause."*

e) Press **[Ctrl]+[F10]** to save the macro.

Following these steps, we will create a macro for double spacing.

    a)  Press **[Ctrl]+[F10]**.

    b)  Define the macro. Press **[Alt]+[D]**.

    c)  Enter a brief description. The description of our macro will be "Double Spacing." Press the **[Enter]** key to continue.

    d)  Input the keystrokes. **Macro Def** will be flashing in the lower left-hand corner of the screen. As we press the keys for our macro, you will see that we move through the WordPerfect menu screens just as though we were working without creating a macro.

        Press **[Shift]+[F8]**, select **1** for line, select **6** for line spacing, select **2** for two line spacing and press **[Enter]**. Now, leave the menu by pressing the **[F7]** key.

    e)  Press **[Ctrl]+[F10]**.

Double spacing may now be activated at any time by pressing **[Alt]+[D]**.

Another use for macros is to record boilerplate language that you need to repeat throughout a document. For example, in responding to a discovery request, you may find yourself using the following objection repeatedly in your responses:

    Plaintiff objects to this discovery request on the ground that the information sought is not relevant to the subject matter of this lawsuit.

Creating a macro that will automatically type in this objection can save you a lot of time when drafting the responding document.

To set up this macro, follow steps **a** through **e** in Creating a Macro. When you input the keystrokes for the macro, type the entire objection. Pressing **[Ctrl]+[F10]** will end the macro creation. The macro may then be retrieved anywhere within the document by pressing **[Alt]+[given letter]** or by pressing **[Alt]+[F10]** and identifying the macro name.

## 2.  Executing a Macro

Executing a macro is accomplished by pressing **[Alt]+[given letter]** or by pressing **[Alt]+[F10]** and typing the macro name. Since we went through the keystrokes to create double spacing in making our **[Alt]+[D]** macro, the document on the screen will be in double spacing. Type a few lines to see the double spacing. Return to single spacing (**[Shift]+[F8], 1, 6, 1, [Enter], [F7]**), and type a few lines. Now execute the macro by pressing **[Alt]+[D]**. Type a few lines to see that you have switched back to double spacing. Many firms also set up a macro for single spacing and call it **[Alt]+[S]**. When these two macros are in place, it is very easy to switch from single to double spacing and back again.

If you create a macro and identify it with a name, instead of using **[Alt]+[any letter]**, the macro is executed by pressing **[Alt]+[F10]**, typing the macro name, and pressing the **[Enter]** key. The macro files are stored with your WordPerfect program files and are available in any document that you create.

---

*If you receive the message* **"ERROR: File not found—ALTD.WPM"** *when you try to execute your macro, you may need to change the location of your macro files in the Setup Menu. Check* **[Shift]+[F1], 6,** *and look at item* **2 Keyboard/Macro Files.** *This will tell you where WordPerfect is looking for the macro files. You may need to change the location to the WordPerfect directory (i.e., C:\wp51) or another directory. Try it yourself and, if the error message continues, seek help from the person in charge of the computer system, or telephone WordPerfect's 800 support number.*

---

### 3. Editing a Macro

To edit the keystrokes within a macro, follow the steps below:

a) Press **[Ctrl]+[F10]**.

b) Select the macro to edit. Type the macro name or press the keys which correspond to the macro, e.g., [Alt]+[D]. WordPerfect will tell you that the macro already exists and will ask you if you want to replace it or edit it.

c) Select **2** for edit. You may now edit the macro and make any desired corrections.

---

*[Ctrl]+[Page Up] will give you access to a number of macro commands that do not correspond to keys—for example, "pause."*

*[Ctrl]+[F10], used within the macro editor, will allow you to add [Enter] symbols and cursor movement characters into the macro. [Ctrl]+[F10], again, returns you to normal editing.*

---

d) When you are finished editing the macro, press **[F7]** to save your changes.

## 4. Creating a Memorandum Macro

There are macros that not only execute commands, but also pause and wait for the user to enter information before continuing with their execution.

A memorandum is a document that is created often by legal professionals. It is used to document telephone conferences, record the contents of conversations with witnesses, report on case status, and prepare legal memoranda. A macro can be created to type the memorandum headings and to pause for entry of data, making the memorandum creation process very easy.

Follow the steps below from a blank screen to create the memorandum macro. To get to a blank screen, press **[F7]**, respond **Y** or **N** to the prompt and respond **N** to the Exit prompt.

a) Press **[Ctrl]+[F10]**.

b) Define the macro as **[Alt]+[M]** by holding down the **[Alt]** key and pressing the letter **M**. If there is already a macro with this letter, try another.

c) Describe the macro as **Memorandum**

d) Input the keystrokes.

1) Press **[Shift]+[F6]** to center, **[F6]** to bold, **[F8]** to underline, and the **[Caps Lock]** key.

2) Type the word *MEMORANDUM* with a space between each letter so that it appears like this:

<u>M E M O R A N D U M</u>

3) Press **[F8]** again to end the underlining.

4) Press **[Enter]** three times.

5) Type **TO:**. Tab twice and press **[Ctrl]+[Page Up]** and select **1** for pause. Press **[Enter]** to end the pause.

6) Press **[Enter]** twice.

7) Type **FROM:**. Tab once and press **[Ctrl]+[Page Up]** and select **1** for pause. Press **[Enter]** to end the pause.

8) Press **[Enter]** twice.

9) Type **DATE:**. Tab once and press **[Shift]+[F5]** and select **2** (Date Code).

10) Press **[Enter]** twice.

11) Type **RE:**. Tab twice, press **[Ctrl]+[Page Up]** and select **1** for pause. Press **[Enter]** to end the pause.

12) Press **[Enter]** twice.

13) Press **[F8]** to underline and press the **Space Bar** until the position marker reaches the right margin: 7.5". If you go too far, backspace some of the underline out.

14) Press **[F6]** to end the bold and **[F8]** to end the underline.

15) Press **[Enter]** twice.

16) Press **[Ctrl]+[F10]** to save the macro.


Your completed macro should look like this, but with a different date.


## M E M O R A N D U M


**TO:**

**FROM:**

**DATE:**     **April 12, 1993**

**RE:**

_____


To run the memorandum macro, press **[Alt]+[M]** or the name or key combination under which it was recorded. When the macro pauses, enter the appropriate information and press **[Enter]** to continue.


## C. STORING BLOCKS OF TEXT


When creating legal documents, you will often repeat the same phrase or sentence throughout the document. An example would be a deposition summary where you are repeating a person's name throughout the summary.

You may record up to ten blocks of text, consisting of 128 characters or less, for use during a work session (the blocks are erased when you exit WordPerfect). To record a block, use **[Alt]+[F4]** or **[F12]** to block the text you desire to record and press **[Ctrl]+[Page Up]**. You will be prompted for a variable and you may enter a number between 0 and 9, and then press **[Enter]**. When you want to paste this block in your text, you may retrieve it by pressing the **[Alt]** key and the number you gave to the block (e.g., [Alt]+[1]).

## D. FOOTNOTES

Footnotes are used often in the drafting of legal memoranda and pleadings. WordPerfect's footnote feature sequentially numbers the footnotes, and automatically adjusts your page lengths to make room for the footnotes.

To create a footnote within your document follow the steps below.

a) Position the cursor at the point where you would like the reference number of the footnote to appear.

b) Press **[Ctrl]+[F7]**. The following options will appear in the lower left-hand corner of the screen.

> **1 Footnote; 2 Endnote; 3 Endnote Placement: 0**

c) Select **1** for footnote. The following options are then displayed.

> **Footnote: 1 Create; 2 Edit; 3 New Number; 4 Options: 0**

d) Select **1** for Create. A blank edit screen with the footnote number then appears.

e) Type the footnote. When you are finished, the **[F7]** (Exit) key will return you to your document.

The footnote reference number will appear where you placed the cursor when you began. You cannot see the footnote unless you view your document through the Print menu: **[Shift]+[F7], 6**.

To practice creating a footnote, type the sentence below.

**The parents of a legitimate unmarried minor child, acting jointly, may maintain an action for injury to such child caused by the wrongful act or neglect of another.**

This is a quote from California Code of Civil Procedure, Section 376. To reference this section with a footnote, follow the steps below.

    a)   Position the cursor at the space just after the period in the sentence.

    b)   Press **[Ctrl]+[F7]** to access the Footnote options.

    c)   Select **1** for Footnote.

    d)   Select **1** for Create.

    e)   Press the **[Space Bar]** once and type **CCP Section 376**. Press **[F7]** to return to your document.

You will see the footnote reference number at the end of the sentence. To see how the footnote will appear on the page, use **[Shift]+[F7], 6**. The footnote should appear like the one shown in Figure 1.19. When you are finished, pressing the **[Space Bar]** twice will return you to your document from View.

The parents of a legitimate unmarried minor child, acting jointly, may maintain an action for injury to such child caused by the wrongful act or neglect of another.[1]

---

[1] CCP Section 376.

**Figure 1.19** A Footnote

# E. COLUMNS

WordPerfect offers three types of columns, Parallel, Parallel with Block Protect, and Newspaper. For the most part, legal professionals use Parallel columns as shown in Figure 1.20. Parallel columns are used to create pleading captions, deposition summaries, and other documents that require columns of text that can be read from left to right.

### SUMMARY OF THE DEPOSITION OF

### HUBERT M. SMITH

### Taken November 9, 1991

| Page:Line | Summary |
|---|---|
| 1:3 | Opening statements. |
| 2:4 | Mr. Smith was born in Walla Walla, Washington on December 12, 1945. He currently resides at 345 Main Street, Seattle, Washington 00990. |
| 3:27 | Mr. Smith obtained a Bachelor of Science degree in Economics from the University of Washington in 1967. He is presently employed by the State of Washington as an Economist. |

Figure 1.20  Parallel Columns

Parallel with Block Protect columns are parallel columns. However, if any part of a row of column entries continues to the next page of the document, the entire row of entries will be moved to the next page.

Newspaper columns differ from parallel columns in that when the left-most column reaches the bottom of the page, it goes back up to the top of the same page. Instead of reading these columns from left to right, you read the first column to the bottom of the page and then read the second column as shown in Figure 1.21.

## Parallel Columns

WordPerfect offers two types of columns, parallel and newspaper. For the most part, legal professionals use parallel columns. This type of column is used to create pleading captions, deposition summaries and other documents which require columns of text which are read from left to right.

## Newspaper Columns

Newspaper columns differ from parallel columns in that when the left-most column reaches the bottom of the page, it goes back up to the top of the same page. Instead of reading these type of columns from left to right, you read the first column to the bottom of the page and then read the second column.

**Figure 1.21** Newspaper Columns

To learn about columns, we will use an example of a deposition summary. Follow the steps below from a blank screen.

a) Type in the specifics about the deposition at the top of the document as shown below.

**SUMMARY OF THE DEPOSITION OF
HUBERT M. SMITH
Taken November 9, 1992**

b) Press the **[Enter]** key to move down a few lines.

c) Access the Columns feature with **[Alt]+[F7]**. Select **1** for Columns. Select **3** for Define. We must define the columns before we can use them. The Columns Definition screen is shown in Figure 1.22.

```
Text Column Definition

      1 - Type                                Newspaper

      2 - Number of Columns                   2

      3 - Distance Between Columns

      4 - Margins

   Column      Left       Right     Column      Left        Right
     1:        1"         4"          13:
     2:        4.5"       7.5"        14:
     3:                               15:
     4:                               16:
     5:                               17:
     6:                               18:
     7:                               19:
     8:                               20:
     9:                               21:
    10:                               22:
    11:                               23:
    12:                               24:


Selection: 0
```

**Figure 1.22**  The Columns Definition Screen

A default setting for newspaper columns is already present when you enter the Columns Definition Screen.

d)  At the Columns Definition screen, change the type of columns to parallel by selecting **1** for **Type**, and then **2** for **Parallel**. Check to see that item 2, **Number of Columns**, is **2**. If it is not, change it to 2.

e)  Define your margins. Select **4** for **Margins** and enter the following margins:

| Column | Left | Right |
| --- | --- | --- |
| 1: | 1" | 2.5" |
| 2: | 3" | 7.5" |

When you have pressed **[Enter]** after the right margin entry for column 2, your cursor will be blinking at the Selection prompt at the bottom of the screen. Press **[Enter]** once to leave this menu.

f)  The next screen will display:

**Columns: 1 On; 2 Off; 3 Define: 0**

Select **1** to turn the columns **On**. When the columns are on, the column number will appear in the Status Line.

g) Type **Page:Line** at the left-hand margin and go to column 2 by pressing **[Ctrl]+[Enter]**. Under normal circumstances this would create a hard page break. If you do get a hard page break (============), then your columns are not turned on. Check your Reveal Codes to make sure that you are typing after the **[Col On]** code. If you do not see a **Col On** code, then you need to turn the columns on with **[Alt]+[F7], 1, 1**.

h) At the second column, type **Summary**, press **[F8]** to turn the underline off, and press **[Ctrl]+[Enter]** to get back to column 1 and begin your summary.

Try entering the summary in Figure 1.20 into your document. To change columns, use **[Ctrl]+[Enter]**. **[Ctrl]+[Home], [Left Arrow]** and **[Ctrl]+[Home], [Right Arrow]** will move you quickly back and forth between your columns when editing the column text.

When you have finished using Columns in your document, they may be turned off with **[Alt]+[F7],1,2**.

# F. DOCUMENT MERGING

Mass mailings and frequently used forms can be produced quickly using WordPerfect's merge features.

In a large litigation case, there may be 25 or more opposing counsel. Creating a separate letter for each counsel, inputting their name and address and a salutation, can be very time consuming. It is much easier to create a merge letter and address list than to type each individual letter. By merging the merge letter with the address list, a personalized letter can be created for each individual.

## 1. Primary and Secondary Files

Merging documents involves the use of primary and secondary files. The primary file is the shell document, into which information will be merged. The secondary file is the list of information to be merged into the primary file document.

For our first example, we will create a simple letter acknowledging an extension of time to respond to a complaint. This letter will be the primary file. The list of addresses for each of the plaintiffs' counsel will be the secondary file.

## 2. The Merged Document

A merge will combine the information from the primary and secondary files, creating a copy of the primary file for each of the records in the secondary file. After our merge is completed, the merged document will contain a letter for each counsel with a hard page break created between each letter. This makes it easy to send all of the letters to the printer at one time.

## 3. Example

For our example, we will create a letter and make it into our primary file. Type the letter shown in Figure 1.23 into a blank WordPerfect screen. Use the centering, underline and bold features where applicable. Use **[Shift]+[F6]** to center the headings and the date. Use **[Shift]+[F5], 1** to insert today's date into the letter. The closing and signature line should not be centered. Use the **[Tab]** key to move the cursor to the middle of the screen to begin typing the closing and signature lines (Pos 4.5"). Use your own name at the signature line.

**SMITH AND SMITH**
**Attorneys at Law**
**1234 Hampton Avenue**
**La Jolla, California  99999**
**(619) 555-1212**

April 1, 1993

Opposing Counsel, Esq.
22 Court Boulevard
San Diego, California  99999

    Re:    Potter, et al. vs. Polluter Co.; Case No. 85549

Dear Mr. Counsel:

Pursuant to a telephone conference of this date, Mr. Johnson of Pote & Tate, on beha of all plaintiffs in this action, has granted our client, Polluter Co., an extension until May 1: 1993, in which to answer or otherwise respond to the complaint on file in this matter.

                    Sincerely,

                    JAMES SMITH
                    SMITH AND SMITH

**Figure 1.23**  The Sample Letter

*Saving the letter.* Before we continue, let's use the **[F10]** Save and Continue option to save our letter. Remember to specify where you wish to save it (e.g., A: or C:), any directory you wish to place it under, and give the letter the name **EXTEND.LTR**. If you are using a floppy disk in the A: drive, save the letter as follows:  **A:EXTEND.LTR**

*Spell checking.* Check the spelling in the letter using the Spell Check feature. Spell checking is accomplished with **[Ctrl]+[F2]**. WordPerfect will give you a number of spelling options; choose **3** for **Document**.

## 4.  Creating the Primary File

In creating our primary file, we will be making three fields:

    1)  Name of the attorney and firm name

    2)  Firm address

    3)  The salutation

In order to do this, we must remove some of the text from our letter and place field names where we wish information to be entered from the secondary file.

    a)  Move the cursor to the "O" in "Opposing Counsel, Esq." Delete to the end of the line using **[Ctrl]+[End]**.

    b)  Press **[Shift]+[F9]** for Merge Codes. Select **1** for **Field**. Type **1** for the field where the name of counsel will be located and press **[Enter]**.

    c)  Remove the entire address by blocking it and pressing the **[Delete]** key.

    d)  Move the cursor to the beginning of the blank line under the first field that you created, and use **[Shift]+[F9], 1** to create a second field **2**.

    e)  The third and final field for our primary file document will be the salutation field. Move the cursor to the "M" in "Mr. Counsel:". Use **[Ctrl]+[End]** to delete to the end of the line. Now, with the cursor remaining after "Dear", use **[Shift]+[F9], 1** to create a third field **3**. Then, place a colon after the field reference number.

Your primary file document is now complete and should look like the one in Figure 1.24.

**SMITH AND SMITH**
**Attorneys at Law**
**1234 Hampton Avenue**
**La Jolla, California  99999**
**(619) 555-1212**


April 1, 1993


{FIELD}1 ~
{FIELD}2 ~


Re:    Potter, et al. vs. Polluter Co.; Case No. 85549

Dear {FIELD}3 ~ :

Pursuant to a telephone conference of this date, Mr. Johnson of Pote & Tate, on behalf of all plaintiffs in this action, has granted our client, Polluter Co., an extension until May 15, 1993, in which to answer or otherwise respond to the complaint on file in this matter.

Sincerely,


JAMES SMITH
SMITH AND SMITH


**Figure 1.24**  The Primary File


Save this document using the **[F7]** Save. Save it under the same name (**EXTEND.LTR**), respond **Y** when asked if you wish to replace the letter, and respond **N** when asked if you would like to exit.

## 5. Creating the Secondary File

The secondary file will be the names, addresses, and salutations for each of the persons who will be receiving a letter. We will be able to use the secondary file for this letter and others that we create in the future for this case.

Although the names of several attorneys would likely be included in this secondary file, we will use only four for this example. They are:

**Marvin Pearce, Esq.**
**Fenner & Pearce**
**64 Honor Avenue, 14th Floor**
**San Diego, California 99999**

**James Franklin, Esq.**
**22 Windship Lane, Suite 3**
**San Diego, California 99999**

**John Simpson, Esq.**
**Sampson, Newberry & Simpson**
**34 Rome Avenue, Suite B**
**La Jolla, California 99999**

**Marsha Mendleson, Esq.**
**Mendleson, Teedlebaum & Mason**
**6552 Main Street, Suite 2003**
**San Diego, California 99999**

Remember, there are three fields in this merge letter. The first field is the attorney and firm name, the second is the address, and the third is the salutation.

To create the secondary file we begin with a blank screen and type each field, pressing the **[F9] End Field** key at the end of each field. A group of fields for a single item is called a record. We have four records in our example. At the end of each record, except the last, we will press **[Shift]+[F9], 2** to let WordPerfect know that this is the end of the record.

The first record in our secondary file will be created as follows:

a)  Type the name of the first attorney, and the firm name if applicable. Press **[F9]**. This puts the merge code **{END FIELD}** at the end of the line and executes a hard return to the next line.

> **Marvin Pearce, Esq.**
> **Fenner & Pearce{END FIELD}**

b)  Type the address. At the end of the complete address, after the zip code, press **[F9]** again.

> **64 Honor Avenue, 14th Floor**
> **San Diego, California  99999{END FIELD}**

c)  Now, type the salutation.

> **Mr. Pearce**

At the end of the salutation line, press **[F9]**.

d)  To tell WordPerfect that you have finished this record, press **[Shift]+[F9]**, **2**. Your first record should look like the one below.

> **Marvin Pearce, Esq.**
> **Fenner & Pearce{END FIELD}**
> **64 Honor Avenue, 14th Floor**
> **San Diego, California  99999{END FIELD}**
> **Mr. Pearce{END FIELD}**
> **{END RECORD}**
> **==========================================**

A hard page break will be created at the end of the record. Following these same procedures, input the remaining three records under the first record. When you are finished, your secondary file should look like the one in Figure 1.25.

Marvin Pearce, Esq.
Fenner & Pearce{END FIELD}
64 Honor Avenue, 14th Floor
San Diego, California  99999{END FIELD}
Mr. Pearce{END FIELD}
{END RECORD}

James Franklin, Esq.{END FIELD}
22 Windship Lane, Suite 3
San Diego, California  99999{END FIELD}
Mr. Franklin{END FIELD}
{END RECORD}

John Simpson, Esq.
Sampson, Newberry & Simpson{END FIELD}
34 Rome Avenue, Suite B
La Jolla, California  99999{END FIELD}
Mr. Simpson{END FIELD}
{END RECORD}

Marsha Mendleson, Esq.
Mendleson, Teedlebaum & Mason{END FIELD}
6552 Main Street, Suite 2003
San Diego, California  99999{END FIELD}
Ms. Mendleson{END FIELD}
{END RECORD}

**Figure 1.25**  The Secondary File

e)  Save the secondary file, using the **[F7]** Save, in the same location as your primary file and give it the name **ADDRESS.MRG** to remind us that these are the addresses for our merge. If you are saving the file to your A: drive the response to "Save as" should be: **A:ADDRESS.MRG**

Respond **N** to the question of whether you wish to exit.

## 6. Merging the Primary and Secondary Files

Merging the addresses into our shell letter involves selecting the merge function, identifying the location and name of our primary file, and identifying the location and name of our secondary file. Follow the steps below from a blank screen.

a) Press **[Ctrl]+[F9]**. Select **1** for **Merge**.

b) When WordPerfect prompts for the **primary file name**, type the location and name of the primary file and press **[Enter]**. Example: **A:EXTEND.LTR**

c) When WordPerfect prompts for the **secondary file name**, type the location and name of the secondary file and press **[Enter]**. Example: **A:ADDRESS.MRG**

WordPerfect will then automatically merge the two documents. You should have a merged document with four letters as shown in Figure 1.26.

```
                    SMITH AND SMITH
                    Attorneys at Law
                  1234 Hampton Avenue
                La Jolla, California  99999
                     (619) 555-1212


                      April 1, 1993



Marvin Pearce, Esq.
Fenner & Pearce
64 Honor Avenue, 14th Floor
San Diego, California  99999


        Re:    Potter, et al. vs. Polluter Co.; Case No. 85549

Dear Mr. Pearce:

        Pursuant to a telephone conference of this date, Mr. Johnson of Pote & Tate, on behalf
of all plaintiffs in this action, has granted our client, Polluter Co., an extension until May 15,
1993, in which to answer or otherwise respond to the complaint on file in this matter.

                        Sincerely,


                        JAMES SMITH
                        SMITH AND SMITH
```

**Figure 1.26** The Merged Documents

SMITH AND SMITH
Attorneys at Law
1234 Hampton Avenue
La Jolla, California 99999
(619) 555-1212

April 1, 1993

James Franklin, Esq.
22 Windship Lane, Suite 3
San Diego, California 99999

Re:    Potter, et al. vs. Polluter Co.; Case No. 85549

Dear Mr. Franklin:

Pursuant to a telephone conference of this date, Mr. Johnson of Pote & Tate, on behalf of all plaintiffs in this action, has granted our client, Polluter Co., an extension until May 15, 1993, in which to answer or otherwise respond to the complaint on file in this matter.

Sincerely,

JAMES SMITH
SMITH AND SMITH

---

SMITH AND SMITH
Attorneys at Law
1234 Hampton Avenue
La Jolla, California 99999
(619) 555-1212

April 1, 1993

John Simpson, Esq.
Sampson, Newberry & Simpson
34 Rome Avenue, Suite B
La Jolla, California 99999

Re:    Potter, et al. vs. Polluter Co.; Case No. 85549

Dear Mr. Simpson:

Pursuant to a telephone conference of this date, Mr. Johnson of Pote & Tate, on behalf of all plaintiffs in this action, has granted our client, Polluter Co., an extension until May 15, 1993, in which to answer or otherwise respond to the complaint on file in this matter.

Sincerely,

JAMES SMITH
SMITH AND SMITH

**Figure 1.26** (continued)

**Figure 1.26**  (continued)

# G.    CREATING A PLEADING CAPTION

WordPerfect for DOS contains a Pleading Style and Pleading Macro (March 1992 releases of WordPerfect 5.1 and later) to create pleading paper (line numbers and border lines) on ordinary bond. If you will be printing on bond, you will want to set up your pleading to print pleading paper. If you are printing on pre-printed pleading bond, you can skip to the section on changing the bottom margin.

## 1.  Selecting the Pleading Style or Macro

The Pleading Style in WordPerfect is an option that numbers the lines on your paper from 1 to 28 lines and places a double vertical line on the left side next to the numbers. The problem with the Pleading Style is that it is set up with margins that you can only change if you are an experienced WordPerfect user. The Pleading Macro is a more sophisticated way to set up your pleading paper, and it allows you to create your own style and margins. Both methods are explained below.

Make sure you are at the very top of the first page of your document by pressing **[Home]**, **[Home]**, **[Home]**, **[Up Arrow]**, and follow part a or b depending on which method will set up your pleading.

a. *Pleading Style*

To choose the Pleading Style for your document, press **[Alt]+[F8]**, move the highlight bar down to **Pleading** and select **1** for **On**. Your document is now set up for pleading paper. You can see the pleading style code with Reveal Codes.

> *If you press [Alt]+[F8] and no styles are listed on the screen, it may be that the style library has not been set up on your computer. To do this, select: [Shift]+[F1], 6, 5. You will need to type in where your Style Files are located (usually where your WordPerfect files are located, e.g., C:\WP51). Then you will need to type in the Library filename: LIBRARY.STY. Exiting out of this menu with [F7], you will then find that your styles are now listed under [Alt]+[F8].*

b. *The Pleading Macro*

The Pleading Macro will allow you to create various pleading styles. The Pleading Macro is accessed by pressing **[Alt]+[F10]**, typing **PLEADING**, and pressing the **[Enter]** key. The screen shown in Figure 1.27 will appear.

```
Pleading Paper Style Macro                              (Press F3 for Help)

    1 - Name                      Pleading

    2 - Top Margin                1"

    3 - Bottom Margin             1"

    4 - Left Margin               1"

    5 - Right Margin              1"

    6 - Left Line (0,1,2)         2

    7 - Right Line (0,1)          0

    8 - Starting Number           1

    9 - Ending Number             28

    0 - Create Style


Selection: 0
```

**Figure 1.27** The Pleading Macro Screen

This macro will create a new pleading style called "Pleading." Since one with this name came with my WordPerfect program, I will name this style "Pleading1." Many pleadings require a 1.5" left margin, so I will make this change. I will also change the right margin to .5". The left line I will leave as a double line, and I will change the right line to a single line. My screen will now look like the one in Figure 1.28. Pressing the **[Enter]** key will save the new style under **[Alt]+[F8]**, and will place it into my document.

If you want to save the new style as part of the style library, in the Styles screen (**[Alt]+[F8]**) select **6** for Save and type the location and file name of the style library (e.g., C:\WP51\LIBRARY.STY).

```
Pleading Paper Style Macro                              (Press F3 for Help)

    1 - Name                          Pleading1

    2 - Top Margin                    1"

    3 - Bottom Margin                 1"

    4 - Left Margin                   1.5"

    5 - Right Margin                  0.5"

    6 - Left Line (0,1,2)             2

    7 - Right Line (0,1)              1

    8 - Starting Number               1

    9 - Ending Number                 28

    0 - Create Style


Selection: 0
```

**Figure 1.28**  Changing the Style Settings

## 2.  Changing the Bottom Margin

In order to accommodate page numbers at the bottom of each page, the bottom margin must be changed to .5". If we had made this change in the Pleading Macro, line 28 would have been placed .5" from the bottom. We want line 28 to remain 1" from the bottom and the page number to be placed .5" from the bottom. The Pleading Style contains a .883" bottom margin.

To change the bottom margin, make sure that your cursor is after the Pleading Style code in the document by using Reveal Codes. Select **[Shift]+[F8], 2, 5** and change the bottom margin to **.5"**. Press **[Enter]** and then press **[F7]**. Your document codes should look similar to Figure 1.29.

```
▲   {   ▲    ▲    ▲    ▲    ▲    ▲    ▲       ▲    Doc 2 Pg 1 Ln 1" Pos 1.5"
[Open Style:pleading1][T/B Mar:0.67",0.5"]    ▲     ▲    ▲    ▲    ▲    }    ▲
```

```
Press Reveal Codes to restore screen
```

**Figure 1.29**  The Pleading Style and Margin Codes

### 3.  Page Numbering

To number the pages of your pleading, begin the command with your cursor directly after the Margin code we created above. Select **[Shift]+[F8], 2, 6, 4, 6** and press **[F7]**. This will place the page number at the bottom center of your pleading.

### 4.  Attorney Address

Immediately following your Pleading Style, bottom margin, and page numbering selections, type the attorney's name, address, telephone number, and representation designation as shown below. Make sure that the attorney name is on the first line of the document. (In some states a Bar Number is also required).

**Attorney Name**
**Attorney at Law**
**Address**
**Telephone Number**

**Attorney for (Plaintiff, Defendant, etc.)**

## 5. Court Designation

Different jurisdictions will have different ways that they want their pleadings to be created. In many jurisdictions, the court designation should begin at line 8 on the pleading paper. This is line 3.33" if you are using WordPerfect's Pleading Style. If you created a pleading style using the Pleading macro, line 8 of the pleading paper is located at line 3.29". Press the **[Enter]** key until you reach the correct line. You may use View in the Print Menu (**[Shift]+[F7],6**) to check to see that the Court Designation begins on line 8.

The court designation should be centered, capitalized and double spaced. (Use the **[Enter]** key to insert a blank line. Do not change to double spacing.) For example:

**SUPERIOR COURT OF THE STATE OF CALIFORNIA**

**IN AND FOR THE COUNTY OF SAN DIEGO**

## 6. Caption

Double space down from the Court Designation to begin the caption.

Change the line justification from **Full** to **Left** so that the caption and pleading title are not spread to the right margins. To do this press **[Shift]+[F8], 1, 3, 1** and press **[F7]**.

Prepare 3 columns following these steps.

a) Press **[Alt]+[F7]**, select **1** for **Columns**, select **3** for **Define**.

b) At the Column Definition Screen, select **1** to change the column type, select **2** for **Parallel**.

c) Select **2** for **Number of Columns**, type **3** and press **[Enter]**.

d) Select **4** for **Margins** and select one of the following margin settings depending upon whether you used the Pleading Style or the Pleading Macro:

**WordPerfect Pleading Style**

**Column 1**   1"   4.5"

**Column 2**   4.5"   4.6"

**Column 3**   5"   7.5"

### <u>Pleading Macro Style with Margins L-1.5", R-.5"</u>

Column 1    1.5"    4.7"

Column 2    4.7"    4.8"

Column 3    5.3"    8.0"

Press **[Enter]** to exit the Column Definition Screen. Then, select **1** to turn the columns **On**.

In the first column, type the plaintiff and defendant names.

**JOHN SMITH and MARY SMITH,**

      **Plaintiffs,**

**vs.**

**ABCD CORPORATION, and DOES 1
through 100, Inclusive,**

      **Defendants.**

After typing the word ***Defendants***, press the **[Enter]** key to return to the left margin.

Using the underline character, create an underline from the left margin to the right margin of Column 1 (4.5" or 4.7").

Press **[Ctrl]+[Enter]** to move to the second column and insert ")" characters until they are even with the underline in the first column.

| | |
|---|---|
| **JOHN SMITH and MARY SMITH,** | ) |
| | ) |
|     **Plaintiffs,** | ) |
| | ) |
| **vs.** | ) |
| | ) |
| **ABCD CORPORATION, and DOES 1** | ) |
| **through 100, Inclusive,** | ) |
| | ) |
|     **Defendants.** | ) |
| _____ | ) |

When the second column is completed, press **[Ctrl]+[Enter]** to move to the third column and enter the case number and pleading name.

| | |
|---|---|
| **JOHN SMITH and MARY SMITH,** ) | **CASE NO. 567320** |
| ) | |
| **Plaintiffs,** ) | **TITLE OF PLEADING AND** |
| ) | **HEARING INFORMATION IF** |
| **vs.** ) | **NECESSARY** |
| ) | |
| **ABCD CORPORATION, and DOES 1** ) | |
| **through 100, Inclusive,** ) | |
| ) | |
| **Defendants.** ) | |
| ) | |

When the third column is completed, turn the columns off by pressing **[Alt]+[F7]**, **1** for **Columns** and **2** for **Off**. This will return you to the left margin.

Turn the full justification back on by pressing:

**[Shift]+[F8], 1, 3, 4, [F7]**

## 7. Text

The text of the pleading should follow the caption and should be double spaced. To make sure that the text will line up with the pleading line numbers on the printed document, your first line of text must begin on a line inch ending in .00, .33, or .67 for the WordPerfect Pleading Style. For the pleading style created with the Pleading Macro, you will need to type some text and View the document in the Print Menu to see if it is aligned (**[Shift]+[F7], 6**).

After positioning the cursor on a correct line, select double spacing with **[Shift]+[F8], 1, 6, 2, [Enter], [F7]**.

You may view your document before you send it to the printer by pressing **[Shift]+[F7], 6**. A sample pleading is shown in Figure 1.30.

```
 1 | JOE ATTORNEY
   | Attorney at Law
 2 | 101 Broad Street, Suite 200
   | San Diego, California  99999
 3 | (619) 555-1212
   |
 4 | Attorney for Defendant
   |
 5 |
   |
 6 |
   |
 7 |
   |
 8 |             SUPERIOR COURT OF THE STATE OF CALIFORNIA
   |
 9 |              IN AND FOR THE COUNTY OF SAN DIEGO
   |
10 | THE ABC CORPORATION, a          )     Case No. 100111
   | California Corporation,         )
11 |                                 )     ANSWER OF DEFENDANT JOE
   |                Plaintiff,       )     SMITH
12 |                                 )
   |          vs.                    )
13 |                                 )
   | JOE SMITH, and DOES 1 through   )
14 | 50,                             )
   |                                 )
15 |                Defendants.      )
   |_____)
16 |
   |       The text will begin at this point.  It will use the entire
17 |
   | page and be fully justified.
18 |
19 |
20 |
21 |
22 |
23 |
24 |
25 |
26 |
27 |
28 |
```

1

**Figure 1.30**  A Sample Pleading

# *Summary*

WordPerfect is a word processing software program that allows you to create and edit documents. WordPerfect features are accessed through the function keys or the pull-down menus. The pull-down menus may be accessed by pressing the right mouse button or **[Alt]+[=]**.

There are two typing modes within WordPerfect, Insert and Typeover. Insert inserts new text at the point of the cursor, pushing existing text to the right. Typeover types over the existing text. You may switch between Insert and Typeover by pressing the **[Insert]** key.

Deleting text can be accomplished with the **[Delete]** or **[Backspace]** key. Blocks of text may be deleted by first blocking the text, and then pressing the **[Delete]** key. A block of text is a group of characters or words that is marked by turning on the Block feature with **[Alt]+[F4]** or **[F12]**, and highlighting the text of the block. The marked block may be deleted, copied, moved, printed, bolded, underlined, centered, or acted upon in many other ways.

WordPerfect is equipped with spell check, thesaurus and search features. Other features allow you to create columns, footnotes, and macros. The wide range of features, WordPerfect's user support, and the ease in using the program itself make WordPerfect the leading choice for legal word processing.

# *Exercise*

Using the pleading caption instructions in Part G, Section 2, draft a complaint, using WordPerfect, with one cause of action (count) for breach of contract. You may make up the parties and the facts of the case.

Save the pleading onto a disk. Spell check and print the document.

# Chapter Index

*WordPerfect for DOS*

# CHAPTER 2

# WORDPERFECT® FOR WINDOWS

# Chapter Preface

WordPerfect is the word processing software used by the majority of law offices. Its popularity is due to its wide range of features and its user support. This chapter will acquaint you with WordPerfect for the Windows operating environment and some of its features. The exercises at the end of the chapter will instruct you in how to perform several law office-related word processing functions. The commands used in this chapter are based upon WordPerfect for Windows version 5.2. The commands for version 5.1 are identical or very similar to the commands for versions 5.2.

# Section One—The Basics

## A. ENTERING WORDPERFECT FOR WINDOWS

To enter WordPerfect for Windows, double click on the WordPerfect for Windows icon. Upon entering the program, you will see the WordPerfect for Windows screen shown in Figure 2.1.

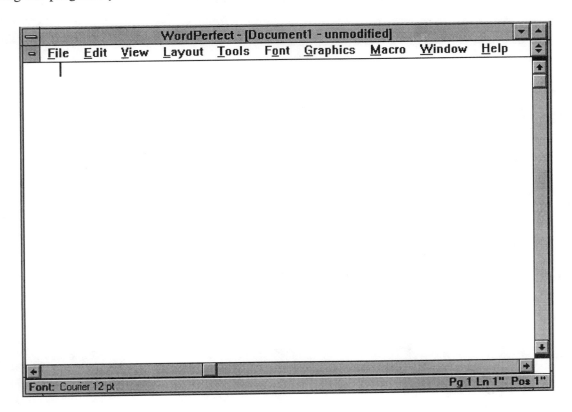

**Figure 2.1** The WordPerfect Windows Screen

## B. THE WORDPERFECT FOR WINDOWS ENVIRONMENT

### 1. Windows and Dialog Boxes

When you enter WordPerfect for Windows, you will see a typical Windows window with a Title Bar, Control Menu Box, and Scroll Bars. In Windows, a window will contain menu options, a dialog box will not.

The Title Bar is at the top of the screen and contains the title of the window or dialog box. The Title Bar of a WordPerfect document window will contain the name of the file you are editing.

The Control Menu Box is in the upper left-hand corner of a window or dialog box and appears as a small square button. When you click on this box, a menu opens that will allow you to close the window or dialog box. You may quickly close a window or dialog box by double-clicking on the Control Menu Box.

The Scroll Bars are seen at the right, and sometimes the bottom, of a window. By clicking on the up or down arrow of a Scroll Bar, you may scroll through a window or dialog box. Also on the Scroll Bar is a square button. By clicking on and dragging the button up or down the Scroll Bar, you may scroll very quickly to a new location.

---

*If you find that your document is extending beyond the right side of your monitor, click on and drag the box on the Scroll Bar at the bottom of the document window to the right. If the Scroll Bar is hidden, you may bring it onto the window by selecting **View, Horizontal Scroll**. You can also try **View, Zoom, To Page Width**.*

---

In the WordPerfect document window, you will also see the Pull-Down Menus, and possibly a Ruler or Button Bar, if they have been selected to be displayed in the **View** menu.

### 2. The Status Bar

At the bottom of the document window is the Status Bar. The Status Bar displays the current font (typeface) and the page number, line number, and position of the cursor.

### 3. Executing Commands

WordPerfect for Windows commands can be accessed with function keys, Pull-Down menu options, and the Button Bar. In this chapter, when a command is referenced, it will be referred to by its function key combination and Pull-Down Menu commands.

In this chapter, the function keys necessary to access a command will be referred to in brackets. For example, the function key for underlining will be referred to as [F8]. The key combination for centering will be referred to as [Shift]+[F6]. The plus symbol (+) indicates that the [Shift] key is to be held down while pressing [F6]. When a function key or key combination evokes further menu choices, the access letter for the options to be selected will follow the function keystrokes and be separated by commas. For example, to change from single spacing to double spacing you select the **Layout** function with **[Shift]+[F8]**. You then must select **Line**, and then **Spacing**. Then you must type a **2** to change to double spacing. This all would be referred to as:

### Keyboard: [Shift]+[F8], L, S, 2

Commands using Pull-Down menus will state the menu selections separated by commas. For example, switching to double spacing would be shown as:

### Mouse: Layout, Line, Spacing, 2

When a command is shown as separated by commas, such as [Home], [Up Arrow], you will press the **[Home]** key and release it, and then press the **[Up Arrow]** key. WordPerfect will remember that you have pressed the first key.

Button Bar commands will not be referenced in this workbook. The commands available on the Button Bar are limited, and many people remove the Button Bar from the screen display. The Button Bar can be displayed or hidden in the View menu.

---

*Sometimes when you select a command, an hourglass graphic will appear on the screen. This symbol means that WordPerfect is working. Wait until it disappears to continue.*

---

### 4. Selecting a Keyboard

WordPerfect for Windows allows you to select from a number of different keyboard types. The keyboard you select will determine the actions of the function keys and other key combinations. The default setting for the keyboard is Common User Access (CUA). This keyboard assigns functions to the keys that are similar to those used in other Windows programs. The WordPerfect 5.1 for DOS keyboard assigns functions to the keys that are similar to those in WordPerfect for DOS (the only difference being that F1 is the Help key and F3 is the Undelete key). This chapter will refer to the function keys based upon the WordPerfect 5.1 for DOS keyboard, because many WordPerfect for Windows users are converts from WordPerfect for DOS and will be familiar with this keyboard. (This keyboard selection is available in all WordPerfect for Windows versions dated after April 30, 1992. If you have an earlier version, you may contact WordPerfect Corporation and request the April 30, 1992, interim upgrade.)

You can check to see which keyboard your WordPerfect for Windows is set up for by selecting:

**Keyboard: [Shift]+[F1], K**
**Mouse: File, Preferences, Keyboard**

The filename of the keyboard selection will be displayed. To change the keyboard selection, press the **Select Button**, highlight the desired keyboard (**wpdos51.wwk**), and press the **Select Button**. Click on the **OK Button** to complete the selection.

## 5. Units of Measure

The line and position measurements within the Status Line are usually set in inches. The inch measurement is based upon the actual measurements from the borders of the paper in your printer. This allows you to measure where you would like text placed upon a page and then move the cursor to that measurement to begin typing.

The other units of measure available in WordPerfect for Windows are:

- **centimeters**
- **points**
- **1200ths of an inch**

The units of measure can be changed with:

**Keyboard: [Shift]+[F1], D**
**Mouse: File, Preferences, Display**

## 6. The Function Keys

The function keys are the keys at the top or left-hand side of the keyboard labeled F1 through F10 or F12. WordPerfect for Windows utilizes all of these function keys. The way the function keys operate depends on the keyboard selected by the user.

With the WordPerfect 5.1 for DOS keyboard, a function key can perform up to six different functions. A function key can perform one function when pressed by itself, and others when the

[Shift], [Alt], [Alt]+[Shift], [Ctrl], or [Ctrl]+[Shift] keys are held while pressing them. The [Alt], [Shift], and [Ctrl] keys do not perform any task when they are pressed alone.

It is important when you press a function key that you depress the key and immediately release it. Holding down a function key will cause it to repeat the function. The only keys that should be held down are the [Alt], [Shift], and [Ctrl] keys. When a function is accessed with [Alt]+[Shift] or [Ctrl]+[Shift] and the function key, both of these keys are held down while the function key is pressed and released.

Figure 2.2 displays the function keys and key combinations of the WordPerfect 5.1 for DOS keyboard.

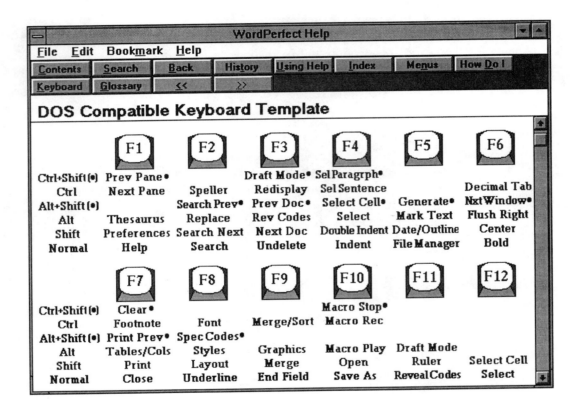

**Figure 2.2** The Function key functions using the WordPerfect for DOS keyboard selection

## 7. The Pull-Down Menus

The Pull-Down menus can be accessed with a mouse or the keyboard. These Menus offer an alternative way to perform the WordPerfect commands. A Pull-Down menu is accessed by pointing to the menu desired and pressing the left mouse button. Using the keyboard, a menu can be opened by pressing the **[Alt]** key and the underlined letter for the menu, such as **[Alt]+[F]** to open the **File Menu**. You may also access the menus by pressing and releasing the **[Alt]** key and then using the **[Arrow]** keys to move among the options. The options available under the **File** menu are shown in Figure 2.3. An arrow to the right of an option indicates the existence of a submenu for that option.

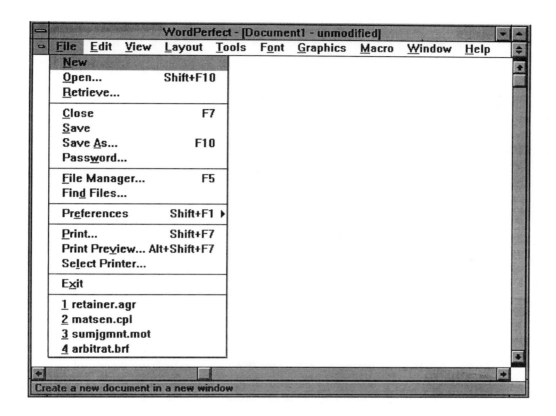

**Figure 2.3**  The Pull-Down Menus

To select an option from one of the Pull-Down menus, point to the option and press the left mouse button. A menu can be closed by clicking the left mouse button with the mouse pointer outside of the menu. To select an option using the keyboard, use the **[Arrow]** keys to highlight an option and press the **[Enter]** key or press the underlined letter of the option. A menu can be closed by pressing the **[Esc]** key. Pressing the **[Esc]** key again will leave the Menu Bar.

## 8. WordPerfect Help

WordPerfect has one of the best Help facilities available in a word processor. Help can be accessed with:

**Keyboard: [F1]**
**Mouse: Help, Contents**

The Help Contents screen is shown in Figure 2.4.

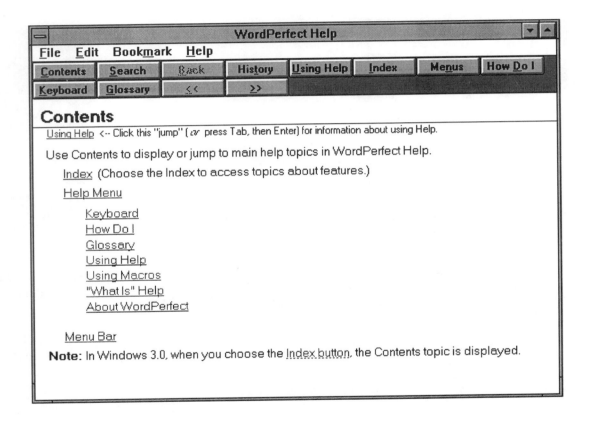

**Figure 2.4** The Help Contents

The Buttons at the top of the Help window perform the following functions.

| | |
|---|---|
| **Contents** | Takes you back to the Help Contents screen. |
| **Search** | Opens the Search dialog box that allows you to search for a topic by typing in a search word or selecting from an alphabetical list of terms. |
| **Back** | Moves backward through the topics you have previously selected. |
| **History** | Opens the Help History dialog box and lists the help topics you have traveled through in Help. Double clicking on a listed topic will take you to that Help window. |
| **Using Help** | Gives you basic assistance in using the Help facility. |
| **Index** | Provides an index to Help topics. |
| **Menus** | Explains the Pull-Down menus found on the Menu Bar. |
| **How Do I** | Explains the most commonly asked questions. |
| **Keyboard** | Provides help on using keyboards and key combinations. |
| **Glossary** | Provides an alphabetical list of terms. The definition for the term is found by clicking on the term. |
| **<<  >>** | The Browse Buttons. They will move you back and forth between topics that have been grouped together with the topic you are viewing. When a button appears shadowed, it is no longer available to select. |

The Help Index is a good tool for help on a specific topic. You may click upon any of the letters within the index to receive a list of topics for that letter. Items may be selected in any of the Help screens when the pointer arrow appears as a hand.  For example, pointing to and clicking on the letter T brings up the list of topics shown in Figure 2.5.

Any of the topics may be selected by clicking upon the topic. The topic Tab Set has been selected in Figure 2.6.

Some terms or topics in the Help screens will appear with a solid underline, and some will appear with a hashed underline. Clicking on a term or topic with a solid underline will take you to a window with an explanation of the term or topic. Clicking on a term or topic with a hashed

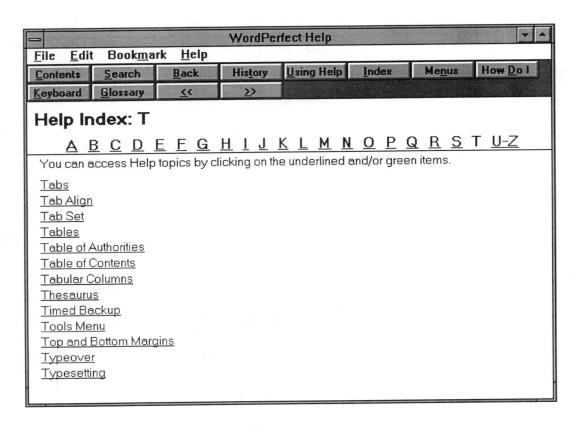

**Figure 2.5**  The Help Index topics listed under the letter T

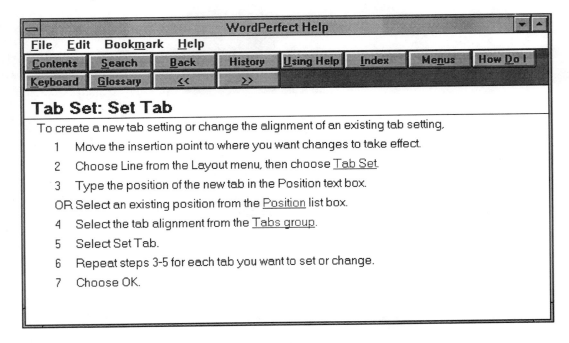

**Figure 2.6**  Help for Tab Set

underline will give you a boxed definition as shown in Figure 2.7. To remove the box, click the left mouse button.

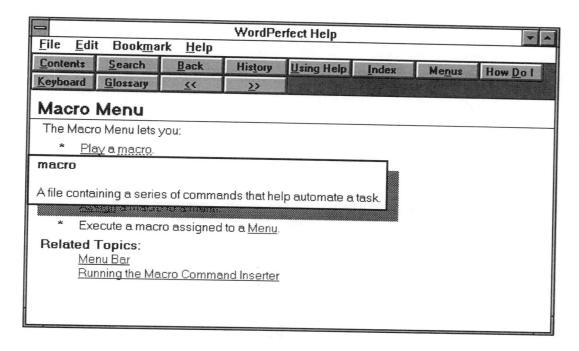

**Figure 2.7**  A Definition Box

To leave the Help facility, select **File, Exit**.

## 9.  Cursor Movement—The Insertion Point and Mouse Pointer

The cursor is the flashing bar that appears on the screen. In WordPerfect for Windows, the cursor is called the "insertion point." The insertion point indicates where characters will be entered as you type them on the keyboard. The "mouse pointer" appears as a large capital I when pointing within a document, an arrow when pointing at menu selections, and a hand and other graphic in other places in the program. The mouse pointer is moved by moving the mouse.

To move the insertion point you may use the **[Arrow]** keys on your keyboard, or the mouse pointer. The insertion point may be moved to any position in your document, except to a position where you have not yet entered any text.

In addition to using the [Arrow] keys and the mouse, the keystrokes below may be used to move the insertion point. Type a couple of lines into the document window and experiment with these keystrokes.

| | |
|---|---|
| [End] or [Home], [Rt. Arrow] | To move to the end of a line. |
| [Home], [Lft. Arrow] | To move to the beginning of a line. |
| [Ctrl], [Rt. or Lft. Arrow] | To move one word to the left or right. |
| [Home], [Up Arrow] | To move to the top of the screen. |
| [Home], [Down Arrow] | To move to the bottom of the screen. |
| [Home], [Home], [Up Arrow] | To move to the top of the document. |
| [Home], [Home], [Down Arrow] | To move to the bottom of the document. |
| [Home], [Home], [Home], [Up Arrow] | To move to the top of the document in front of all codes. |
| [Page Up] | To move up one page. |
| [Page Down] | To move down one page. |
| [Ctrl]+[Home] | The Go To key combination. To move to a specific page. You will be prompted for a page number in the Go To dialog box. |

## 10. Insert Versus Typeover

There are two typing modes in WordPerfect, Insert and Typeover. When you enter WordPerfect, the program is in the Insert mode.

In the Insert mode, text that already exists will be pushed to the right as you enter new text. In the Typeover mode, text that is typed will overwrite existing text and spaces.

To "toggle" between Insert and Typeover, press the **[Insert]** key. When you are in the Typeover mode, the word "Typeover" will appear on the Status Bar.

## 11. Switching Between Documents

WordPerfect for Windows allows you to open up to nine separate documents at one time into the program. You can identify the documents by the name in the Title Bar at the top of each window. The Window menu will display a list of the current open documents as shown in Figure 2.8. A check is placed next to the current document on the screen.

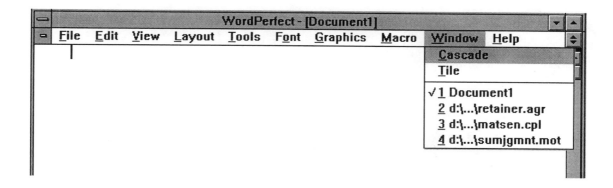

**Figure 2.8** The Window menu displays the documents currently open in WordPerfect

You may switch to another document while in the Window menu by clicking on the document name. You may also choose to have all of your document windows appear on the screen by selecting **Cascade** or **Tile**. You may then switch between documents by clicking in the window of the document you wish to edit. You may also switch between documents using the function keys:

**Keyboard:** [Alt]+[Shift]+[F3] (Previous Doc)
**Mouse:** [Shift]+[F3] (Next Doc)

Switching between documents becomes useful when you are drafting a new document from an old document. The two documents can both be open and text can be moved or copied from the old into the new document. Moving and copying text will be covered in a later section.

## C. EDITING A DOCUMENT

### 1. Deletions

When editing a document, deletions of a character or a group of characters will need to be made. WordPerfect offers a variety of ways to delete text. The two keys that perform deletions are [Delete] and [Backspace].

| KEYSTROKES | ACTION |
| --- | --- |
| [Delete] | Deletes the character immediately to the right of the insertion point. |
| [Backspace] | Deletes the character immediately to the left of the insertion point. |

To delete more than one character at a time, the **[Delete]** and **[Backspace]** keys may be held down, or the following key combinations may be used.

| KEYSTROKES | ACTION |
| --- | --- |
| [Ctrl]+[Backspace] | Deletes the word currently containing the insertion point, or the word to the immediate left of the insertion point. |
| [Ctrl]+[End] | Deletes all characters from the right of the insertion point to the end of the current line. |
| [Ctrl]+[Page Down] | Deletes all text to the bottom of the current page. |

## 2. Selecting (Blocking) Text

Selecting text (referred to as "blocking" in WordPerfect for DOS) is the marking of text prior to performing some action upon the text. Selecting text can be accomplished using the function keys, the Mouse, or the Pull-Down menus.

a. *Using the Function Keys*

To use the function keys to select text, place the insertion point at the beginning of the text to be selected and press:

**Keyboard:  [Alt]+[F4] or [F12]**

Either of these keys will cause the words "Select Mode" to appear in the Status Bar. The text to be selected is highlighted using any keys you normally would use to move the insertion point. You may also press keys on the keyboard to move the highlight to the next occurrence of that key within the document. For example, pressing a period will move the highlight to the end of the sentence. Pressing the **[Enter]** key will move to the end of a paragraph. When the desired text is highlighted, actions such as deleting, copying, moving, saving, and printing may be performed upon the selected text.

Select can be turned off by pressing the Select function key or clicking the left mouse button outside of the highlight.

*WordPerfect for Windows*

b.  *Using the Mouse*

An easy method to select text is to use the mouse. Click and hold the mouse pointer at the beginning of the text to be selected, and drag the highlighting until the desired text is selected. Clicking the left mouse button outside of the highlight will cancel the selection.

You may also use the mouse to select a word, sentence, or paragraph by clicking within the word, sentence, or paragraph and using multiple clicks of the left mouse button as shown below.

> **Select a Word:**       **Double click**
> **Select a Sentence:**   **Triple click**
> **Select a Paragraph:**  **Quadruple click**

c.  *Using the Pull-Down Menus*

You may use the Pull-Down menus to select a sentence or paragraph with the following menu selections.

> **Mouse:  Edit, Select, Sentence**
> **Mouse:  Edit, Select, Paragraph**

## 3.  Deleting Selected Text

If you wish to delete selected text, select the text and press the **[Delete]** key. WordPerfect will automatically delete the text.

## 4.  Retrieving Deleted Text (Undelete)

WordPerfect saves you if you have erroneously deleted text that you wanted to keep. The Undelete feature will restore up to three previous deletions of text from your document. Move the insertion point to where you want the text to return and select:

> **Keyboard:  [F3]**
> **Mouse:  Edit, Undelete**

The last deletion will appear at the insertion point, and the dialog box shown in Figure 2.9 will appear.

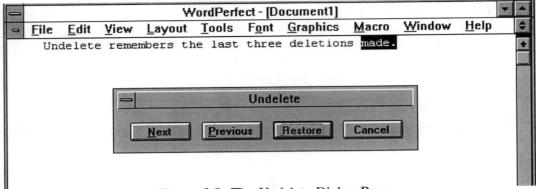

**Figure 2.9** The Undelete Dialog Box

You may restore the displayed deletion, or toggle through the previous two deletions, with the **Next** and **Previous Buttons**. Press the **Restore Button** to retrieve the deleted text.

## 5. Centering

Centering a word or phrase can be performed before or after the text has been entered.

a. *Before Typing Text*

Document titles and pleading headings often need to appear in the center of the printed page. To center the text that you will be typing, select either:

**Keyboard: [Shift]+[F6]**
**Mouse: Layout, Line, Center**

Either command places the insertion point in the middle of the document screen. Type the text to be centered, and then press the **[Enter]** key.

b. *After Typing Text*

If the text to be centered has been typed at the left margin, move the insertion point to the beginning of the text and select either:

**Keyboard: [Shift]+[F6]**
**Mouse: Layout, Line, Center**

Moving the insertion point to the next line of the document will complete the centering. You may need to press the **[End]** key and then **[Enter]** to move to the next line.

c. *Selecting Text and Centering*

Another way of centering more then one line is to type the lines at the left margin, Select the lines with the arrow keys or the mouse and press:

**Keyboard:  [Shift]+[F6]**
**Mouse:  Layout, Line, Center**

The Select is then turned off by pressing the Select function key or clicking the mouse outside of the highlight. Try typing the text below, and then Select and center the text.

**ARTICLES OF INCORPORATION**
**OF**
**XYZ CORPORATION**

## 6. Bold Type

Occasionally, you will want a word, or sequence of words, to stand out in **bold type**. For example, points and authorities can appear more authoritative when the heading for each point stands out from the rest of the text as shown below.

**B.**

**DEFENDANT HAS THE BURDEN OF**
**SHOWING THAT THE COUNTY IN WHICH**
**THE ACTION IS BROUGHT IS IMPROPER**

It is the Defendant's burden to offer sufficient facts to show to this court that San Diego County is not the proper court to hear the case. *Massae v. Superior Court* (1981) 118 Cal. App. 3d 527, 530, 173 Cal. Rptr. 527.

Bolding can be performed while the text is being entered or, later, by selecting the text and accessing the Bold command.

a. *Before Typing Text*

To type in bold print, use any of the options below prior to typing the text:

**[F6]**
**Font, Bold**
**[Ctrl]+[B]**

When you wish to stop bolding, select any of these options again or press **[Ctrl]+[N]** to return to normal type.

b.  *After Typing Text*

If you have already typed the text you desire to be bolded, Select the text, and use:

**[F6]**
**Font, Bold**
**[Ctrl]+[B]**

Then, turn the Select off by clicking the left mouse button outside of the highlight,  or press **[Alt]+[F4]** or **[F12]**.


## 7.  Underlining

**Underlining** is used to <u>emphasize</u> a character, word, or block of text. As you can see in the points and authorities example, case names are usually underlined (or italicized). Underlining is performed in the same manner as bolding.

a.  *Before Typing Text*

To underline a word or passage, select any of the options below prior to typing the text:

**[F8]**
**Font, Underline**
**[Ctrl]+[U]**

When you wish to stop the underlining, select any of these options again or press **[Ctrl]+[N]** to return to normal type.

b.  *After Typing Text*

If you have already typed the text you desire to be underlined, Select the text, and then use:

**[F8]**
**Font, Underline**
**[Ctrl]+[U]**

Then, turn the Select off by clicking the mouse button outside of the Select highlight, or press **[Alt]+[F4]** or **[F12]**.


## PRACTICE EXERCISE

Using some of the commands covered thus far, let's revise a portion of an old complaint, conforming it to the set of facts of a new case.

The preliminary paragraphs of the old complaint are shown below. These are the paragraphs that establish the venue for a complaint. Type these paragraphs into WordPerfect. (You do not need to start with a blank screen to perform this exercise.)

**Plaintiff JOHN PORT alleges:**

**1.   Plaintiff, JOHN PORT, is, and at all times herein mentioned was, a resident of San Diego County, California.**

**2.   Plaintiff is informed and believes, and on that basis alleges, that Defendant, MARK SAMPSON, is, and at all times herein mentioned was, an individual, residing in San Diego County, California, within the North County Judicial District.**

Now, using the WordPerfect commands we learned above, we will revise these opening paragraphs to conform to the new facts. Our client Joe Smith is suing ABCD Corporation, a California Corporation. The new plaintiff and defendant reside within the same jurisdiction as the old parties.

a)   Begin the revision by moving the insertion point to the beginning of the first mention of "JOHN PORT." Using the **[Delete]** key, delete the entire name. Then, type the name of our new plaintiff **JOE SMITH** in this space.

b)   Next, move to the "J" at the second "JOHN PORT" and use **[Ctrl]+[Backspace]** to remove both words. Then, type in **JOE SMITH,**.

c)   Now, move to paragraph 2 of the complaint and remove the name of the old defendant. Replace the name with: **ABCD CORPORATION,**.

d)   The capacity of this defendant needs to be changed to reflect its status as a corporation. Move the insertion point to the "a" at the beginning of "an individual" and turn on Select with **[Alt]+[F4]** or **[F12]** so that you may delete the selected text. Extend the highlight to the end of the sentence using the **[Right Arrow]** key, or by pressing the **[.]** key. Then, press the **[Delete]** key. You could also highlight the text with the mouse and press the **[Delete]** key.

e)   Now, type in the following: **a corporation organized pursuant to the laws of the State of California, having its principal office in San Diego County, California, within the North County Judicial District.**

Your new paragraphs should look as follows:

**Plaintiff JOE SMITH alleges:**

  **1.   Plaintiff, JOE SMITH, is, and at all times herein mentioned was, a resident of San Diego County, California.**


  **2.   Plaintiff is informed and believes, and on that basis alleges, that Defendant, ABCD CORPORATION, is, and at all times herein mentioned was, a corporation organized pursuant to the laws of the State of California, having its principal office in San Diego County, California, within the North County Judicial District.**


## D. SAVING AND RETRIEVING FILES


To save a document, you must store it on some type of secondary storage device (magnetic disk, tape, etc.) and give it a name. To retrieve a document, you must identify where the document is stored and its name. Remember, as you are typing a document in WordPerfect, the document is temporarily stored in RAM. If your computer is turned off, if a power outage occurs, or if the computer or network suddenly crashes, your RAM and your document are erased.

There are three methods for saving documents in WordPerfect for Windows:

- **Save As**
- **Save**
- **Close**

There are four methods for retrieving documents in WordPerfect for Windows:

- **Open**
- **Retrieve**
- **File Manager**
- **File Menu**


### 1.  Save As

Save As allows you to give a document a name, store it to a disk and then return for further editing. You will use **Save As** the first time you save your document, or if you desire to save your document under another name. The command can be accessed with either:

**Keyboard:  [F10]**
**Mouse:  File, Save As**

The Save As dialog box is shown in Figure 2.10.

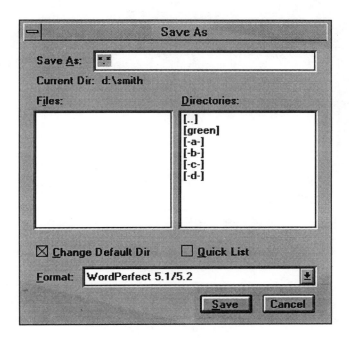

**Figure 2.10** The Save As Dialog Box

At this point, you may type the drive and directory where you would like the file to be stored, and give the file a name. You may also click on drives or directories listed under "Directories:" before giving the document a name. In WordPerfect the document name can be 1 to 8 characters with an optional period and 1 to 3 character extension. An example of an arbitration brief being stored in the **\Smith\Green** directory on the **D:** drive is shown in Figure 2.11.

If you would like to practice saving your current document, type in a drive letter and file name in the **Save As** dialog box. You may also type in a file name without a drive letter. If you do so, the document will be saved to the current directory listed under "Current Dir:".

After typing the document name, pressing the **[Enter]** key or clicking on the **Save Button** saves the document. The document path and name will then be displayed in the Title Bar at the top of the document window.

*If the document has previously been saved,* your file name will already be displayed when you access the Save As dialog box. Pressing the **[Enter]** key or clicking on the **Save Button** will replace the file stored on the disk with the one currently on your screen. You will be prompted to confirm the replacement.

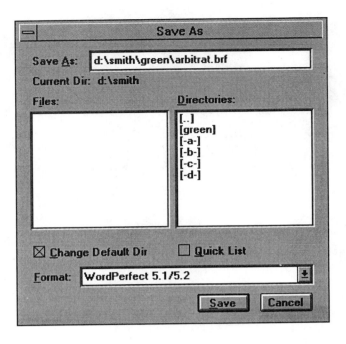

**Figure 2.11**  Entering a File Name

## 2.  Save

The Save option stores your document without opening any dialog box or otherwise prompting you. It is accessed with:

**Mouse:  File, Save**

I recommend that you use the Save option often while drafting a document. In the event of a loss of power to the computer, only text that has not yet been saved will be lost.

## 3.  Close

The Close option allows you to save and exit your document to a new WordPerfect screen or another open document. Close is accessed with:

**Keyboard:  [F7]**
**Mouse:  File, Close**

When you select this option, the document will be closed or the dialog box shown in Figure 2.12 will appear. Click on the appropriate button. The Close option closes a file but does not exit WordPerfect.

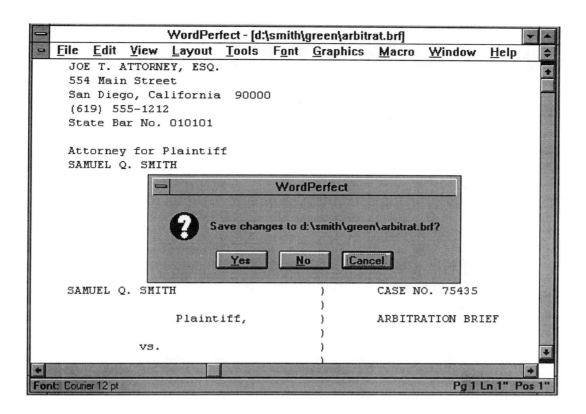

Figure 2.12  The Close Dialog Box

---

***Automatic Backup***

*WordPerfect for Windows offers a feature which automatically backs up your document.  This backup occurs according to a time which is set with:*

**[Shift]+[F1], Backup** *or*
**File, Preferences, Backup**

*The backup file is erased if you exit WordPerfect properly.  However, in the event that the computer is accidentally turned off, or loses power for any reason, the backup file is saved to the drive and directory indicated in Preferences, Location of Files.  This can be accessed with:*

**[Shift]+[F1], Location of Files** *or*
**File, Preferences, Location of Files**

*When you reenter WordPerfect after a failure the Timed Backup window will appear and you will be given the option to open, rename, or delete the file or files in the Backup.*

---

## 4. Open

The Open option allows you to open a file stored on a disk. This option is accessed with:

**Keyboard: [Shift]+[F10]**
**Mouse: File, Open**

The Open File dialog box shown in Figure 2.13 will appear when Open is selected.

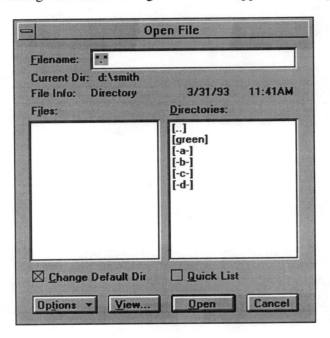

**Figure 2.13** The Open File Dialog Box

You may at this point:

**Type in a location and file name** of the file to retrieve.

**Click on a file name** listed at the left side of the dialog box.

**Double Click on a drive letter** to see the files at that location. Then, you can click on a file name listed at the left side of the dialog box.

**Click on a directory** to see the Files within the directory and then click on a file name.

After entering or selecting a file name, clicking on the Open Button will open the file onto your screen. You may look at a file before opening it by clicking on its name, and then clicking on the View Button.

## 5. Retrieve

The Retrieve option retrieves a file stored on a disk <u>into</u> the current document on the screen. This option is accessed with:

**Mouse: File, Retrieve**

The Retrieve File dialog box, very similar to the Open File dialog box, will appear when this option is selected. This box operates in the same manner as the Open File dialog box. After you have selected a file, click on the **Retrieve Button** to retrieve the file into your document. You may be prompted to confirm that you wish to insert the file into the current document.

## 6. File Manager

The File Manager option allows you to open or retrieve a file, but it also gives you the option to copy, move, delete, print, and perform many other actions upon files. The File Manager window shown in Figure 2.14 is accessed with:

**Keyboard: [F5]**
**Mouse: File, File Manager**

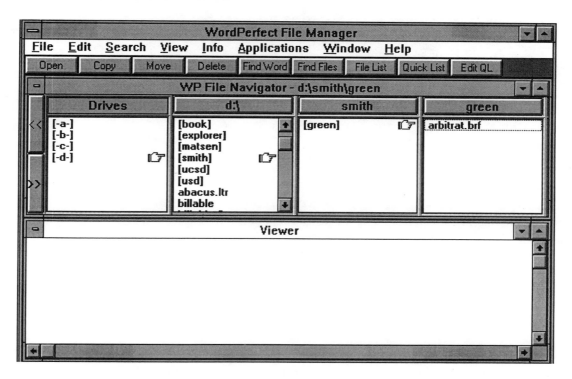

**Figure 2.14** The File Manager

You may act upon any file by clicking on the file name and clicking on one of the displayed buttons. You may also use the Pull-Down menus to perform windows commands. Some of the features of this window are explained below.

The WP File Navigator box displays the drives, directories, and files stored on the computer. Double clicking on a drive letter will display the directories and files for that drive. Double clicking on a directory name will display the files located in that directory.

The Viewer allows you to view a document without retrieving. Clicking on a file name in one of the WP File Navigator columns will bring that file into the Viewer.

The Find Files Button will open a dialog box to search for a specific file name.

The Find Word Button will open a dialog box to search for a word pattern in the listed files. This is helpful when you have a long list of files but cannot remember what you named the file you wish to act upon. If you remember a word pattern that exists in the document for which you are searching, such as "Merger Agreement," you may use Find Word to locate the document.

The **File Manager** is exited by selecting **File, Exit**.

### 7. File Menu

The File Menu is the last method for opening files. This menu keeps a list of the last four documents opened into WordPerfect (see Figure 2.15). You may open any one of these files by clicking on its file name.

## E. MOVING AND COPYING TEXT

When editing a document, it is often necessary to move or copy text from one position to another. Moving or Cutting text removes it from its old location and pastes it in a new location that you select. Copying leaves the original text in place and copies that text to a new location. To move or copy text, you may Select the text and use the **Cut** or **Copy** option in the **Edit** menu or you may drag it to a new location with the mouse.

### 1. Cutting and Pasting

Cutting and pasting involves moving text from one location to another. To perform this action, Select the text to be moved and cut it from the document with:

> **Keyboard:** [Shift]+[Delete] or [Ctrl]+[X]
> **Mouse:** Edit, Cut

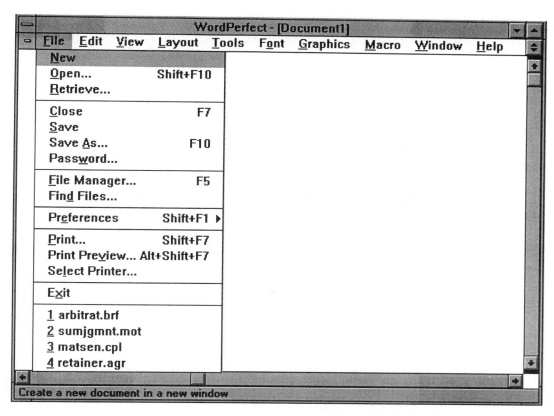

**Figure 2.15** The File Menu keeps a list of the last four files opened into WordPerfect. Any one of these may be retrieved by clicking on the file name.

This removes the text from the document and places it on the Windows Clipboard. Text placed onto the Clipboard may be copied into the current document, another open document, or any other Windows application program. This text will remain on the Clipboard until it is replaced with something else, or until you exit the Windows operating environment. Therefore, you may continue to work in your document, or do anything else in Windows, before you paste the text to the new location. You can also paste the text into more than one location, because the text remains on the Clipboard until it is replaced.

To paste the text into a new location, move the insertion point to the new location and select:

**Keyboard: [Shift]+[Insert] or [Ctrl]+[V]**
**Mouse: Edit, Paste**

*You may restore text you have cut out of the document by pasting it back in the same location, or by selecting **Edit, Undo**. Your insertion point is not required to be in the location from where the text was cut when using **Undo**.*

## 2. Copying and Pasting

Copying and pasting involves copying the text from one location, and pasting the same text in another location. To perform this action, select the text to be copied and select:

> **Keyboard:** [Ctrl]+[Insert] or [Ctrl]+[C]
> **Mouse:** Edit, Copy

Then, move the insertion point to the new location and select:

> **Keyboard:** [Shift]+[Insert] or [Ctrl]+[V]
> **Mouse:** Edit, Paste

## 3. Dragging Selected Text to Move or Copy

As an alternative to selecting text and then using the keyboard or menus to perform a move or copy, you may drag selected text to a new location. To do this select the text and either:

**Move** the text by clicking and holding the left mouse button within the highlight, drag the text to the new location, and release the mouse button.

**Copy** the text by clicking and holding the left mouse button within the highlight, hold down the **[Ctrl]** key, drag the text to the new location, and release the mouse button.

When you drag the selected text, a square icon will move with you as you position the text with the mouse pointer. Behind the square will be either another square with a hashed border, or a black square. These squares indicate whether you are moving the text or copying the text. The square with the hashed border is displayed when you are moving the text. The black square indicates that you are copying the text. You will also see an insertion point following the arrow and squares. This is where the text will actually be placed when you release the left mouse button.

## F. USING OTHER WINDOWS APPLICATIONS WHILE IN WORDPERFECT

While you are using WordPerfect for Windows, you may move to any other Windows applications program without exiting your document or the program. From WordPerfect, hold down the **[Alt]** key and press the **[Tab]** key. While you continue to hold down the **[Alt]** key, a dialog box for the Program Manager window will appear. If you release the **[Alt]** key at this time, you will move to the Program Manager window. Your WordPerfect window and document are still intact.

From the Program Manager window, you can enter any other program by double-clicking on its icon. For example, there may be a spreadsheet that you wish to look at in Lotus 1-2-3 for Windows. You may enter Lotus and retrieve the spreadsheet. You can edit the spreadsheet, and at any time move back to your WordPerfect window and document by holding down the **[Alt]** key and pressing the **[Tab]** key. As you press the **[Tab]** key, you will see dialog boxes for the Program Manager window and your WordPerfect window. Release the **[Alt]** key when the dialog box for your WordPerfect window is displayed. The spreadsheet window is still open, as is the Program Manager window. You may continue to use **[Alt]+[Tab]** to move between these windows when necessary.

## G. OTHER WORDPERFECT FEATURES

### 1. Margins and Line Spacing

Margins, line spacing, and a number of other page and document settings are altered in the Layout Menu. The Layout Menu can be accessed with the mouse or **[Shift]+[F8]**. Any change that you make in margins or line spacing will affect all text after the location of the code, so place your insertion point where you would like the change to begin before selecting the option.

a. *Margins*

Margins are set in the Margins dialog box shown in Figure 2.16. This box is accessed with:

**Keyboard: [Shift]+[F8], M**
**Mouse: Layout, Margins**

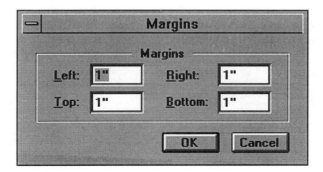

**Figure 2.16** The Margins Dialog Box

You can set your top, bottom, left and right margins in this dialog box. Click within the margin boxes you wish to change, and click on the **OK Button** to return to your document.

You may also set your margins using the Ruler (**View, Ruler**) shown in Figure 2.19. Simply use the mouse to drag the left or right margin arrows, shown above the numbers on the Ruler, to the desired new margins.

b. *Line Spacing*

Line spacing is altered with:

**Keyboard: [Shift]+[F8], L, S**
**Mouse: Layout, Line, Spacing**

With this selection, the Line Spacing dialog box, shown in Figure 2.17, will appear. Select the desired line spacing, and click on the **OK Button**.

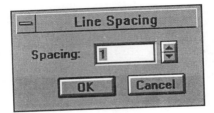

**Figure 2.17** The Line Spacing Dialog Box

c. *Selecting Text for Specific Margins or Line Spacing*

Another way to change the margins or line spacing of a specific block of text is to select the text with the mouse or **[Alt]+[F4]** or **[F12]**, and then access the **Margins** or **Line Spacing** dialog box to change the settings.

## 2. Setting Tabs

The [**Tab**] key and the [**F4**] key serve the functions of tab and indent, respectively. Indent can also be selected from the menu with **Layout, Paragraph.**

The spacing for tabbing and indenting are pre-set at every one-half inch. If you wish to change the tab set, you may do so in the **Tab Set** dialog box, or with the WordPerfect for Windows **Ruler**. The change in tabs will affect all text after the location of the code, so place your insertion point where you would like the change to begin before making the change.

a. *Tab Set*

The **Tab Set** dialog box, shown in Figure 2.18, is accessed with:

**Keyboard: [Shift]+[F8], L, T**
**Mouse: Layout, Line, Tab Set**

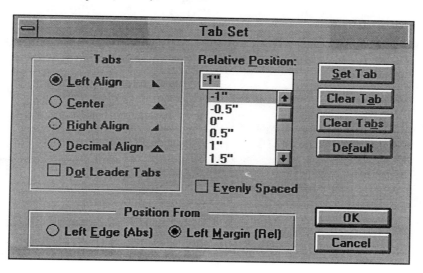

**Figure 2.18** The Tab Set Dialog Box

The current tab settings are listed in the **Relative Position** box. The Position From box indicates whether the tabs are measured from the Left Edge of the page or the Left Margin (the common selection).

**Delete unwanted tabs** by clicking on the tab setting in the **Relative Position** box and pressing the **Clear Tabs Button.**

**Delete all current tab settings** by pressing the **Clear Tabs Button.**

**Set new tabs** by typing a new position in the **Position** box and clicking on the **Set Tab Button**.

Leave the **Tab Set** dialog box by clicking on the **OK Button**.

b. *The Ruler*

The WordPerfect for Windows **Ruler** shown in Figure 2.19 is either displayed or hidden at the top of your document. If the Ruler is hidden, you may display it with **View, Ruler**.

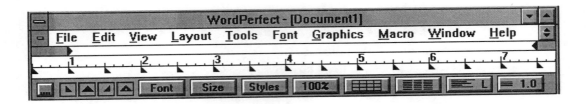

**Figure 2.19** The WordPerfect for Windows Ruler

On the Ruler, tabs are displayed as triangles.

**Delete unwanted tabs** by dragging them off the Ruler. Click on the tab triangle, hold down the left mouse button, and drag the icon off of the Ruler.

**Delete all current tab settings** by double-clicking on any tab icon to open the **Tab Set** dialog box and pressing the **Clear Tabs Button**. Click on the **OK Button** to leave the dialog box.

**To set new tabs** you may drag any tab icon to a new location, or drag one of the Tab Buttons at the bottom of the Ruler to a new location.

The default tab set of every one-half inch can be returned by double-clicking on a tab icon to access the **Tab Set** dialog box, clicking on the **Default Button**, and then clicking on the **OK Button**.

c. *Selecting Text for Specific Tab Settings*

Another way to change the tab settings of a specific block of text is to select the text and then access the **Tab Set** dialog box or change the settings on the **Ruler**. The changes will apply only to the selected text. All text before and after the selected text will remain with the previous tab settings.

## 3. Tabbing and Indenting

After you have set the tabs, you may tab with the **[Tab]** key, or indent with the **[F4]** key. The [Tab] key indents the first line of the text to a tab stop. After the first line, the text will word wrap back to the left margin similar to the text in this paragraph.

The **[F4]** Indent key, or **Layout, Paragraph, Indent,** indents the entire paragraph to the tab stop. The text will word wrap to the tab stop until the **[Enter]** key is pressed at the end of the paragraph.

The **[Shift]+[F4]** key combination, or **Layout, Paragraph, Double Indent,** indents both the right and left margins to a tab stop. The text will word wrap within the indent until the **[Enter]** key is pressed at the end of a paragraph.

The **[F4], [Shift]+[Tab]** key combination, or **Layout, Paragraph, Hanging Indent,** leaves the first line of the paragraph at the left margin. Subsequent text word wraps to the tab stop until the **[Enter]** key is pressed at the end of the paragraph.

The tab and indent features are used frequently when typing long quotations from code sections or case reporters. An example is shown below using the **[Tab]** key and **[Shift]+[F4]** or **Layout, Paragraph, Double Indent**.

**Rule 373 states in pertinent part:**

> **In ruling on the motion the court shall consider all matters relevant to a proper determination of the motion, including the court's file in the case and the affidavits and declarations and supporting data submitted by the parties and, where applicable, . . . the diligence of the parties in pursuing discovery or other pretrial proceedings, . . . the nature of any extensions of time or other delay attributable to either party, . . . whether the interests of justice are best served by dismissal or trial of the case; and any other fact or circumstance relevant to a fair determination of the issue.**

**The interests of justice would best be served by a trial on the merits in this action. Therefore, plaintiff herein should be allowed to proceed to trial.**

## 4. Reveal Codes

WordPerfect hides its formatting codes to allow you to work with a clean screen. To view the formatting codes, WordPerfect provides the Reveal Codes feature. Reveal Codes is accessed with:

**Keyboard: [Alt]+[F3]**
**Keyboard: [F11]**
**Mouse: View, Reveal Codes**

When accessed, Reveal Codes divides the screen, displaying the normal text at the top, and the same text with its codes at the bottom as shown in Figure 2.20. You may change the size of the Reveal Codes portion of the screen by dragging the bar separating the two portions of the screen up or down.

Revealing codes is useful when you wish to delete a **bold**, underline, tab or other code which has been inserted into a document. It is also useful when your document suddenly

begins to do something
that you did not intend
it to do.

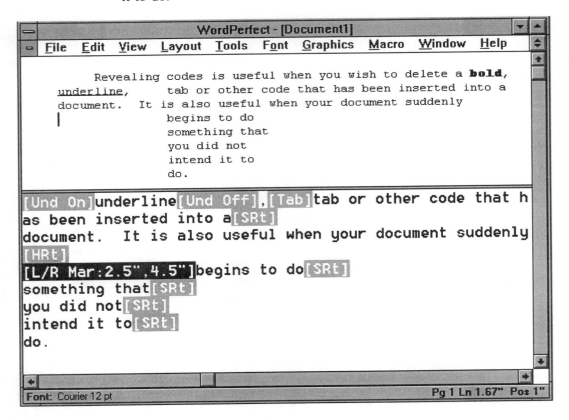

**Figure 2.20**  The hidden codes of a document revealed with Reveal Codes

The Reveal Codes feature displays the actual codes present within the text. A bolded word is preceded by the words **[Bold On]** and followed by **[Bold Off]**. This indicates where the bold begins and where it ends. An underlined word is indicated in the same manner with **[Und On]** and **[Und Off]** codes. Where the **[Enter]** key has been pressed is indicated by a hard return (**[Hrt]**). A word wrap is indicated by a soft return (**[Srt]**). Our margin problem begins with a margin code (**[L/R Mar:2.5",4.5"]**), which has inadvertently made its way into the text.

The [Arrow] keys, which are used to move the insertion point in the upper half of the screen, also move a highlight bar in the lower half of the screen. To remove any of the codes, move the highlight bar to the code with the [Arrow] keys or the mouse pointer and press the **[Delete]** key. With a bold or underline, deleting either the uppercase or lowercase code will remove both codes.

## 5. Page Breaks

When you reach the bottom of a page in your document, a single line appears across the screen. This single line shown in Figure 2.21 is called a "soft page break." WordPerfect automatically ends a page with a soft page break, according to the preset page length of your document.

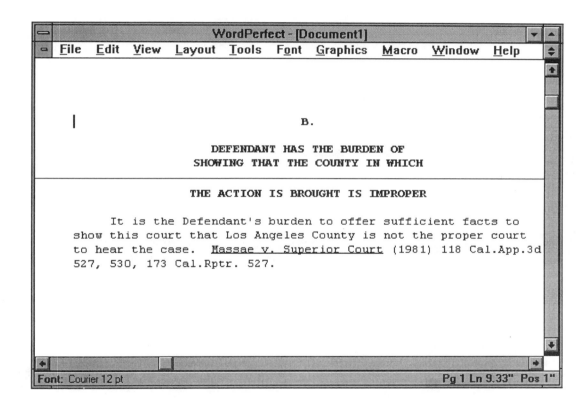

**Figure 2.21** A single line appears where WordPerfect automatically ends a page

When you wish to end a page in a place other than where the soft page break occurs, you can create a "hard page break." In the example shown in Figure 2.21, a hard page break could be placed before the "B." so that this point will begin on the next page. To create a hard page break, place the insertion point where you want the new page to begin and press: **[Ctrl]+[Enter]**.

A double line indicates the location of a hard page break as shown in Figure 2.22.

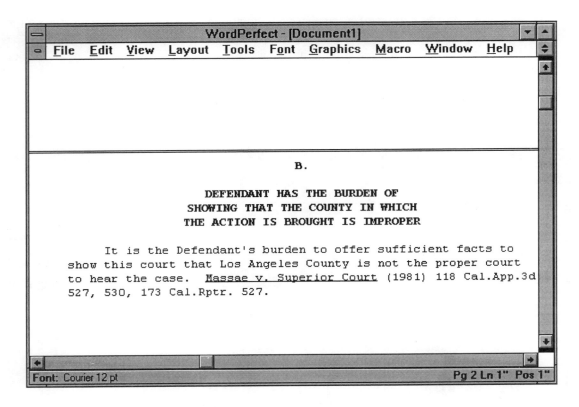

**Figure 2.22** A hard page break is created with [Ctrl]+[Enter]

A hard page break is indicated by a **[HPg]** code in Reveal Codes. A soft page break is indicated by a **[SPg]** code.

## 6. Text Appearances and Sizes

Different appearances and sizes for your text can add emphasis, significance, and originality.

a. *Appearance*

In addition to bolding and underlining, text may be <u>double underlined</u>, *italicized*, redlined, or ~~stricken out~~, with selections in the **Font Menu**. Italics may also be selected with **[Ctrl]+[I]**.

The text appearances listed above, and other appearances (outline, shadow, and SMALL CAPS) may be selected within the **Font** dialog box shown in Figure 2.23 and accessed with:

**Keyboard: [Ctrl]+[F8]**
**Mouse: Font, Font**

The desired appearance may be selected by clicking on its name in the **Appearance** box and clicking on the **OK Button**. To turn off the appearance, after you have typed the text, simply press the **[Right Arrow]** key to move outside of the code, press **[Ctrl]+[N]**, or access the **Font** dialog box again and click on the appearance to turn it off.

b. *Size*

Text may also be printed in different sizes. The sizes, <sup>superscript</sup>, <sub>subscript</sub>, fine, small, large, very large, and extra large, are selected in the **Font Menu**. Subscript and superscript are found directly on the menu. The other options are found in the **Size** submenu by selecting:

**Keyboard: [Ctrl]+[S]**
**Mouse: Font, Size**

As with the appearances, sizes may also be selected in the **Size** box of the **Font** dialog box accessed with:

**Keyboard: [Ctrl]+[F8]**
**Mouse: Font, Font**

To turn off the size, press the **[Right Arrow]** key to move outside of the code, press **[Ctrl]+[N]**, or access the **Font** dialog box again and click on the size to turn it off.

If text has already been typed, it can be selected prior to accessing the **Font menu** or **Font** dialog box to select an appearance or size.

## 7. Changing Fonts

A font is the typeface of a document. The initial font of your document is displayed in the Status Bar. You may change the initial font by accessing the **Initial Font** dialog box with:

**Keyboard:  [Shift]+[F8], D, F**
**Mouse:  Layout, Document, Initial Font**

Click on the font you want for your document. If it is a scalable font, you will need to select a point size in the **Point Size** box. Click on the **OK Button** to complete the selection.

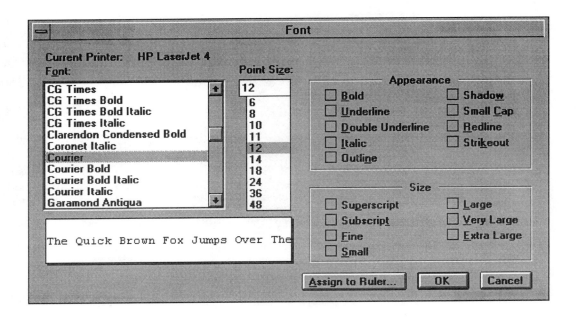

**Figure 2.23**  The Font Dialog Box

Subsequent font changes in your document may be made in the **Font** dialog box shown in Figure 2.23. Place your insertion point where you would like the new font to begin and access the **Font** dialog box with:

**Keyboard:  [Ctrl]+[F8]**
**Mouse:  Font, Font**

You may change the font by clicking on the font you want. If the font is scalable, you will need to select a point size in the **Point Size** box. Click on the **OK Button** to complete the selection.

A code indicating where a new font begins can be seen in **Reveal Codes**.

## 8.  The Date Feature

WordPerfect provides a way to incorporate the date from your computer's internal clock into your documents. The Date feature allows you to place the current date or a date code within a document. The Date feature is accessed with:

**Keyboard:  [Shift]+[F5], D**
**Mouse:  Tools, Date**

Selecting **Text** inserts the current date; selecting **Code** inserts a date code. Both options place the current date within a document. However, the date code will place the current date into the document each time the document is retrieved into WordPerfect. The date code option is used primarily with form documents and form letters.

## 9.  Spell Checking

Checking the spelling within a document is one of the great features of a word processor. The spell checking feature will read each word within a document and compare each word to words contained within its dictionary. When it finds a word that does not match, the spell checker will stop and give you alternative spellings and/or allow you to edit your spelling.

WordPerfect's Spell Check feature is accessed with:

**Keyboard:  [Ctrl]+[F2]**
**Mouse:  Tools, Speller**

> *I recommend that you save your document with **File, Save** (or **Save As**) prior to spell checking your document. The Spell Check feature has been known to freeze computers, requiring that the computer be restarted, thus erasing RAM.*

When you access the Spell Check feature, the Speller dialog box appears as shown in Figure 2.24.

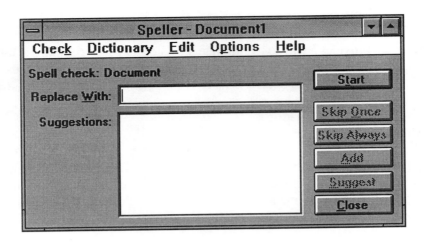

**Figure 2.24** The Speller Dialog Box

In the **Speller** dialog box, you can begin the Spell Check from the beginning of the document forward by clicking on the **Start Button**. If you wish to check a word, check forward in the document from the insertion point, check backward in the document from the insertion point, check the current page, or check to the end of the current page, you may select one of these options from the **Check** menu.

When you click on the **Start Button** to begin the Spell Check, WordPerfect will stop at words that it does not recognize and offer alternatives as shown in Figure 2.25. The most likely replacement is displayed in the Replace With box. Other possibilities are listed in the Suggestions box. You may place a word from the **Suggestions** box into the **Replace With** box by clicking on the word. To complete the replacement, click on the **Replace Button**.

If the word is spelled correctly but not recognized by the dictionary, you can:

- **Add** the word to the dictionary
- **Skip** the word **Once**
- **Skip** the word **Always**

If a proper spelling is not given for a misspelled word, you may type the correct spelling in the **Replace With** box and press the **Replace Button**. You can also click the mouse back within your document, correct the word, and then click on the **Resume Button** (changes from the **Start Button**) within the Speller dialog box.

When the Spell Check is completed, you will be prompted to close the Speller. Click on the **Yes Button** to return to your document.

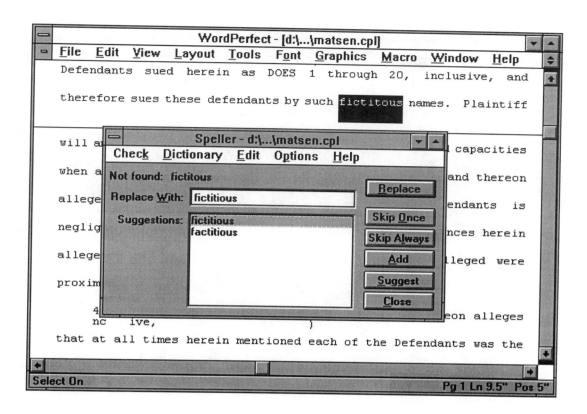

**Figure 2.25** The Spell Check suggests alternatives for the misspelled word

## 10. The Thesaurus

WordPerfect contains a thesaurus to assist you in drafting your documents. A thesaurus supplies synonyms for a variety of words. To use the Thesaurus feature, place the insertion point within a word and select:

**Keyboard:** [Alt]+[F1]
**Mouse:** Tools, Thesaurus

The Thesaurus for the word *press* is shown in Figure 2.26.

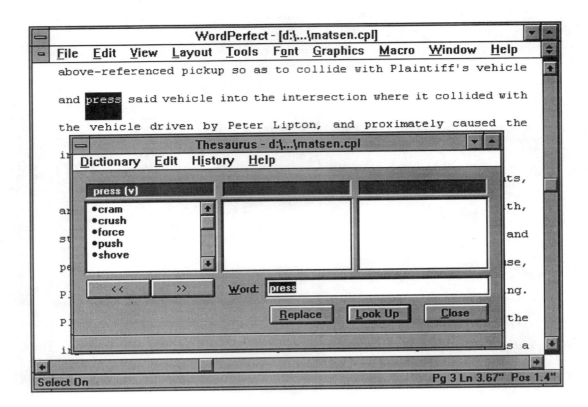

**Figure 2.26** WordPerfect's Thesaurus for the word *press*

Further synonyms may be seen for words with a filled dot next to them. To see further synonyms for those words, double-click on the desired word. For example, double-clicking on the word *push* displays its synonyms in the second column as shown in Figure 2.27.

You may select any one of the words by clicking on the word and clicking on the **Replace Button**. The insertion point is left at the end of the word to enable you to add any necessary ending.

## 11. Searching

WordPerfect contains a Search feature that can search for words, characters, or codes within your document. To begin a search, select:

**Keyboard:  [F2]**
**Mouse:  Edit, Search**

The Search dialog box, shown in Figure 2.28, will then appear.

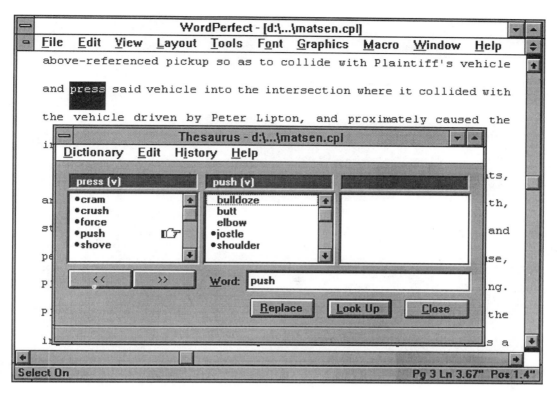

**Figure 2.27** Synonyms for the word *push*

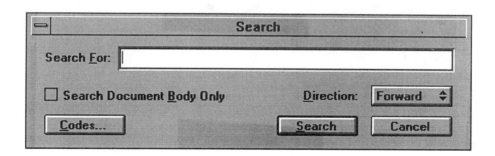

**Figure 2.28** The Search Dialog Box

Clicking on the **Direction** box will allow you to change from the default forward search to a backward search. The search will begin from the position of the insertion point. Type what you wish to search for in the **Search For** box, and click on the **Search Button**.

Clicking on the **Codes Button** opens the **Codes** dialog box, shown in Figure 2.29, and allows you to search for WordPerfect codes within the document. Clicking on a code and clicking on the **Insert Button** places the code in the **Search For** box.

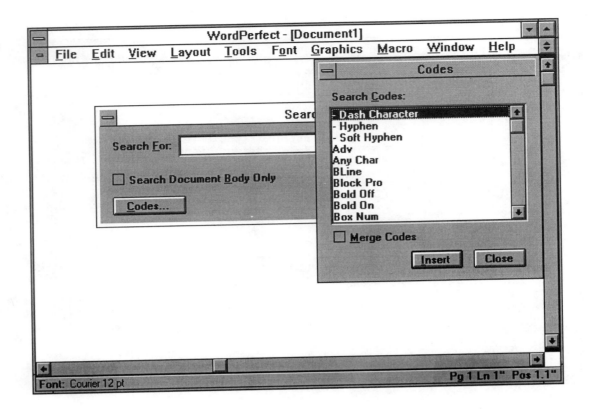

**Figure 2.29** The Codes Button will open the Codes dialog box to allow you to search for a WordPerfect code within the document.

## 12. Search and Replace

Search and Replace is very similar to Search. You use Search and Replace when you wish to replace a word with a different word throughout your document. For example, you have typed a 25-page legal memorandum and find that you have spelled the plaintiff's name, "Kerrigan," as "Carrigan" throughout the document. The Search and Replace feature can fix this error very quickly. You access the feature with:

**Keyboard:** [Alt]+[F2]
**Mouse:** Edit, Replace

The **Search and Replace** dialog box, shown in Figure 2.30, contains boxes for the search and replace words. The word *Kerrigan* would be entered in the **Search For** box. The word *Carrigan* would be entered in the **Replace With** box.

You may choose the direction in which to search, from the position of the insertion point, by clicking in the **Direction** box. The **Codes Button** will allow you to enter WordPerfect codes into the **Search For** and **Replace With** boxes. The **Replace All Button** will conduct the search and replace without pausing. The **Replace Button** will stop at each instance of the search terms and wait for you to either replace by clicking on the **Replace Button**, or move on to the next instance by clicking on the **Search Next Button**.

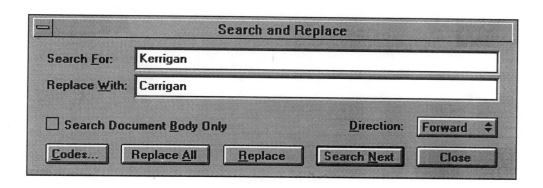

**Figure 2.30** The Search and Replace Dialog Box

## H. PRINTING

To receive a hard copy of a document, you must send it to a printer. Save your document prior to printing as a safety measure.

The **Print** dialog box, shown in Figure 2.31, is accessed with:

**Keyboard: [Shift]+[F7]**
**Mouse: File, Print**

You may select any one of the following within the **Options** box:

- **The Full Document**
- **The Current Page**
- **Multiple Pages (5-10 or 1,3,5-10)**
- **A Document on Disk**
- **Selected Text (if text has been selected prior to accessing the dialog box)**

Other print options are provided in the **Copies** box and the **Document Settings** box.

To print, click on the **Print Button**.

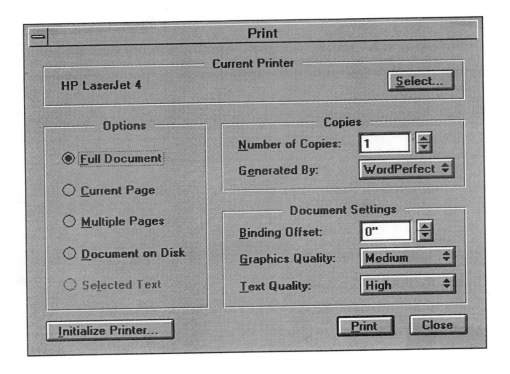

**Figure 2.31** The Print Dialog Box

To view your document prior to sending it to the printer, you may select:

> **Keyboard:** [Alt]+[Shift]+[F7]
> **Mouse:** File, Print Preview

Your document will be shown as it will appear when printed. You may increase the size of the view by clicking on the **100%** or **200% Buttons** in the **Print Preview** window, or you may **Zoom In** or **Zoom Out** of text. To return to your document, click on the **Close Button**.

To print the document currently on the screen without using the dialog box, press **[Ctrl]+[P]**.

## I. EXITING WORDPERFECT FOR WINDOWS

Exiting WordPerfect for Windows is accomplished by selecting:

> **File, Exit**

If any documents are currently open, you will be asked if you would like to save them. It is a good idea to Close all of your documents before you exit.

# Section Two—Advanced WordPerfect Features

## A. BULLETS AND SPECIAL CHARACTERS

There are many special characters, not available on the keyboard, that can be accessed from WordPerfect using:

**Keyboard: [Ctrl]+[W]**
**Mouse: Font, WP Characters**

Either method will access the **WordPerfect Characters** dialog box shown in Figure 2.32. WordPerfect has a number of different character sets. You may change character sets by clicking and holding on the button in the **Set** box, highlighting the desired set, and releasing the mouse button.

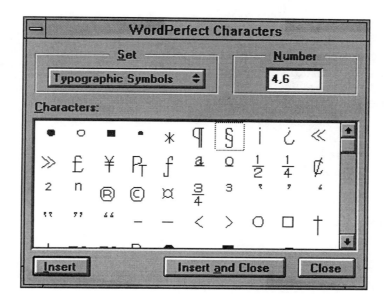

**Figure 2.32** The WordPerfect Characters Dialog Box

The **Typographic Symbols** character set will be the one most often used in legal documents. It contains bullets, the section symbol, the registered trademark and copyright symbols, and many other characters you may find useful. You may select any one of the symbols by clicking on it and either pressing:

- The **Insert Button** to place it into the document and remain in the dialog box.
- The **Insert and Close Button** to place it into the document and close the dialog box.

# B. MACROS

A Macro allows you to program a single keystroke combination to record several keystrokes. For example, you will be switching from single-spaced type to double-spaced type quite frequently when drafting legal documents. The WordPerfect keystrokes necessary to switch from single spacing to double spacing are:

**Keyboard:** [Shift]+[F8], L, S, 2, [Enter]
**Mouse:** Layout, Line, Spacing, 2, OK

You can create a macro which, when you play it, will perform all of these keystrokes for you.

## 1. Creating a Double-Spacing Macro

When you create a macro, you may identify it by holding down the **[Ctrl]** and **[Shift]** keys and pressing a letter of the alphabet (**[Ctrl]+[Shift]+[Letter]**), or by giving it a name. If you use the [Ctrl]+[Shift] key combination, the macro will be played by pressing the **[Ctrl]** and **[Shift]** keys and pressing the letter of the macro. If you give the macro a name, you will play the macro by selecting **Play** from the **Macro** menu. The **Play Macro** dialog box will prompt for the name of the macro. Our first macro example will use the [Ctrl]+[Shift]+[Letter] combination to create a double-spacing macro.

Creating a macro in WordPerfect for Windows involves the following steps:

a) Press **[Ctrl]+[F10]** or select **Macro, Record**. The **Record Macro** dialog box shown in Figure 2.33 will appear.

b) With the cursor flashing in the **Filename** box, hold down the **[Ctrl]** and **[Shift]** keys and press a letter on the keyboard. For this macro use the letter **D** (**[Ctrl]+[Shift]+[D]**). The file name **ctrlsftd.wcm** will appear in the **Filename** box.

> *If the name already exists, you will be prompted to either replace the stored macro file with your macro, or enter another name.*

c) Click in the **Descriptive Name** box and enter a brief description of the macro for reference purposes. A longer description, if needed, may be entered in the **Abstract** box.

d) Click on the **Record Button** to record the keystrokes of the macro. You will be returned to your document and the message **Recording Macro** will appear in the Status Bar. The mouse pointer will appear as a slashed circle.

e) Input the keystrokes you wish to use. Every key that you press at this point will be recorded in the macro. As we press the keys for our macro, you will see that we move through the WordPerfect menu screens just as though we were working without creating a macro. Using the mouse, open the **Layout** menu, select **Line**, select **Spacing**, type a **2**, and click on the **OK** Button. We are finished with the keystrokes for our macro.

f) Press **[Ctrl]+[Shift]+[F10]** or select **Macro, Stop** to save the macro.

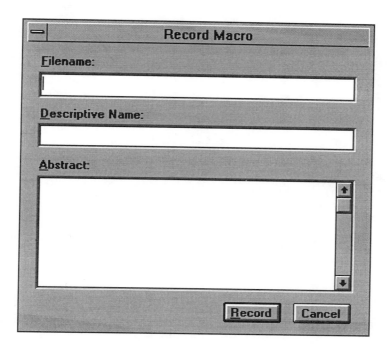

**Figure 2.33** The Record Macro Dialog Box

The double-space macro is now complete. If you type a few lines in your document, you will see that in creating the macro we changed to double spacing. To return to single spacing so we can try our macro, select **Layout, Line, Spacing, 1, OK**. Type a few lines to see that the document is single spacing, and press **[Enter]** to return to the left margin. Then, press **[Ctrl]+[Shift]+[D]** to change to double spacing and type a few lines to see that the macro has worked. You will probably want to create another macro to quickly change to single spacing and call it **[Ctrl]+[Shift]+[S]**.

## 2. Creating a Macro to Store Boilerplate Text

The next macro that we will create will be one for boilerplate text that will be included in all of our firm's complaints. Our firm uses two standard paragraphs in every complaint to identify the fictitious DOE defendants. Rather than typing this text every time a new complaint is created, we would like to be able to have a macro insert this text for us. We will give this macro a name, and then add it to the **Macro** menu so that it will be easily accessible. Follow the instructions below to create the DOE Paragraphs macro.

a) Press **[Ctrl]+[F10]** or select **Macro, Record**. The **Record Macro** dialog box will appear.

b) Type a file name for the macro. The name may be 1 to 8 characters. Call this macro: DOE.

c) Click in the **Descriptive Name** box and enter a brief description of the macro for reference purposes. Type: **DOE paragraphs for complaints**. A longer description may be entered in the **Abstract** box if you wish.

d) Click on the **Record Button** to record the keystrokes of the macro. You will be returned to your document and the message **Recording Macro** will appear in the Status Bar. The mouse pointer will appear as a slashed circle.

e) Input the keystrokes you wish to use. Every key that you press at this point will be recorded in the macro. Type the following two paragraphs into your document.

**Plaintiff is ignorant of the true names and capacities of defendants sued herein as DOES 1 through __, inclusive, and therefore sues these defendants by such fictitious names. Plaintiff will amend this complaint to allege their true names and capacities when ascertained. Plaintiff is informed and believes and thereon alleges that each of the fictitiously named defendants is negligently responsible in some manner for the occurrences herein alleged, and that Plaintiff's injuries as herein alleged were proximately caused by that negligence.**

**Plaintiff is informed and believes and thereon alleges that at all times herein mentioned each of the defendants was the agent and employee of the remaining defendants, and in doing the things hereinafter alleged, was acting within the course and scope of such agency and employment.**

f) Press **[Ctrl]+[Shift]+[F10]** or select **Macro, Stop** to save the macro.

> ***Pausing the Macro Recording:*** *You may pause in the recording of your macro, to experiment with a function or perform some other action, by selecting **Macro, Pause**. When you are ready to resume the macro recording, select **Macro, Pause** again. This pause is not to be confused with the pause command, which can be used when creating a macro.*

The DOE macro is now complete. To play the macro, press **[Alt]+[F10]** or select **Macro, Play**. The **Play Macro** dialog box, shown in Figure 2.34, will appear.

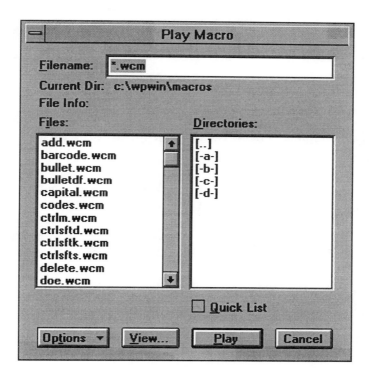

**Figure 2.34** The Play Macro Dialog Box

You may select a macro by clicking on its name or typing the macro name in the **Filename** box. Type the name **DOE** in the **Filename** box, and click on the **Play Button**. You may also double-click on a macro name to cause it to play. The first time you play a macro, WordPerfect will take a few seconds to compile it. When you use the macro thereafter, it will operate much faster.

There are some macros that WordPerfect includes with its program files, such as the Memo.wcm macro that prepares a memorandum for you. These are also accessed with **Macro, Play** and can be selected by clicking on their name and clicking on the **Play** button.

### 3. Assigning a Macro to the Macro Menu

To allow you to quickly access a named macro, WordPerfect for Windows lets you assign a macro to the Macro menu or the Button Bar. Assigning a macro to the Macro menu is explained below. To assign a macro to the Button Bar see your WordPerfect for Windows Manual.

You may assign nine of your most frequently used macros to the **Macro** menu. Macros such as the DOE macro that we just created, and a macro to create the columns for a pleading caption would be good macros to place in this menu. When you wish to play any one of these macros, you will simply select the **Macro** menu and then click on the macro name.

To assign a macro to the **Macro** menu, follow the steps below.

a) Open the **Assign Macro to Menu** dialog box, shown in Figure 2.35, by selecting **Macro, Assign to Menu**. The macros currently assigned to the menu will be listed. (There may not be any.)

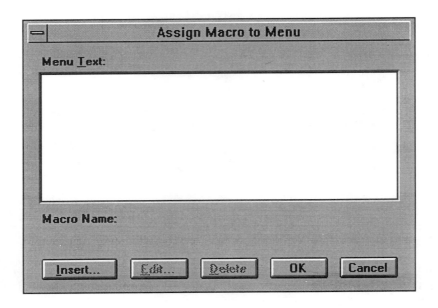

**Figure 2.35** The Assign Macro to Menu Dialog Box

b) To add our macro, click on the **Insert Button**. This will open the **Insert Macro Menu Item** dialog box shown in Figure 2.36.

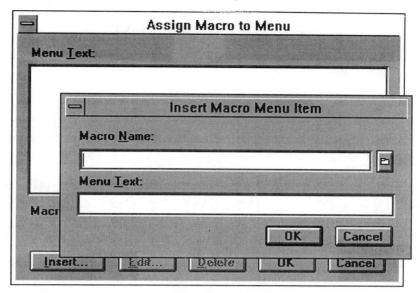

**Figure 2.36** The Insert Macro Menu Item Dialog Box

c) In the **Insert Macro Menu Item** dialog box, type the macro name in the **Macro Name** box. To assign our DOE macro, type **DOE**. If you do not specify an extension, WordPerfect for Windows will automatically assume a .WCM extension. If you cannot remember the macro name, click on the button to the right of the **Macro Name** box. A list of the macro files will be displayed. Clicking on one of these file names will place it into the **Macro Name** box.

d) Click in the **Menu Text** box and type the name that you want listed in the **Macro** menu to represent this macro. The macro file name will be automatically displayed. For a more descriptive title, type **DOE Paragraphs** in this box. Click on the **OK Button** to return to the **Assign Macro to Menu** dialog box. Click on the **OK Button** in this box to return to your document.

The macro has now been added to the **Macro** menu. Open the **Macro** menu to see your listed macro. Clicking on the macro name will play the macro.

## 4. Editing a Macro

Macros are edited in the same manner as ordinary WordPerfect documents. Simply open the macro document with **File, Open** and make any necessary changes. You will find the macros in the **Macros** subdirectory of the **wpwin** directory. There will be many codes in this document. Be careful that you do not delete necessary codes such as the **WP;WPWP** code that is present at the beginning of all macros. Save and close the document when you are finished.

## C. FOOTNOTES

**Footnotes** are used often in the drafting of legal memoranda and pleadings. WordPerfect for Windows' Footnote feature sequentially numbers the footnotes, and automatically adjusts your page lengths to make room for them.

To create a footnote within your document follow the steps below.

  a)  Position the insertion point at the point where you would like the reference number of the footnote to appear.

  b)  Press **[Ctrl]+[F7]**, **F**, **C** or select **Layout, Footnote, Create**. The **Footnote** window will appear on your screen displaying the footnote number.

  c)  Type the footnote in the Footnote window. When you are finished, press **[F7]** or click on the **Close Button** to return to your document.

The footnote reference number will appear in your text where you placed the insertion point when you began. You cannot see the footnote unless you view your document in the **File** menu by selecting **Print Preview**.

To practice creating a footnote, type the paragraph below into your document.

> **The parents of a legitimate unmarried minor child, acting jointly, may maintain an action for injury to such child caused by the wrongful act or neglect of another.**

This is a quote from California Code of Civil Procedure, Section 376. To reference this section with a footnote, follow the steps below.

  a)  Position the insertion point at the space just after the period in the sentence.

  b)  Press **[Ctrl]+[F7]**, **F**, **C** or select **Layout, Footnote, Create**. The **Footnote** window will appear displaying the number of the footnote.

  c)  Type the text of the footnote. For our footnote the text will be **CCP Section 376**. When you are finished, press **[F7]** or click on the **Close Button** to return to your document.

You will see the footnote number at the end of the sentence, but the footnote will not appear on the screen. To see how the footnote will appear on the page, use **File, Print Preview**. Your footnote should be similar to the one in Figure 2.37.

The parents of a legitimate unmarried minor
child, acting jointly, may maintain an action
for injury to such child caused by the
wrongful act or neglect of another.[1]

_____

[1]  CCP Section 376.

**Figure 2.37** A Footnote

## D. COLUMNS

WordPerfect offers three types of columns, Parallel, Parallel with Block Protect, and Newspaper. For the most part, legal professionals use Parallel columns. Parallel columns are used to create pleading captions, deposition summaries and other documents that require columns of text that can be read from left to right. An example of parallel columns is shown in Figure 2.38.

```
          SUMMARY OF THE DEPOSITION OF

              HUBERT M. SMITH

            Taken November 9, 1991


Page:Line              Summary

1:3                    Opening statements.

2:4                    Mr. Smith was born in Walla Walla, Washington
                       on December 12, 1945.  He currently resides at
                       345 Main Street, Seattle, Washington 00990.

3:27                   Mr.  Smith  obtained  a  Bachelor  of  Science
                       degree  in  Economics  from  the  University  of
                       Washington in 1967.  He is presently employed
                       by the State of Washington as an Economist.
```

**Figure 2.38** Parallel Columns

Newspaper columns differ from parallel columns in that when the left-most column reaches the bottom of the page, it goes back up to the top of the same page in the next column. Instead of reading these columns from left to right, you read the first column to the bottom of the page and then read the next column. An example of newspaper columns is shown in Figure 2.39.

### Parallel Columns

WordPerfect offers two types of columns, parallel and newspaper. For the most part, legal professionals use parallel columns. This type of column is used to create pleading captions, deposition summaries and other documents which require columns of text which are read from left to right.

### Newspaper Columns

Newspaper columns differ from parallel columns in that when the left-most column reaches the bottom of the page, it goes back up to the top of the same page. Instead of reading these type of columns from left to right, you read the first column to the bottom of the page and then read the second column.

**Figure 2.39** Newspaper Columns

Parallel with Block Protect columns are parallel columns with an added feature. If any part of a row of column entries continues to the next page of the document, the entire row of entries will be moved to the next page.

To learn about columns, we will use an example of a deposition summary. Follow the steps below.

a) In a new document, type in the heading of the deposition as shown below.

**SUMMARY OF THE DEPOSITION OF**
**HUBERT M. SMITH**
**Taken November 9, 1992**

b) Press the [Enter] key to move down a few lines.

c) Press [Alt]+[F7], C, D or select **Layout, Columns, Define** to access the **Define Columns** dialog box shown in Figure 2.40.

d) In the **Number of Columns** box, type **2**. This is the default setting, so it may already be typed for you.

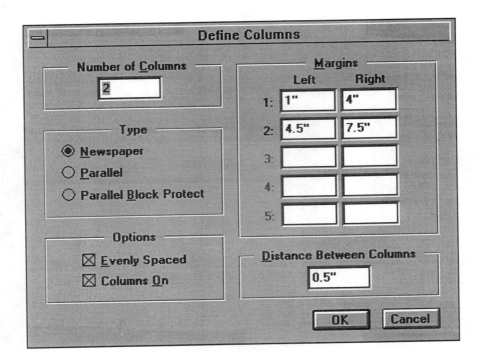

**Figure 2.40** The Define Columns Dialog Box

e) In the **Type** box, click on **Parallel**.

f) Define your margins in the **Margins** box by clicking on the boxes with margins that need to be changed, deleting the existing entry, and then typing in the new entry. The margins are shown below.

|    | Left | Right |
|----|------|-------|
| **1:** | 1" | 2.5" |
| **2:** | 3" | 7.5" |

g) If Columns On is checked in the Options box, the columns will be turned on when you exit. Click on the **OK Button** to record the columns and return to your document. The column number will be displayed in the Status Bar.

h) Type <u>PAGE:LINE</u> in column 1 at the left margin and move to column 2 by pressing **[Ctrl]+[Enter]**. Under normal circumstances this would create a hard page break. If you do get a hard page break (===========), then your columns are not turned on. Check your Reveal Codes to make sure that you are typing after the **(Col On)** code. If you do not see a **(Col On)** code, then you need to turn the columns on in **Layout, Columns**.

i) At the second column, type <u>SUMMARY</u>, press **[F8]** to turn off the underline, and press **[Ctrl]+[Enter]** to get back to column 1 and begin your summary.

Try entering the summary in Figure 2.38 into your document. To change columns, use **[Ctrl]+[Enter]**. **[Alt]+[Left Arrow]** and **[Alt]+[Right Arrow]** will move you quickly back and forth between your columns when you need to edit the column text.

When you have finished using columns in your document, turn them off with **[Shift]+[F8]**, **C, F** or **Layout, Columns, Columns Off**.

## E. DOCUMENT MERGING

Mass mailings and frequently used forms can be produced quickly using WordPerfect's merge features.

In a large litigation case, there may be as many as 25 opposing counsel. Creating a separate letter for each counsel can be very time consuming. It is much easier to create a merge letter and address list than to type each individual letter. The address list can then be used for future mailings in the case. By merging the merge letter with the address list, a personalized letter will be created for each individual.

### 1. Primary and Secondary Files

Merging documents involves the use of primary and secondary files. The primary file is the shell document, into which information will be merged. The secondary file is the list of information to be merged into the primary file document.

To practice using merge, we will create a simple letter acknowledging an extension of time to respond to a complaint. This letter will be the primary file. The list of addresses for each of the plaintiffs' counsel (in this case, there are four separate law firms representing the plaintiffs) will be the secondary file.

### 2. The Merged Document

A merge will combine the information from the primary and secondary files, creating a copy of the primary file for each of the records in the secondary file. After our merge is completed, the merged document will contain a letter for each counsel with a hard page break created between each letter. Sending the merged document to the printer will print all of the letters.

### 3. Example

For our example, we will create a letter and make it into our primary file. Type the letter shown in Figure 2.41 into a blank WordPerfect screen. Use the centering, underline and bold features where applicable. Use **[Shift]+[F6]** to center the headings and the date. Use **[Shift]+[F5], D, T** or **Tools, Date, Text** to insert today's date into the letter. The closing and signature line should not be centered. Use the **[Tab]** key to move the insertion point to the middle of the screen to begin typing the closing and signature line (Pos 4.5"). Use your own name at the signature line.

**SMITH AND SMITH**
**Attorneys at Law**
**1234 Hampton Avenue**
**La Jolla, California  99999**
**(619) 555-1212**

April 1, 1993

Opposing Counsel, Esq.
22 Court Boulevard
San Diego, California  99999

    Re:    Potter, et al. vs. Polluter Co.; Case No. 85549

Dear Mr. Counsel:

Pursuant to a telephone conference of this date, Mr. Johnson of Pote & Tate, on behalf of all plaintiffs in this action, has granted our client, Polluter Co., an extension until May 15, 1993, in which to answer or otherwise respond to the complaint on file in this matter.

        Sincerely,

        JAMES SMITH
        SMITH AND SMITH

**Figure 2.41**  The Sample Letter

Before we continue, use **File, Save As** to save the letter. Remember to specify where you wish to save it (i.e., A: or C:), any directory you wish to place it under, and give the letter the name **EXTEND.LTR**. If you are using a floppy disk in the A: drive, save the letter as follows: **A:EXTEND.LTR**

Check the spelling in the letter using the Spell Check feature. Spell checking is accessed with **[Ctrl]+[F2]** or **Tools, Speller**.

### 4. Creating the Primary File

To convert our letter into the primary file, we will create three fields:

1) Name of the attorney and firm name

2) Firm address

3) The salutation

In order to do this, we must remove some of the text from our letter and place field identifiers where we wish information to be entered from the secondary file. To do this, follow the steps below.

a) Move the insertion point in front of the "O" in "Opposing Counsel, Esq." Delete to the end of the line using **[Ctrl]+[End]**.

b) Press **[Shift]+[F9]**. Select **Field**. Type **1** and click on the **OK Button**.

c) Remove the entire address by blocking it and pressing the **[Delete]** key.

d) Move the insertion point to the beginning of the blank line under the first field that you created, and use **[Shift]+[F9], Field** to create a second field **2**.

e) The third and final field for our primary file document will be the salutation field. Move the insertion point in front of the "M" in "Mr. Counsel:". Use **[Ctrl]+[End]** to delete to the end of the line. Now, with the insertion point remaining after "Dear," use **[Shift]+[F9], Field** to create a third field. Then, place a colon after the field identifier.

The primary file document is now complete and should look like the one shown in Figure 2.42.

**SMITH AND SMITH**
**Attorneys at Law**
**1234 Hampton Avenue**
**La Jolla, California  99999**
**(619) 555-1212**


April 1, 1993


{FIELD}1 ~
{FIELD}2 ~


Re:    Potter, et al. vs. Polluter Co.; Case No. 85549

Dear {FIELD}3 ~ :

Pursuant to a telephone conference of this date, Mr. Johnson of Pote & Tate, on behalf of all plaintiffs in this action, has granted our client, Polluter Co., an extension until May 15, 1993, in which to answer or otherwise respond to the complaint on file in this matter.

Sincerely,


JAMES SMITH
SMITH AND SMITH


**Figure 2.42**  The Primary File


Close this document using **File, Close**. Click on **Yes** to save the changes.


## 5.  Creating the Secondary File

In a new document, begin drafting the secondary file. The secondary file will be the names, addresses, and salutations for each of the persons who will be receiving a letter. We will be able to use this secondary file for this letter and any others that we create in the future for this case. The plaintiffs' counsel are as follows:

**Marvin Pearce, Esq.**
**Fenner & Pearce**
**64 Honor Avenue, 14th Floor**
**San Diego, California  99999**

**James Franklin, Esq.**
**22 Windship Lane, Suite 3**
**San Diego, California  99999**

**John Simpson, Esq.**
**Sampson, Newberry & Simpson**
**34 Rome Avenue, Suite B**
**La Jolla, California  99999**

**Marsha Mendleson, Esq.**
**Mendleson, Teedlebaum & Mason**
**6552 Main Street, Suite 2003**
**San Diego, California  99999**

Remember, there are three fields in this merge letter. The first field is the attorney and firm name, the second is the address, and the third is the salutation.

To create the secondary file we begin with a blank screen, and type each field, pressing the **[F9] End Field** key at the end of each field. A group of fields for a single item is called a record. We have four records in our example. At the end of each record we will press **[Shift]+[F9], R** to let WordPerfect know that this is the end of the record.

The first record in our secondary file will be created as follows:

a)  Type the name of the first attorney, and the firm name if applicable. Press **[F9]**. This puts the merge code **{END FIELD}** at the end of the line and executes a hard return to the next line.

> **Marvin Pearce, Esq.**
> **Fenner & Pearce{END FIELD}**

b)  Type the address. At the end of the complete address, after the zip code, press **[F9]** again.

> **64 Honor Avenue, 14th Floor**
> **San Diego, California  99999{END FIELD}**

c) Now, type the salutation and press **[F9]**.

**Mr. Pearce**

d) To tell WordPerfect that you have finished this record, press **[Shift]+[F9], R**.

A hard page break will be created at the end of the record. Following these same procedures, input the remaining three records under the first record. When you are finished, your secondary file should look like the Figure 2.43.

Marvin Pearce, Esq.
Fenner & Pearce{END FIELD}
64 Honor Avenue, 14th Floor
San Diego, California  99999{END FIELD}
Mr. Pearce{END FIELD}
{END RECORD}

James Franklin, Esq.{END FIELD}
22 Windship Lane, Suite 3
San Diego, California  99999{END FIELD}
Mr. Franklin{END FIELD}
{END RECORD}

John Simpson, Esq.
Sampson, Newberry & Simpson{END FIELD}
34 Rome Avenue, Suite B
La Jolla, California  99999{END FIELD}
Mr. Simpson{END FIELD}
{END RECORD}

Marsha Mendleson, Esq.
Mendleson, Teedlebaum & Mason{END FIELD}
6552 Main Street, Suite 2003
San Diego, California  99999{END FIELD}
Ms. Mendleson{END FIELD}
{END RECORD}

**Figure 2.43** The Secondary File

e) Save the secondary file, using **File, Save As**, in the same location as your primary file and give it the name "**ADDRESS.MRG**" to remind us that these are the addresses for our merge. If you are saving the file to your A: drive the response to "Save as" should be: **A:ADDRESS.MRG**. Then, close the file with **File, Close**.

## 6. Merging the Primary and Secondary Files

Merging the secondary file addresses into the primary file letter involves selecting the merge function, identifying the location and name of the primary file, and identifying the location and name of the secondary file. In a new document, follow the steps below.

    a)  Press **[Shift]+[F9], M** or **Select Tools, Merge, Merge**

    b)  The **Merge** dialog box will appear for you to enter the **primary** and **secondary** file names.

        Example:   Primary file:   **A:EXTEND.LTR**
                       Secondary file: **A:ADDRESS.MRG**

    c)  Click on the **OK Button** to begin the merge.

WordPerfect will automatically merge the two documents. You should have a merged document with four letters that appear similar to those shown in Figure 2.44.

---

**SMITH AND SMITH**
Attorneys at Law
1234 Hampton Avenue
La Jolla, California  99999
(619) 555-1212

April 1, 1993

Marvin Pearce, Esq.
Fenner & Pearce
64 Honor Avenue, 14th Floor
San Diego, California  99999

    Re:   Potter, et al. vs. Polluter Co.; Case No. 85549

Dear Mr. Pearce:

    Pursuant to a telephone conference of this date, Mr. Johnson of Pote & Tate, on behalf of all plaintiffs in this action, has granted our client, Polluter Co., an extension until May 15, 1993, in which to answer or otherwise respond to the complaint on file in this matter.

    Sincerely,

    JAMES SMITH
    SMITH AND SMITH

---

**Figure 2.44** The Merged Documents

SMITH AND SMITH
Attorneys at Law
1234 Hampton Avenue
La Jolla, California  99999
(619) 555-1212

April 1, 1993

James Franklin, Esq.
22 Windship Lane, Suite 3
San Diego, California  99999

Re:    Potter, et al. vs. Polluter Co.; Case No. 85549

Dear Mr. Franklin:

Pursuant to a telephone conference of this date, Mr. Johnson of Pote & Tate, on behalf of all plaintiffs in this action, has granted our client, Polluter Co., an extension until May 15, 1993, in which to answer or otherwise respond to the complaint on file in this matter.

Sincerely,

JAMES SMITH
SMITH AND SMITH

---

SMITH AND SMITH
Attorneys at Law
1234 Hampton Avenue
La Jolla, California  99999
(619) 555-1212

April 1, 1993

John Simpson, Esq.
Sampson, Newberry & Simpson
34 Rome Avenue, Suite B
La Jolla, California  99999

Re:    Potter, et al. vs. Polluter Co.; Case No. 85549

Dear Mr. Simpson:

Pursuant to a telephone conference of this date, Mr. Johnson of Pote & Tate, on behalf of all plaintiffs in this action, has granted our client, Polluter Co., an extension until May 15, 1993, in which to answer or otherwise respond to the complaint on file in this matter.

Sincerely,

JAMES SMITH
SMITH AND SMITH

**Figure 2.44** (continued)

```
┌─────────────────────────────────────────────────────────┐
│                                                           │
│                      SMITH AND SMITH                      │
│                      Attorneys at Law                     │
│                    1234 Hampton Avenue                    │
│                  La Jolla, California  99999              │
│                      (619) 555-1212                       │
│                                                           │
│                                                           │
│                      April 1, 1993                        │
│                                                           │
│                                                           │
│                                                           │
│   Marsha Mendleson, Esq.                                  │
│   Mendleson, Teedlebaum & Mason                           │
│   6552 Main Street, Suite 2003                            │
│   San Diego, California  99999                            │
│                                                           │
│            Re:    Potter, et al. vs. Polluter Co.; Case No. 85549 │
│                                                           │
│   Dear Ms. Mendleson:                                     │
│                                                           │
│            Pursuant to a telephone conference of this date, Mr. Johnson of Pote & Tate, on behalf │
│   of all plaintiffs in this action, has granted our client, Polluter Co., an extension until May 15, │
│   1993, in which to answer or otherwise respond to the complaint on file in this matter. │
│                                                           │
│                        Sincerely,                         │
│                                                           │
│                                                           │
│                        JAMES SMITH                        │
│                        SMITH AND SMITH                     │
│                                                           │
└─────────────────────────────────────────────────────────┘
```

**Figure 2.44**  (continued)

# F. CREATING A PLEADING CAPTION

WordPerfect for Windows contains a Pleading Style to create pleading paper (line numbers and border lines) on ordinary bond. WordPerfect for Windows version contains the Pleading Style and a Pleading Macro to create custom pleading styles. Using the Pleading Style or setting up a Pleading Style with the Pleading macro will create the line numbering and border lines of pleading paper on ordinary bond. If you are printing on pre-printed pleading bond, you can skip to the section below on changing the bottom margin.

## 1.  Selecting the Pleading Style or Macro

The Pleading Style in WordPerfect is an option that numbers the lines on your paper from 1 to 28 and places a double vertical line on the left side next to the numbers. The problem with the Pleading Style is that it is set up with margins that can be difficult to change if you are a novice WordPerfect user.  The Pleading Macro is a more sophisticated way to set up your pleading paper, and it allows you to create your own style and margins. Both methods are explained below.

Before you begin creating the pleading, *it is essential* that Auto Code Placement is turned off. To check this, select **File, Preferences, Environment**. In the Settings box you will see a selection for Auto Code Placement. If there is an X in the box next to Auto Code Placement, it is turned on. If it is on, click on the box to remove the X. Then, click on the **OK Button** to complete the change.

To begin the Pleading Style, make sure you are at the very top of the first page of your document by pressing **[Home], [Home], [Home], [Up Arrow]**, and follow the instructions in part a or b below.

a. *Pleading Style*

To choose the Pleading Style for your document, press **[Alt]+[F8]** or select **Layout, Styles**. The **Styles** dialog box will appear. Highlight **Pleading** and click on the **On Button**. The appearance of your document will not change. If you go into reveal codes, you will see that you have selected the pleading style. Your document is now set up for pleading paper.

---

*If you open the **Styles** dialog box and no styles are listed on the screen, it may be that the style library has not been set up on your computer. To set up your styles, select **File, Preferences, Location of Files**. You will need to type in where your Style Files are located in the **Styles** box (usually where your WordPerfect files are located, e.g., C:\WPWIN). Then you will need to type in the Library file name: **LIBRARY.STY**. When you exit out of this menu, you will then find that your styles are listed in the **Styles** dialog box.*

---

b. *The Pleading Macro*

The Pleading Macro will allow you to create several different pleading styles. The Pleading Macro is played by pressing **[Alt]+[F10]** or selecting **Macro, Play**. The **Play Macro** dialog box will appear. Click on the **Pleading** macro in the **Files** box (pleading.wcm) and click on the **Play Button** to play the macro. A dialog box will appear prompting for the specific margins and appearance of your pleading style. To make a change, click in the appropriate box, delete the current entry, and type in a new entry.

Name the style "Pleading1." Many pleadings require a 1.5" Left Margin, so make this change. Also change the Right Margin to .5". Leave the Left Line as a double line, and change the Right Line to a single line by typing **1** in the **Right Line** box. Click on the **Create Button** to create the Pleading1 style. The appearance of your document will not change. If you go into reveal codes you will see that you have selected the Pleading1 style.

## 2. Changing the Bottom Margin

In order to accommodate page numbers at the bottom of each page, the bottom margin must be changed to .5". If we had made this change in the Pleading macro when creating the pleading style, line 28 would have been placed .5" from the bottom. We want line 28 to remain 1" from the bottom and the page number to be placed .5" from the bottom.

To change the bottom margin, make sure that your insertion point is after the Pleading Style code in the document using Reveal Codes. Select **[Shift]+[F8], M** or select **Layout, Margins**, and change the bottom margin to **.5"**. Click on the **OK** button to complete the change.

## 3. Page Numbering

Before you select page numbering, make sure that your insertion point is after the margin code by revealing codes. To page number your pleading, select **[Shift]+[F8], P, N** or **Layout, Page, Numbering**. The **Page Numbering** dialog box will appear. To change the **Position** from **No Page Numbering** to **Bottom Center**, click and hold on the **Position Button**, highlight Bottom Center, and release the mouse button. Click on the **OK Button** to complete the action. This will place the page number at the bottom center of your pleading.

Selecting **File, Print Preview** at this point will show you how your pleading style and page numbering will appear when printed.

## 4. Attorney Address

Immediately following your style, bottom margin, and page numbering selections, type the attorney's name, address, telephone number, and representation designation as shown below. (In some states a state bar number is also required.) Make sure that the attorney name is on the first line of the document.

**Attorney Name**
**Attorney at Law**
**Address**
**Telephone Number**

**Attorney for (Plaintiff, Defendant etc.)**

## 5. Court Designation

Different jurisdictions will have different ways that they wish their pleadings to be created. In many jurisdictions, the court designation should begin at line 8 on pleading paper. This is line 3.33" if you are using WordPerfect's Pleading Style. If you created a pleading style using the Pleading macro, line 8 of the pleading paper is located at line 3.29". The line inches are displayed in the Status Bar. Use the **[Enter]** key to move to the appropriate line.

The court designation should be centered, capitalized and double spaced (do not change your spacing to double spacing, just press the **[Enter]** key between the lines). For example:

**SUPERIOR COURT OF THE STATE OF CALIFORNIA**
**IN AND FOR THE COUNTY OF SAN DIEGO**

### 6. Creating the Caption Columns

Move two or three lines down from the Court Designation to begin the caption.

We will need to set the line justification at left at this point so that the caption and pleading title do not spread to the right margin of their columns. To do so, press **[Ctrl]+[L]**.

Now we will prepare the three columns of the caption following these steps:

a) Press **[Alt]+[F7], C, D** or select **Layout, Columns, Define**.

b) In the **Column Definition** dialog box change the number of columns to **3** and change the type of column to **Parallel**.

c) In the **Margins** box, enter the margins shown below for the pleading style that you have selected.

**WordPerfect Pleading Style**

| | | |
|---|---|---|
| Column 1 | 1" | 4.5" |
| Column 2 | 4.5" | 4.6" |
| Column 3 | 5" | 7.5" |

**Pleading Macro Style with Margins L-1.5", R-.5"**

| | | |
|---|---|---|
| Column 1 | 1.5" | 4.7" |
| Column 2 | 4.7" | 4.8" |
| Column 3 | 5.3" | 8.0" |

Make sure that the **Columns On** option is selected in the Options box and click on the **OK Button** to complete the column definition. The column number indicator will now appear in the Status Bar.

## 7. Entering the Caption

In the first column of the caption, type the plaintiff and defendant names in a similar manner as the example shown below.

**JOHN SMITH and MARY SMITH,**

      **Plaintiffs,**

**vs.**

**ABCD CORPORATION, and DOES 1 through 100, Inclusive,**

      **Defendants.**

After typing **Defendants.**, return to the left margin by pressing the **[Enter]** key and use the underline character to create an underline from the left margin to the right margin of Column 1 (4.5" or 4.7").

Press **[Ctrl]+[Enter]** to move to the second column and insert "**)**" characters until they are even with the underline in the first column. Your caption should now appear similar to the one shown below.

| | |
|---|---|
| **JOHN SMITH and MARY SMITH,** | ) |
| | ) |
|     **Plaintiffs,** | ) |
| | ) |
| **vs.** | ) |
| | ) |
| **ABCD CORPORATION, and DOES 1** | ) |
| **through 100, Inclusive,** | ) |
| | ) |
|     **Defendants.** | ) |
| _____ | ) |

When the second column is completed, press **[Ctrl]+[Enter]** to move to the third column and enter the case number and pleading name. Your caption should now look like the one below.

| | | |
|---|---|---|
| **JOHN SMITH and MARY SMITH,** | ) | **CASE NO. 567320** |
| | ) | |
| **Plaintiffs,** | ) | **TITLE OF PLEADING AND** |
| | ) | **HEARING INFORMATION IF** |
| **vs.** | ) | **NECESSARY** |
| | ) | |
| **ABCD CORPORATION, and DOES 1** | ) | |
| **through 100, Inclusive,** | ) | |
| | ) | |
| **Defendants.** | ) | |
| | ) | |

When the third column is completed, turn the columns off by pressing **[Alt]+[F7]**, **C**, **F** or selecting **Layout, Columns, Columns Off**. This will return you to the left margin.

Turn the full justification back on by pressing **[Ctrl]+[F]**.

## 8. Entering the Text of the Pleading

The text of the pleading should follow the caption and should be double spaced. To make sure that the text will line up with the pleading line numbers on the left-hand side, you must begin the text on the correct line. For the WordPerfect pleading style, your first line of text must begin on a line inch ending in .00, .33, or .67. For the pleading style created with the Pleading Macro, move down one line and type a few characters. Then, use **File, Print Preview** to check to see if the text is aligned with a line number. If it is not, return to your document and insert another line above the characters that you typed. Then, use **File, Print Preview** again to see if you are now aligned.

When you are at a numbered line, make sure that the insertion point is at the beginning of the line and change to double spacing by pressing **[Shift]+[F8]**, **L, S, 2** or selecting **Layout, Line, Spacing, 2**.

You may now begin typing the text of the pleading. To view your document before you send it to the printer select **File, Print Preview**. Figure 2.45 shows how your pleading should appear.

```
 1 │ JOE ATTORNEY
   │ Attorney at Law
 2 │ 101 Broad Street, Suite 200
   │ San Diego, California  99999
 3 │ (619) 555-1212
   │
 4 │ Attorney for Defendant
   │
 5 │
   │
 6 │
   │
 7 │
   │
 8 │           SUPERIOR COURT OF THE STATE OF CALIFORNIA
   │
 9 │             IN AND FOR THE COUNTY OF SAN DIEGO
   │
10 │ THE ABC CORPORATION, a        )     Case No. 100111
   │ California Corporation,       )
11 │                               )     ANSWER OF DEFENDANT JOE
   │                 Plaintiff,    )     SMITH
12 │                               )
   │         vs.                   )
13 │                               )
   │ JOE SMITH, and DOES 1 through )
14 │ 50,                           )
   │                               )
15 │                 Defendants.   )
   │ ──────────────────────────────)
16 │
   │       The text will begin at this point.  It will use the entire
17 │
   │ page and be fully justified.
18 │
   │
19 │
   │
20 │
   │
21 │
   │
22 │
   │
23 │
   │
24 │
   │
25 │
   │
26 │
   │
27 │
   │
28 │
                                      1
```

**Figure 2.45**  A Sample Pleading

# Summary

WordPerfect for Windows is a word processing software program that allows you to create and edit documents. WordPerfect for Windows has many features that are accessed through the function keys or the Pull-Down menus. The mouse is used frequently to select menu items and position the insertion point (cursor). The WordPerfect features covered in this chapter will help you to draft almost any type of document.

There are two typing modes within WordPerfect, Insert and Typeover. Insert inserts new text at the point of the insertion point, pushing existing text to the right. Typeover types over the existing text. You may switch between Insert and Typeover by pressing the **[Insert]** key.

Deleting text can be accomplished with the **[Delete]** or **[Backspace]** keys. Blocks of text may be deleted by first selecting them, and then pressing the **[Delete]** key. A block of text is a group of characters or words that is marked by turning on the Select feature and highlighting the text of the block. The marked block may be deleted, copied, moved, printed, bolded, underlined, centered, or acted upon in many other ways.

WordPerfect is equipped with spell check, thesaurus, and search features. Other features allow you to create columns, footnotes, and macros. An important feature for legal professionals is the pleading style, which creates the numbers and vertical lines of pleading paper on ordinary bond.

The wide range of features, WordPerfect's user support, and the ease in using the program itself make WordPerfect the leading choice for legal word processing.

# Exercise

Using the instructions for creating a pleading caption, draft a complaint using WordPerfect for Windows with one cause of action (count) for breach of contract. You may make up the parties and the facts of the case.

Save the pleading onto a disk. Spell check and print the document.

# Chapter Index

# CHAPTER 3

# LOTUS® 1-2-3®

---

# Chapter Preface

Lotus 1-2-3 is an electronic spreadsheet program. Electronic spreadsheets are similar to an accountant's pad, but much more flexible. There is little difference between electronic spreadsheets, so learning Lotus 1-2-3 will make you proficient in almost any other spreadsheet program.

An electronic spreadsheet can be used to create any type of spreadsheet that can be created on paper. The advantages of the electronic spreadsheet are that you can manipulate the columns and rows, and that the computer calculates the totals for you, eliminating mistakes in calculations (as long as you write the formula correctly). Graphs may be created from the data for visual effects, and database functions may be performed upon data in a spreadsheet.

This chapter will introduce you to the Lotus 1-2-3 environment and commands. The Lotus 1-2-3 commands will be used to act upon sample spreadsheets within the chapter. At the end of the chapter is an exercise and a Lotus 1-2-3 Command List. The Command List provides a quick reference for the most common Lotus 1-2-3 commands.

## A. ENTERING THE PROGRAM

To enter Lotus 1-2-3, type: **lotus [Enter]**

*OR* select the Lotus 1-2-3 option or icon from a menu screen.

Upon entering the program, you will be greeted by the Lotus 1-2-3 Access Menu, shown in Figure 3.1, which displays the Lotus 1-2-3 options.

```
Create worksheets, graphs, and databases
1-2-3        PrintGraph      Translate       Install      Exit
```
```
                              Lotus
                         1-2-3 Access Menu
                           Release 2.4

         Copyright 1990, 1991, 1992 Lotus Development Corporation
                         All Rights Reserved.


   To select a program to start, do one of the following:

      *  Use  →, HOME, or END to move the menu pointer
         to the program you want and then press ENTER.

      *  Type the first character of the program's name.

   Press F1 (HELP) for more information.
```

**Figure 3.1** The Lotus 1-2-3 Access Screen

The options available in the Access Menu are:

**1-2-3**          The Lotus 1-2-3 Worksheet.

**PrintGraph**     The utility that prints graphs from your worksheet information.

**Translate**      The utility that translates files created in other software programs (dBase, Symphony, etc.) so that they may be used in Lotus 1-2-3.

**Install**        The utility used to install the Lotus 1-2-3 program onto your computer system. You will not need to access this utility, unless you are installing the program for the first time, or are changing a material part of your computer system, such as the printer.

**Exit**           Leave the program.

To reach the Lotus 1-2-3 worksheet, highlight **1-2-3** and press **[Enter]**.

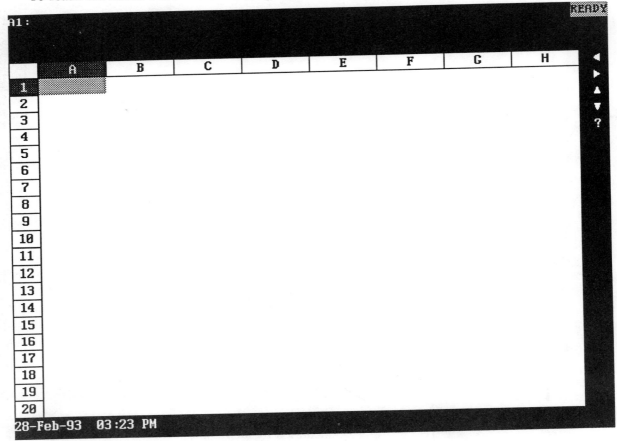

**Figure 3.2** The Lotus Worksheet

## B. THE LOTUS 1-2-3 WORKSHEET

The Lotus 1-2-3 worksheet, shown in Figure 3.2, is the screen in which you create your spreadsheets. The worksheet is made up of columns and rows. The columns are labeled with letters, the rows with numbers.

Lotus 1-2-3 versions 2.4 and later will have icons to the right of the worksheet which are accessed with a mouse. These icons allow you to move left, right, up or down, and access help. If your version of Lotus 1-2-3 has the WYSIWYG ("wi-see-wig" or What You See Is What You Get) add-in attached, you will also see icons that can add, copy, move, and perform many other actions upon the worksheet.

In the Lotus 1-2-3 worksheet, the intersection of a column and a row forms a cell where data is entered. The cells are identified by their cell address, the letter of the column followed by the number of the row. Cell B2 is highlighted in Figure 3.3.

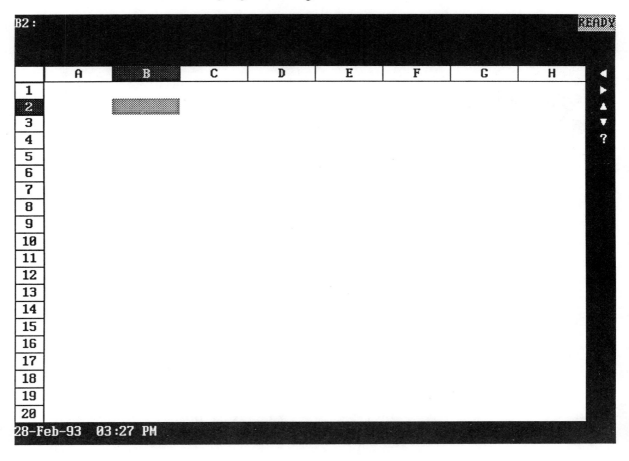

**Figure 3.3** Cells are identified by their column letter
and row number. Cell B2 is highlighted.

## 1. Worksheet Components

The main components of the Lotus 1-2-3 worksheet are explained below:

**Rows**  The horizontal divisions of the worksheet. The rows of the Lotus 1-2-3 worksheet are numbered from 1 to 8,192.

**Columns**  The vertical divisions of the worksheet. The columns of the Lotus 1-2-3 worksheet are labeled A through IV. After Z, the columns begin with AA, AB, AC, continuing to AZ and then beginning BA, BB, BC. There are 230 columns in Lotus 1-2-3.

**Cells**  The intersection of a column and a row.

**Cell Address**  The column letter of the cell followed by the row number. The cell at the top left-hand corner of the worksheet is A1.

**Cell Pointer**  The reverse video bar that is moved around the worksheet using the [Arrow] keys. The cell pointer points to the cell where data will be entered.

**Control Panel**  The portion of the screen above the column labels. This is where the menu selections will be displayed when the menu is accessed.

**Mode Indicator**  The mode indicator is located at the upper right corner of the worksheet screen. The mode indicator displays the current mode of the worksheet. For example, when the worksheet is ready to receive information, the mode indicator will display READY. When the worksheet is busy, the mode indicator will display WAIT.

## 2. Movement Within the Worksheet

The keys that are used to move the cell pointer around within the Lotus 1-2-3 worksheet are explained below.

**Arrow Keys**  The [Arrow] Keys, located to the right of the keyboard, allow you to move the cell pointer around the worksheet one cell at a time. When preceded by the [End] key, they allow you to move in the direction of the [Arrow] key to the boundary of an empty and filled space. For example, in an empty worksheet, press the [End] key, release it, and press the [Right Arrow] key. In a blank worksheet this will take you to column IV. [End], [Down Arrow] will take you to row 8,192.

**Home**  The [Home] key will always return the cell pointer to cell A1.

| Page Up | The [Page Up] key moves the cell pointer up one screen. |
| | |
| Page | The [Page Down] key moves the cell pointer down one screen. |
| | |
| Tab | The [Tab] key moves the cell pointer right one screen. |
| | |
| Shifted Tab | Holding down the [Shift] key and pressing the [Tab] key ([Shift]+[Tab]) moves the cell pointer left one screen. |
| | |
| GoTo [F5] | The GoTo function key, [F5], allows you to move to a specific cell address. After pressing [F5], Lotus 1-2-3 will prompt you to enter the destination cell address. |

## 3. The Function Keys

In Lotus 1-2-3, the function keys F1 through F10, excepting F6, each have two functions. The function keys perform one function when pressed alone, and another when pressed while holding down the [Alt] or [Shift] keys.

Alone, the function keys perform the following functions.

| F1 | Help | Accesses the Help facility. |
| F2 | Edit | Shifts Lotus 1-2-3 into the Edit mode to allow you to alter the contents of a cell without having to retype the entire entry. |
| F3 | Name | Displays a list of the range names in the current worksheet. |
| F4 | ABS | Used while creating or editing a cell entry; will change a relative cell address to an absolute or mixed address. |
| F5 | GoTo | Allows you to move to a specified cell address. |
| F6 | Window | Moves the cursor to the other side of a split screen. You may divide the worksheet screen into two windows with a menu selection. |
| F7 | Query | Repeats the most recent data query operation. |
| F8 | Table | Repeats the most recent data table operation. |
| F9 | Calc | Recalculates the worksheet formulas and functions when in the READY mode. When creating or editing a cell entry, converts the formula or function to its value. |
| F10 | Graph | Draws a graph defined by the current graph settings. |

*Lotus 1-2-3*

When combined with the [Alt] or [Shift] keys, the function keys perform advanced program functions. The beginning to intermediate Lotus 1-2-3 user will not be using most of these functions. If you wish to learn about them, they are explained in the Lotus 1-2-3 Manual and in the Lotus 1-2-3 Help Menu.

## 4. The Help Menu

The Lotus 1-2-3 Help Menu provides information regarding most of the worksheet features. The Help Menu is accessed by pressing the **[F1]** "Help" key. Whenever you press the Help key, Lotus 1-2-3 temporarily suspends the worksheet session and takes you to the Help Menu shown in Figure 3.4.

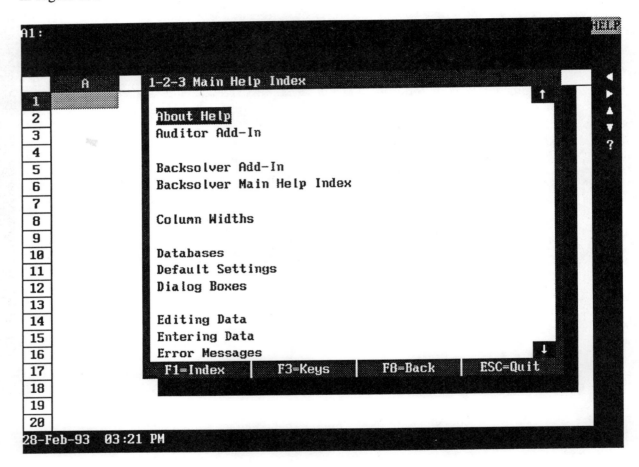

**Figure 3.4** The Help Menu

To review a Help topic, highlight the item and press the **[Enter]** key. To exit help, press the **[Esc]** key. To return to the Help topic you were last reviewing, use **[Ctrl]+[F1]** ("Bookmark") to access Help from the worksheet.

## 5. The Command Menu

Lotus 1-2-3 is traditionally a menu-driven program. This means that commands are selected from a menu. With later versions of the program, you may also access commands with a mouse.

The Lotus 1-2-3 Command Menu is accessed by pressing the forward slash [/] key. When the [/] key is pressed, two lines of commands are displayed above the column letters of the worksheet as shown in Figure 3.5.

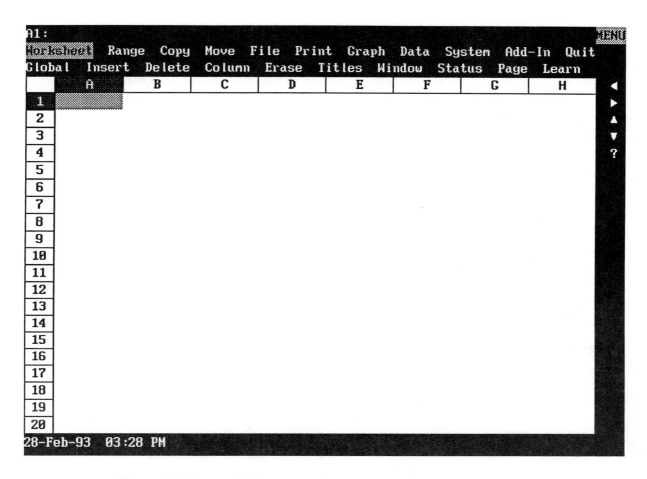

**Figure 3.5** Lotus 1-2-3 command options are displayed above the
column letters when the [/] is pressed

The top line of the Menu indicates the available selections. A highlight bar is moved along the top row with the **[Left Arrow]** and **[Right Arrow]** keys. As you highlight an item in the top row of the Menu, the options available under that item are shown on the bottom line.

a. *Selecting a Command*

To select a command from the Menu, either highlight the command and press **[Enter]**, or type the first character of the command name. Commands will be referred to within this workbook beginning with a " **/** " and followed by the command selections. For example, to save a file, you access the Menu with the forward slash key [/] and select **File** and then **Save**. This will be referred to as /File Save.

b. *The Worksheet and Range Commands*

The first two selections in the Lotus 1-2-3 Menu are Worksheet and Range. Selecting **Worksheet** will take you to commands that are performed upon complete columns and rows of the worksheet. Selecting **Range** will take you to commands that are performed upon a single cell, or a group of cells. Under the Worksheet command is a Global selection. Selecting **Global** will take you to commands that will act upon the entire worksheet.

c. *Exiting the Command Menu*

To leave the Command Menu, you can either complete a command or back out with the **[Esc]** key. The [Esc] key will always take you one step backwards in a Lotus 1-2-3 command.

## C. CELL ENTRIES

The entering of data into a Lotus 1-2-3 cell involves moving the cell pointer to the cell and typing the entry. As you are typing a cell entry, the characters being typed are displayed in the upper left-hand corner of the screen as shown in Figure 3.6.

Pressing the **[Enter]** key or moving the cell pointer with one of the **[Arrow]** keys places the entry, or a calculated result, into the cell as shown in Figure 3.7.

There are two types of cell entries in Lotus 1-2-3, Labels and Values.

## 1. Labels

A Label cell entry begins with a letter or a justification character.

Examples of Label cell entries are:

```
============
John Smith
TOTAL
```

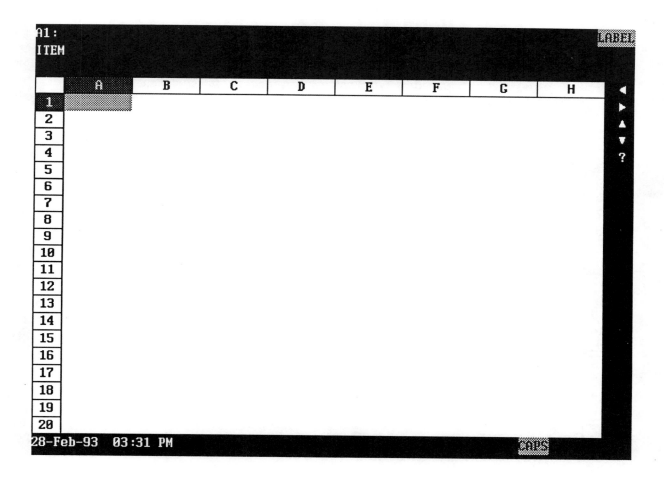

**Figure 3.6** As the word "ITEM" is typed into cell A1, the characters are displayed in the upper left-hand corner of the screen

a.  *Justification Characters*

Justification characters are used to position a Label entry within a cell. The three Lotus 1-2-3 justification characters are:

' **Left justifies the entry**
" **Right justifies the entry**
^ **Centers the entry**

| Left | Right | Center |
|------|-------|--------|
| TOTAL | TOTAL | TOTAL |

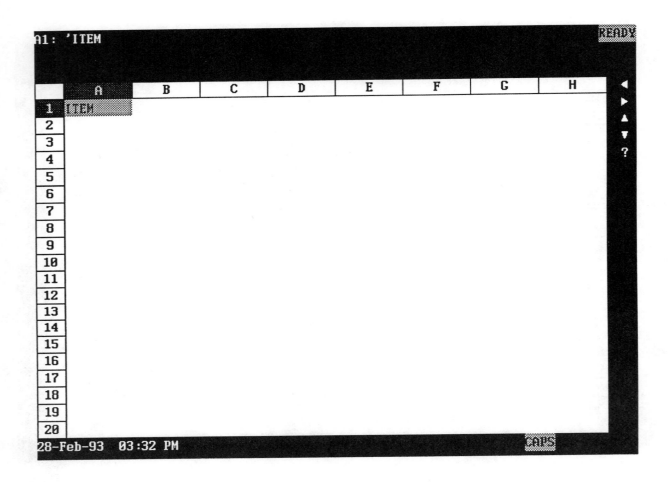

**Figure 3.7** The entry is placed within the cell when the [Enter] key or an [Arrow] key is pressed

Lotus 1-2-3 automatically left justifies Label cell entries. Right or center justifying requires that you type the justification character before you type the entry.

To left justify "TOTAL," you type:     **TOTAL**

To right justify "TOTAL," you type:     **"TOTAL**

To center "TOTAL," you type:     **^TOTAL**

> *Justification characters may only be used with Label cell entries. If they are used with a Value cell entry, Lotus 1-2-3 will read them as a Label, and treat them as such.*

b. *Underlining*

A cell can only contain one entry. Therefore, in order to underline a cell entry, you must, in most cases, put the underline in the cell below as shown in Figure 3.8.

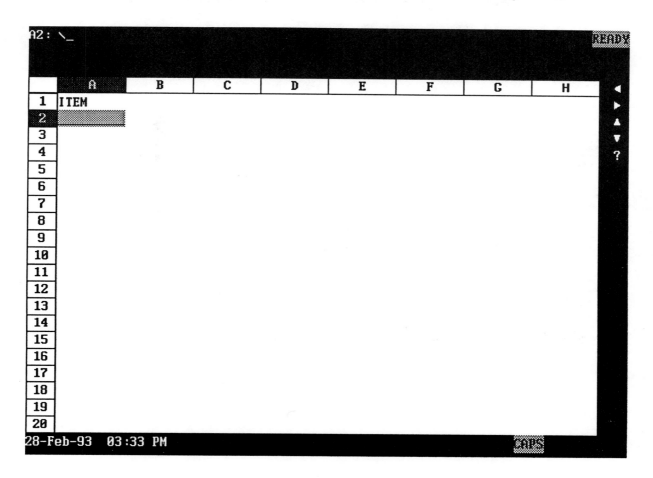

**Figure 3.8** To underline a cell entry, the underline characters
are placed in the cell below

c. *The Repeater*

Underlining is made simple with the Repeater. To make a cell entry full of the underline character "_", you do not need to hold down the underline key. The Repeater, [\], followed by one underline character, will repeat the underline character throughout the cell. Any character(s) which follow the Repeater will be repeated throughout a cell. Below are examples of cell entries using the Repeater and their results.

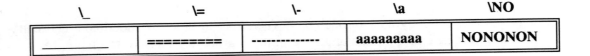

| \L | \= | \- | \a | \NO |
|---|---|---|---|---|
| _____ | ========= | ------------- | aaaaaaaaa | NONONON |

The advantage of using the repeater is that the repeated characters will adjust to increases or decreases in column width. If you type underline characters to fill a cell, and then change the width of that cell, you will need to edit your cell entry to increase or decrease the number of underline characters.

## 2. Values

A Value cell entry is a number to be used for math, a formula, or a Lotus 1-2-3 function.

### a. *Numbers*

Numbers are Value cell entries that begin with a number, a plus or minus sign, a period, a parenthesis, or a dollar sign, and are intended to be used for calculation purposes. Numbers such as addresses and telephone numbers are not considered Values, they are Labels. Lotus 1-2-3 will interpret an address or telephone number *as a Value* unless a justification character is placed in front of them.

Examples of Number cell entries are:

**126**
**199000**
**10E+30**

> *You may not type commas in your numbers as you enter them into a cell. Later, you will learn about the /Range Format command which allows you to add commas and other symbols such as dollar signs and percent symbols.*

### b. *Formulas*

A Formula is a Value cell entry that performs some type of calculation upon a cell or group of cells. In Figure 3.9, the formula +B3+C3+D3+E3 has been entered in cell **F3**. As you can see, the formula is displayed in the upper left-hand corner of the screen. The calculated results are displayed in the cell.

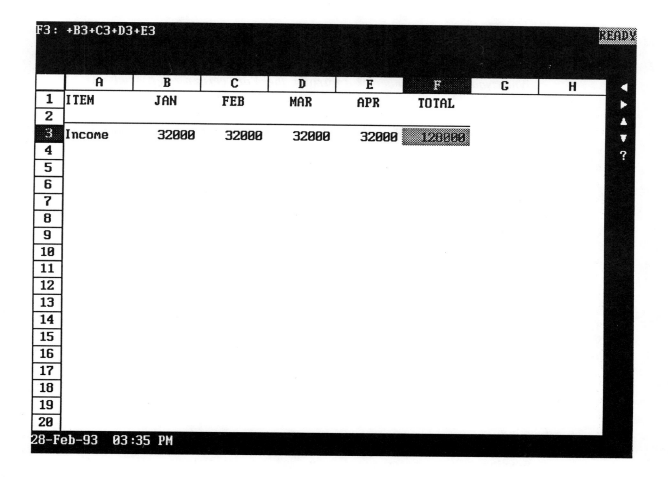

**Figure 3.9** The formula entered into cell F3 is displayed at the top of the screen

Examples of Formula cell entries are:

**+B2+B3+B4**
**123*B6**
**(-C14/C15)+C16**

Formulas that begin with a cell address must be preceded by a plus or minus sign, or a parenthesis. If they are not, Lotus 1-2-3 will receive the letter of the cell address and interpret the entry as a Label instead of a Value.

## ENTERING FORMULAS AND NUMBERS

*When you enter a number or a formula, there are certain rules which must be followed.*

1. *It must begin with 0-9, a plus or minus sign, a period, a parenthesis, or a dollar sign.*

2. *A number may end with a %, which has the same effect as if you entered the number /100.*

3. *Numbers may not contain commas or spaces and may only have one decimal point. (Commas may be added later.)*

4. *"@NA" may be entered into a cell when the information for that cell is not yet available. This will make any calculation which is dependent upon this cell display "NA". This will save you from using a total which does not contain all necessary information.*

c.  *Functions*

A function is a pre-programmed Lotus 1-2-3 formula. Lotus 1-2-3 functions are sometimes called "at functions" because they begin with the @ symbol.

Examples of Function cell entries are:

**@SUM(B3..E3)**
**@AVG(B3..E3)**

The three characters after the @ symbol indicate the function type. The addition and average functions are shown as examples above. Within the parentheses is the cell range to be acted upon. "B3..E3" is interpreted as "cell B3 through E3." An @SUM Function could be entered in cell F3 in Figure 3.10 in place of the formula which was entered in Figure 3.9.

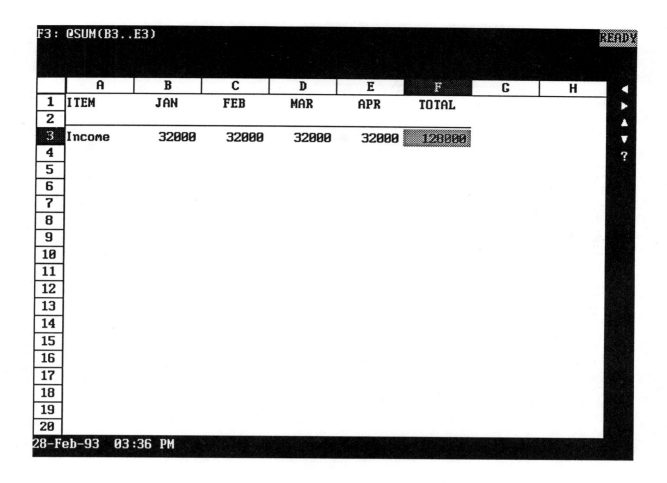

**Figure 3.10** An @SUM Function entered in cell F3 produces the same result as the formula previously entered in Figure 3.9

The question often arises "When should I use @SUM(B3..E3) as opposed to +B3+C3+D3+E3?" Well, in this example you could use either one. However, when you are adding cells B3 through Z3, you can see that the @SUM Function is a better method.

## 3. Ranges of Cells

A Range is a cell or a group of cells identified by the cell address in the upper left-hand corner of the range and the cell address in the lower right-hand corner of the range. In identifying the two corners of the range, Lotus 1-2-3 uses two periods to indicate "through." Some range examples will be explained using the spreadsheet in Figure 3.11.

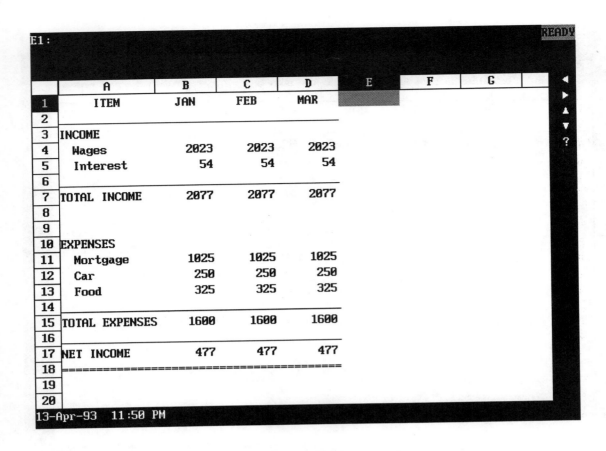

**Figure 3.11** A Sample Worksheet

The headings "ITEM," "JAN," "FEB," and "MAR," are shown in cells A1 through D1. This range would be identified as:

**A1..D1**

The Expense Item amounts for January through March are shown in columns B, C, and D, and in rows **11** through **13**. This range would be identified as:

**B11..D13**

The **entire** spreadsheet range shown here would be identified as:

**A1..D18**

The phrase "NET INCOME" is in the single cell identified as:

**A17..A17**

## 4. Editing a Cell Entry

Changing the contents of a cell can be accomplished in two ways. With the cell pointer in the cell to be changed, either:

- Type a new entry into the cell and press **[Enter]**; or

- Press the **[F2]** (Edit) key. This places your cursor in the upper left corner of the screen where the contents of the cell are displayed. After any changes have been made, pressing the **[Enter]** key will place the new entry into the cell.

## 5. Erasing a Cell Entry

Lotus 1-2-3 versions 2.3 and later allow you to erase the contents of a single cell by moving the cell pointer to the desired cell and pressing the **[Delete]** key. To erase a range of cells, or to erase a single cell in versions before 2.3, you must use **/Range Erase** and specify the range of cells to be erased.

# D. USING LOTUS 1-2-3 COMMANDS

Lotus 1-2-3 commands are accessed through the Lotus 1-2-3 Command Menu with the **[/]** key. To illustrate how commands are executed, we will walk through the **/Move** command with the spreadsheet shown in Figure 3.11. Take a few minutes and enter this spreadsheet into Lotus 1-2-3 if you would like to follow along.

## 1. The Command Process (Using /Move)

The /Move command will be used with the spreadsheet in Figure 3.11 to illustrate a typical command process. For this example, all of the Expense and Net Income items will be moved up one row so that they will begin in Row 9.

### a. *Accessing the Menu*

Accessing the menu with the [/] key displays the Menu options as shown in Figure 3.12. Remember, the first line lists the options available. The second line lists the options available under the highlighted option on the first line.

```
E1:                                                                    MENU
Worksheet  Range  Copy  Move  File  Print  Graph  Data  System  Add-In  Quit
Global  Insert  Delete  Column  Erase  Titles  Window  Status  Page  Learn
        ┌─────────┬───────┬───────┬───────┬───────┬───────┬───────┬─────┐  ◄
        │    A    │   B   │   C   │   D   │   E   │   F   │   G   │     │  ►
    1   │  ITEM   │  JAN  │  FEB  │  MAR  │       │       │       │     │  ▲
    2   │         │       │       │       │       │       │       │     │  ▼
    3   │INCOME   │       │       │       │       │       │       │     │  ?
    4   │  Wages  │ 2023  │ 2023  │ 2023  │       │       │       │     │
    5   │  Interest│  54  │   54  │   54  │       │       │       │     │
    6   │         │       │       │       │       │       │       │     │
    7   │TOTAL INCOME│2077 │ 2077  │ 2077  │       │       │       │     │
    8   │         │       │       │       │       │       │       │     │
    9   │         │       │       │       │       │       │       │     │
   10   │EXPENSES │       │       │       │       │       │       │     │
   11   │  Mortgage│ 1025 │ 1025  │ 1025  │       │       │       │     │
   12   │  Car    │  250  │  250  │  250  │       │       │       │     │
   13   │  Food   │  325  │  325  │  325  │       │       │       │     │
   14   │         │       │       │       │       │       │       │     │
   15   │TOTAL EXPENSES│1600│1600  │ 1600  │       │       │       │     │
   16   │         │       │       │       │       │       │       │     │
   17   │NET INCOME│ 477  │  477  │  477  │       │       │       │     │
   18   │=========================================│       │       │     │
   19   │         │       │       │       │       │       │       │     │
   20   │         │       │       │       │       │       │       │     │
        └─────────┴───────┴───────┴───────┴───────┴───────┴───────┴─────┘
28-Feb-93  03:40 PM
```

**Figure 3.12** The Menu options are displayed when the [/] key is pressed

Moving the highlight bar to "Move," we see in Figure 3.13 that the second line displays a description of the /Move command.

b. *Selecting a Command*

A command is selected by highlighting it and pressing the **[Enter]** key, or by typing the first character of the command name. Selecting **Move** by highlighting it and pressing the **[Enter]** key brings up either of the following two messages depending upon your Lotus 1-2-3 version.

**Enter range to move FROM:**

or

**Move what?**

The range of the cell containing the cell pointer at the time the Move command is accessed is specified in the command message as shown in Figure 3.14.

*Lotus 1-2-3*

At this point, you can either type in the range to be moved, A10..D18, or point at the range with the cell pointer. Pointing involves anchoring the cell pointer and spreading it to highlight the range. Anchoring will be explained in the next section. For this example, type in the range:

**A10..D18**

Pressing the **[Enter]** key displays one of the following two messages.

**Enter range to move TO:**

or

**To where?**

```
E1:                                                                      MENU
Worksheet  Range  Copy  Move  File  Print  Graph  Data  System  Add-In  Quit
Move a cell or range of cells
           A           B         C         D        E        F       G
  1       ITEM        JAN       FEB       MAR
  2
  3  INCOME
  4    Wages         2023      2023      2023
  5    Interest        54        54        54
  6
  7  TOTAL INCOME    2077      2077      2077
  8
  9
 10  EXPENSES
 11    Mortgage      1025      1025      1025
 12    Car            250       250       250
 13    Food           325       325       325
 14
 15  TOTAL EXPENSES  1600      1600      1600
 16
 17  NET INCOME       477       477       477
 18  =========================================
 19
 20
28-Feb-93  03:44 PM
```

**Figure 3.13** Highlighting the Move item displays a description of the /Move command

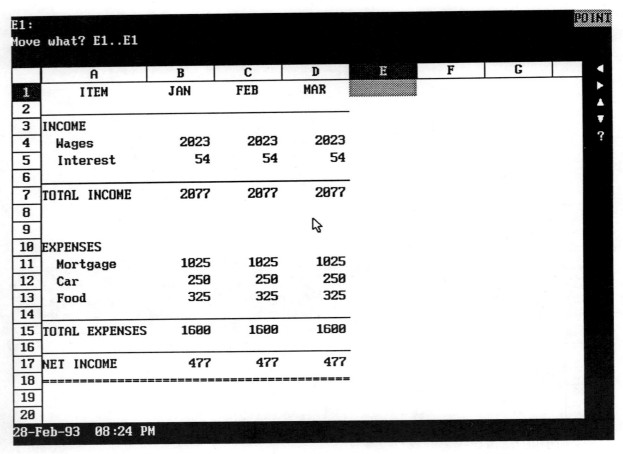

**Figure 3.14** Upon selecting the /Move command, Lotus 1-2-3 prompts you for the Range that you wish to move

The address of the cell in which the cell pointer was located at the time the command was accessed is displayed in the command as shown in Figure 3.15.

To move the entire range up one row, only the upper left-hand corner of the new range needs to be specified. So, we type **A9**. Pressing the **[Enter]** key completes the command and moves the range as shown in Figure 3.16.

> *When using the [/Move] command, be careful that you do not move your range over other cells containing data. If you do, those cell entries will be lost.*

```
E1:                                                                    POINT
Move what? a10..d18                        To where? E1

        │     A     │   B   │   C   │   D   │    E    │   F   │   G   │   │  ◄
   1    │   ITEM    │  JAN  │  FEB  │  MAR  │░░░░░░░░░│       │       │   │  ►
   2    │           │       │       │       │░░░░░░░░░│       │       │   │  ▲
   3    │INCOME     │       │       │       │                                ▼
   4    │  Wages    │ 2023  │ 2023  │ 2023  │                                ?
   5    │  Interest │   54  │   54  │   54  │
   6    │           │       │       │       │
   7    │TOTAL INCOME│ 2077 │ 2077  │ 2077  │
   8    │           │       │       │       │
   9    │           │       │       │       │
  10    │EXPENSES   │       │       │       │
  11    │  Mortgage │ 1025  │ 1025  │ 1025  │
  12    │  Car      │  250  │  250  │  250  │
  13    │  Food     │  325  │  325  │  325  │
  14    │           │       │       │       │
  15    │TOTAL EXPENSES│1600 │ 1600  │ 1600  │
  16    │           │       │       │       │
  17    │NET INCOME │  477  │  477  │  477  │
  18    │===========================================│
  19    │           │       │       │       │
  20    │           │       │       │       │
28-Feb-93  08:27 PM
```

**Figure 3.15**  After entering the range to be moved, Lotus 1-2-3 prompts for the new location


## 2. Pointing and Anchoring

As an alternative to typing ranges, you may point to the range to be acted upon by anchoring the cell pointer and then highlighting the cells. The anchor is what holds the cell pointer in one place and allows you to spread the pointer to highlight other cells.

In commands like the /Move command, the cell pointer is anchored at the cell containing the cell pointer at the time the command is selected. You can tell it is anchored, because the "through" periods ".." are present. See Figure 3.14.

*Lotus 1-2-3*

To demonstrate pointing and anchoring, we will move the range of cells used in the previous example back down to Row 10. To begin the command, access the Menu and select **Move.** The prompt for the range to move will appear, followed by the range of the cell that contained the cell pointer at the time the command was accessed. Moving the cell pointer around the worksheet with the **[Arrow]** keys will expand the cell pointer.

We want to move the range A9..D17. To point to this range, we need to release the anchor so that we may re-anchor at cell A9. The **[Esc]** key will release the anchor. When the **[Esc]** key is pressed, the "through" periods and ending cell address are removed from the prompt as shown in Figure 3.17.

```
E1:                                                             READY

        A           B        C        D        E      F      G       ◄
  1     ITEM        JAN      FEB      MAR                              ►
  2     ─────────────────────────────────────────                    ▲
  3  INCOME                                                           ▼
  4    Wages        2023     2023     2023                            ?
  5    Interest       54       54       54
  6     ─────────────────────────────────────────
  7  TOTAL INCOME   2077     2077     2077
  8
  9  EXPENSES
 10    Mortgage     1025     1025     1025
 11    Car           250      250      250
 12    Food          325      325      325
 13     ─────────────────────────────────────────
 14  TOTAL EXPENSES 1600     1600     1600
 15     ─────────────────────────────────────────
 16  NET INCOME      477      477      477
 17  ==========================================
 18
 19
 20
28-Feb-93  08:28 PM
```

**Figure 3.16** The Worksheet After the Move

|      |    A          |   B   |   C   |   D   |   E   |   F   |   G   |      |
|------|---------------|-------|-------|-------|-------|-------|-------|------|
| 1    |    ITEM       | JAN   | FEB   | MAR   |       |       |       |      |
| 2    |               |       |       |       |       |       |       |      |
| 3    | INCOME        |       |       |       |       |       |       |      |
| 4    |    Wages      | 2023  | 2023  | 2023  |       |       |       |      |
| 5    |    Interest   | 54    | 54    | 54    |       |       |       |      |
| 6    |               |       |       |       |       |       |       |      |
| 7    | TOTAL INCOME  | 2077  | 2077  | 2077  |       |       |       |      |
| 8    |               |       |       |       |       |       |       |      |
| 9    | EXPENSES      |       |       |       |       |       |       |      |
| 10   |    Mortgage   | 1025  | 1025  | 1025  |       |       |       |      |
| 11   |    Car        | 250   | 250   | 250   |       |       |       |      |
| 12   |    Food       | 325   | 325   | 325   |       |       |       |      |
| 13   |               |       |       |       |       |       |       |      |
| 14   | TOTAL EXPENSES| 1600  | 1600  | 1600  |       |       |       |      |
| 15   |               |       |       |       |       |       |       |      |
| 16   | NET INCOME    | 477   | 477   | 477   |       |       |       |      |
| 17   | =============================================== |       |       |       |       |       |
| 18   |               |       |       |       |       |       |       |      |
| 19   |               |       |       |       |       |       |       |      |
| 20   |               |       |       |       |       |       |       |      |

28-Feb-93   08:30 PM

**Figure 3.17** Pressing the [Esc] key removes the anchor

The cell pointer is moved to cell A9 and re-anchored by pressing the period key once. This will display the newly anchored range A9..A9 as shown in Figure 3.18.

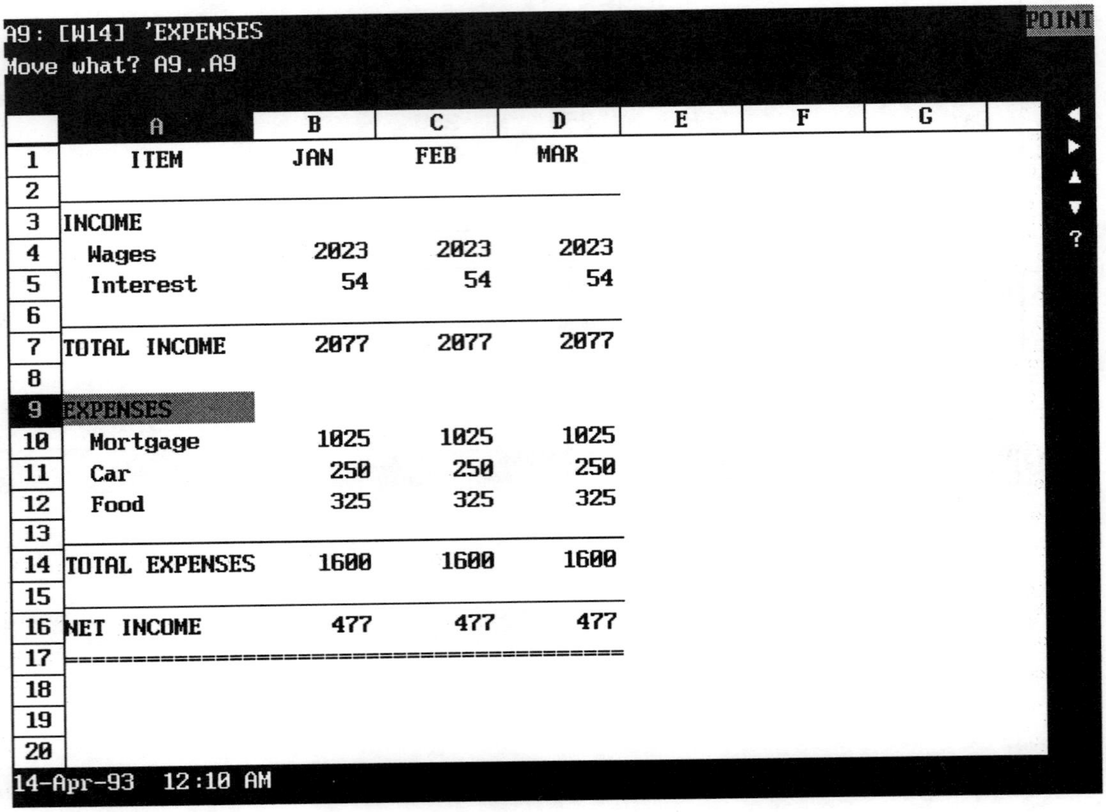

```
A9: [W14] 'EXPENSES                                                    POINT
Move what? A9..A9

               A           B        C        D       E      F      G
     1       ITEM         JAN      FEB      MAR
     2  ─────────────────────────────────────────────
     3  INCOME
     4      Wages         2023     2023     2023
     5      Interest        54       54       54
     6
     7  TOTAL INCOME      2077     2077     2077
     8
     9  EXPENSES
    10      Mortgage      1025     1025     1025
    11      Car            250      250      250
    12      Food           325      325      325
    13
    14  TOTAL EXPENSES    1600     1600     1600
    15
    16  NET INCOME         477      477      477
    17  ════════════════════════════════════════════
    18
    19
    20
14-Apr-93  12:10 AM
```

Figure 3.18  Re-anchoring is accomplished by pressing the period key one time

The cell pointer may now be moved to highlight the range of cells to be moved, A9..D17, as shown in Figure 3.19.

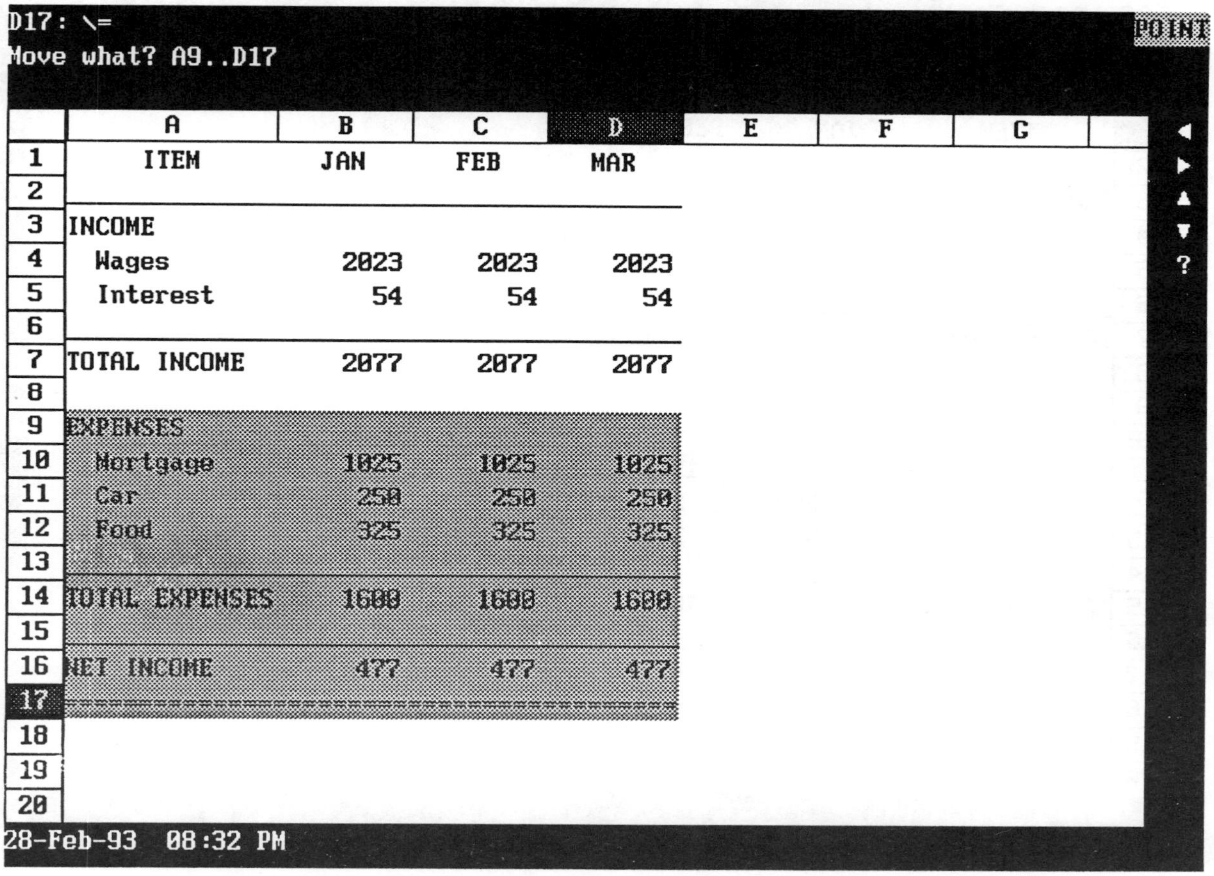

```
D17: \=                                                                    POINT
Move what? A9..D17
        ┌───────────┬──────────┬─────────┬─────────┬────────┬────────┬────────┬───┬───┐
        │     A     │    B     │    C    │    D    │   E    │   F    │   G    │   │ ◄ │
   ┌────┼───────────┼──────────┼─────────┼─────────┼────────┼────────┼────────┼───┤ ► │
   │ 1  │   ITEM    │   JAN    │   FEB   │   MAR   │        │        │        │   │ ▲ │
   │ 2  │           │          │         │         │        │        │        │   │ ▼ │
   │ 3  │INCOME     │          │         │         │        │        │        │   │ ? │
   │ 4  │  Wages    │   2023   │  2023   │  2023   │
   │ 5  │  Interest │     54   │    54   │    54   │
   │ 6  │           │
   │ 7  │TOTAL INCOME   2077      2077      2077
   │ 8  │
   │ 9  │EXPENSES
   │ 10 │  Mortgage     1025      1025      1025
   │ 11 │  Car           250       250       250
   │ 12 │  Food          325       325       325
   │ 13 │
   │ 14 │TOTAL EXPENSES 1600      1600      1600
   │ 15 │
   │ 16 │NET INCOME      477       477       477
   │ 17 │
   │ 18 │
   │ 19 │
   │ 20 │
28-Feb-93   08:32 PM
```

**Figure 3.19**  Highlighting the Range of Cells

*Lotus 1-2-3*

Pressing the **[Enter]** key displays the prompt for the new location of the range. To point to this new location, move the cell pointer to cell A10 with the **[Arrow]** keys. To complete the move, press the **[Enter]** key. The move results are shown in Figure 3.20.

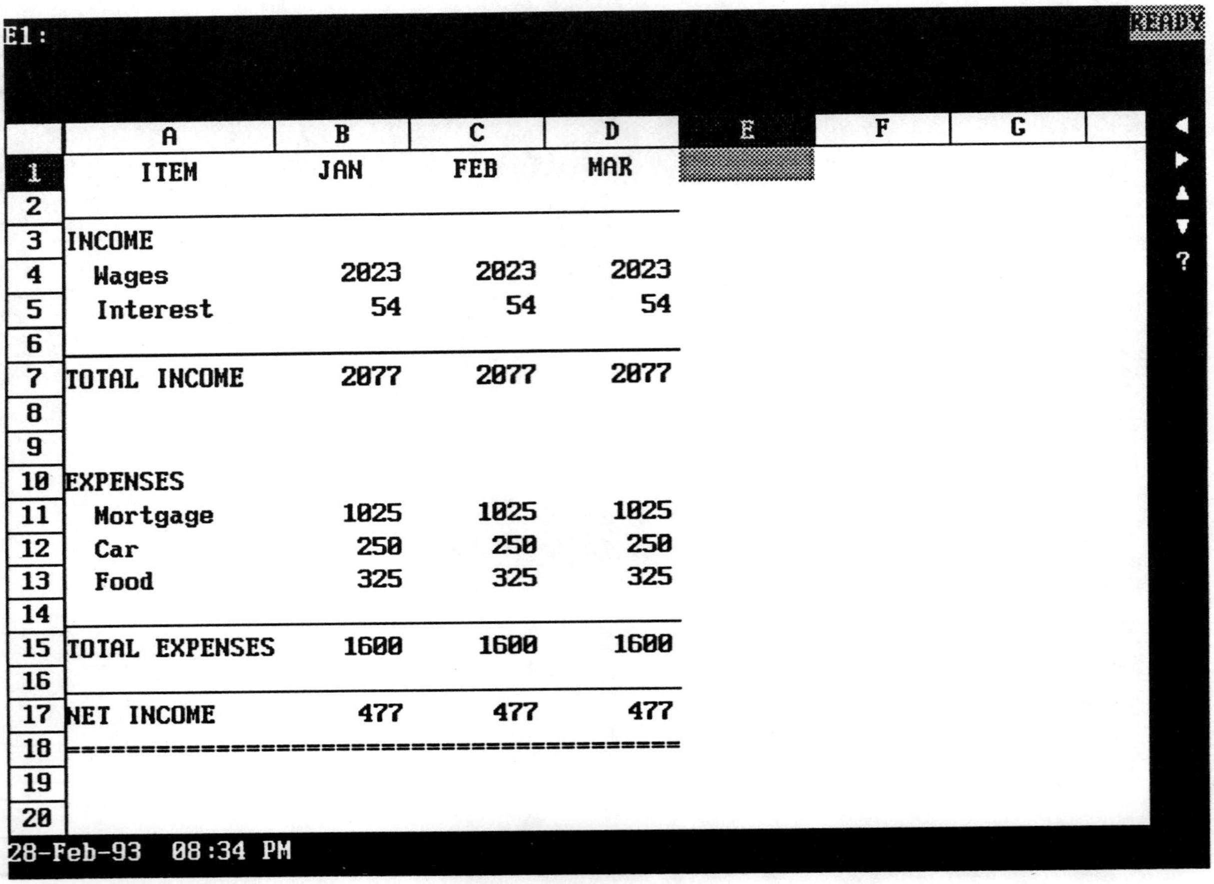

```
E1:                                                                    READY

           A         B         C         D       E       F       G     ◄
                                                                       ►
  1     ITEM       JAN       FEB       MAR                              ▲
  2    ─────────────────────────────────────────                       ▼
  3   INCOME                                                            ?
  4     Wages      2023      2023      2023
  5     Interest     54        54        54
  6
  7   TOTAL INCOME 2077      2077      2077
  8
  9
 10   EXPENSES
 11     Mortgage   1025      1025      1025
 12     Car         250       250       250
 13     Food        325       325       325
 14    ─────────────────────────────────────────
 15   TOTAL EXPENSES 1600    1600      1600
 16    ─────────────────────────────────────────
 17   NET INCOME    477       477       477
 18   ==========================================
 19
 20
28-Feb-93   08:34 PM
```

Figure 3.20  The Move Results

## EXAMPLE 1

Using what you have learned so far, try entering the spreadsheet below into Lotus 1-2-3. If you need a clean worksheet screen, select **/Worksheet Erase**. The formulas and functions are displayed to assist you. When you enter the formulas and functions, the calculated totals will appear in the "Total Amount" column and "Totals" row.

Begin the heading "JANUARY REVENUE" in Column B, and leave Row 2 blank. You will notice t at this heading will overlap into cell C1. This will not create a problem unless there is an entry in C1.

|   | A | B | C | D |
|---|---|---|---|---|
| 1 |   | JANUARY REVENUE | | |
| 2 |   |   |   |   |
| 3 | BILLER | HOURS | RATE | TOTAL AMT |
| 4 |   |   |   |   |
| 5 | JLD | 160 | 250 | +B5*C5 |
| 6 | STR | 176 | 245 | +B6*C6 |
| 7 | MMD | 125 | 245 | +B7*C7 |
| 8 |   |   |   |   |
| 9 | Totals | @sum(B5..B7) | | +D5+D6+D7 |

When you are finished, your worksheet should look like the one shown in Figure 3.21.

## 1. Formatting a Range [/Range Format]

To improve the appearance of our worksheet, we need to add commas and dollar signs to the numbers in Columns C and D. The /Range Format command allows you to format a range of values in a variety of ways. Accessing the /Range Format command displays the options shown below in Figure 3.22.

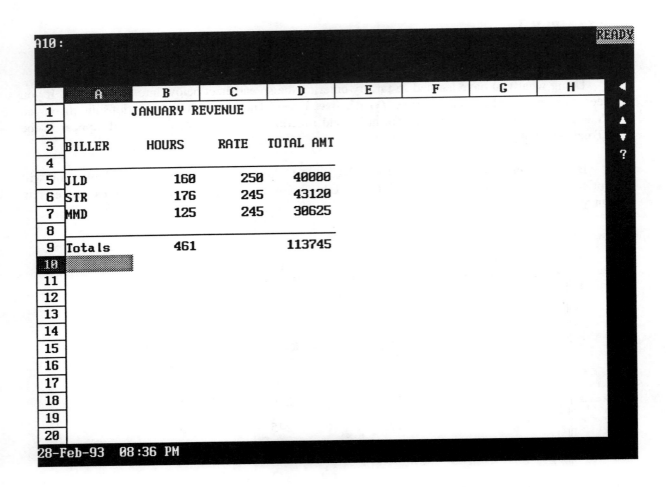

**Figure 3.21** Example 1

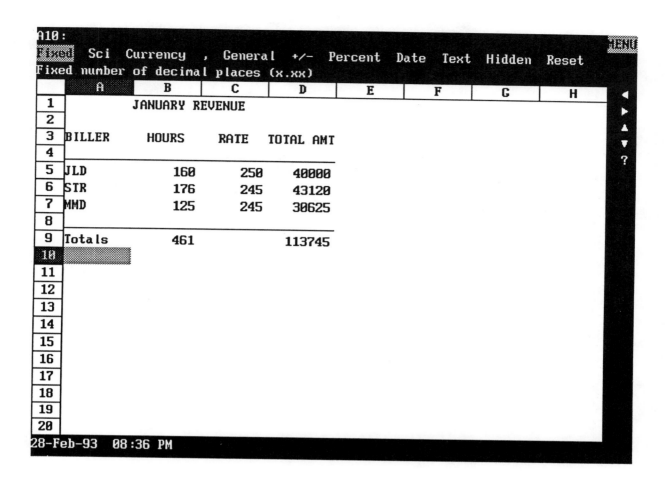

**Figure 3.22** /Range Format Options

The three types of formats most often used by legal professionals are the Fixed, Currency, and Comma (,) formats. These three formats are explained below using the number "12345." We will assume that we want two decimal places in this number.

> *The Comma format is represented by the comma character ([,]), because "currency" and "comma" both begin with a "c". This way, the Currency format may be selected by pressing the letter [c], and the Comma format may be selected by pressing [,].*

**Fixed**       Displays a number *without commas*, and lets you set the number of decimal places.

                                    **12345.00**

**Currency**    Displays a number preceded by a dollar sign ($), *with commas*, and lets you set the number of decimal places.

                                    **$12,345.00**

,               Displays a number *with commas*, and lets you set the number of decimal places.

                                    **12,345.00**

For our example, we will select the **Currency** format. After **Currency** has been selected, Lotus 1-2-3 prompts for the number of decimal places for the numbers. For this example, type 0 and press the **[Enter]** key. Lotus 1-2-3 will then prompt for the range to be formatted. At this point, you can either type **C5..D9**, or point to the range to be formatted with the cell pointer. If you have trouble with pointing to the range, refer to Section D, Item 2, regarding Pointing and Anchoring. Your spreadsheet should now look like the one in Figure 3.23.

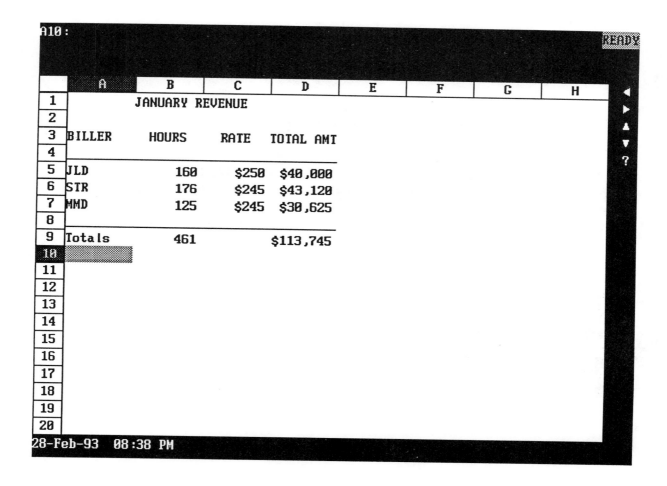

**Figure 3.23** The Formatted Spreadsheet

## 2. Saving the Worksheet [/File Save]

The /File Save command is used to save a worksheet. Upon accessing the command, Lotus 1-2-3 prompts for the name of the file:

**Enter name of file to save:**

To name the file, specify the disk drive, directory and a 1- to 8-character name for the file. Lotus 1-2-3 will provide the file with an extension.

Lotus 1-2-3 often displays a preset drive and directory where files will be saved:

**Enter name of file to save: C:\LOTUS\**

If this is not where you wish to save your files, press the **[Esc]** key to remove the directory and the disk drive designation before typing your selection. Type the location and name of the file and press the **[Enter]** key.

### 3. Clearing the Lotus 1-2-3 Worksheet Screen [/Worksheet Erase]

When you have finished using a worksheet and want to begin another, you need to clear the worksheet screen. To do this, you use the /Worksheet Erase command. You will be prompted with a **No Yes** to confirm that you wish to erase the worksheet. Highlight **Yes** and press the **[Enter]** key. This will erase the worksheet. If you have not saved the worksheet, a warning message will appear asking if you really wish to erase the worksheet.

## EXAMPLE 2

The spreadsheet in Figure 3.24 is a law firm's income forecast for the first quarter of the year. Since this is a forecast, the amount of revenue from each legal professional is an estimate. This

F1:                                                                    READY

| | A | B | C | D | E | F | G |
|---|---|---|---|---|---|---|---|
| 1 | | INCOME FORECAST – First Quarter | | | | | |
| 2 | | | | | | | |
| 3 | ITEM | JAN | FEB | MAR | TOTALS | | |
| 4 | | | | | | | |
| 5 | INCOME | | | | | | |
| 6 | Partners | | | | | | |
| 7 | MDL | 40,000 | 40,000 | 40,000 | $120,000 | | |
| 8 | JKK | 32,000 | 32,000 | 32,000 | $96,000 | | |
| 9 | TLM | 28,800 | 28,800 | 28,800 | $86,400 | | |
| 10 | Associates | | | | | | |
| 11 | WBB | 28,800 | 28,800 | 28,800 | $86,400 | | |
| 12 | DLS | 24,000 | 24,000 | 24,000 | $72,000 | | |
| 13 | JMG | 24,000 | 24,000 | 24,000 | $72,000 | | |
| 14 | DGA | 22,400 | 22,400 | 22,400 | $67,200 | | |
| 15 | Paralegals | | | | | | |
| 16 | James | 12,800 | 12,800 | 12,800 | $38,400 | | |
| 17 | Susan | 12,800 | 12,800 | 12,800 | $38,400 | | |
| 18 | | | | | | | |
| 19 | TOTAL INCOME | $225,600 | $225,600 | $225,600 | $676,800 | | |
| 20 | | | | | | | |

28-Feb-93  08:42 PM

**Figure 3.24**  The Income Forecast Worksheet

section will follow the creation of this worksheet. Lotus 1-2-3 commands which help in creating the worksheet will be explained as they are needed.

- To create the Income Forecast worksheet, begin by entering the **title** of the spreadsheet in Cell **B1**.

- In Row **3**, center the headings in their respective columns. Remember that typing the [^] character before you type the heading will center it within the cell.

- In Cell A4, use the Repeater to place an underline throughout the cell (\_).

At this point, your worksheet should look like Figure 3.25. To proceed to the next step in the worksheet creation, you need to learn about the /Copy command.

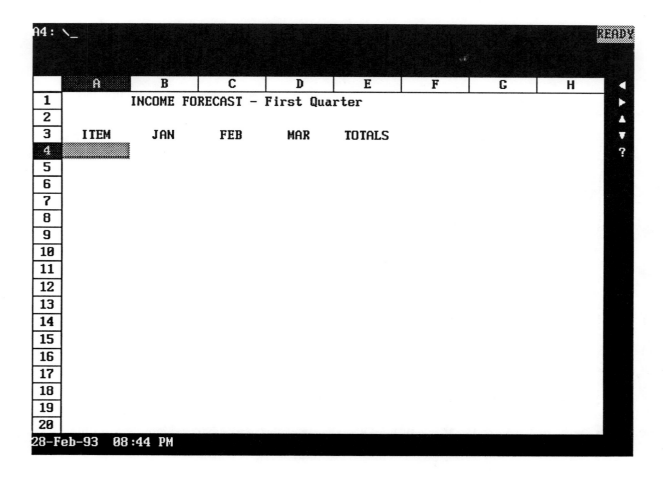

**Figure 3.25** The Income Forecast Worksheet with Title and Headings

## 1.  Copying a Cell Entry [/Copy]

Copying a cell entry is accomplished with the /Copy command. Instead of entering a repeating underline in Cells B4, C4, D4, and E4, we can copy the entry in **A4** to the range B4..E4. The following steps make up the /Copy command.

• Access the Menu with the [/] key and select **Copy**.

Lotus 1-2-3 will display one of the following messages:

> **Enter range to copy FROM:**

or

> **Copy what?**

• Type the range of the cell to be copied,  **A4..A4,** or highlight the range with the cell pointer (if you need to release the anchor, press **[Esc]**). Pressing the **[Enter]** key completes this portion of the command.

• After entering the range to copy a prompt will appear asking where to copy the range:

> **Enter range to copy TO:**

or

> **To where?**

• Type the range of cells you wish to copy this entry to, **B4..E4,** or highlight the range with the cell pointer. Pressing the **[Enter]** key completes the copy as shown in Figure 3.26.

> *Hint: Move the cell pointer to the cell you wish to copy before accessing the Menu to begin the copy. This will make it easier to enter the range to be copied.*

## 2.  Changing the Width of a Column [/Worksheet Column Set-Width]

The Items in Column A will be the next part of the worksheet we will enter. Lotus 1-2-3 pre-sets the width of all worksheet columns at nine spaces. We will need to increase the width of Column A to accommodate the item names.

To increase or decrease the width of a column, the /Worksheet Column Set-Width command is used. To use this command, the cell pointer must be within the desired column before acces-

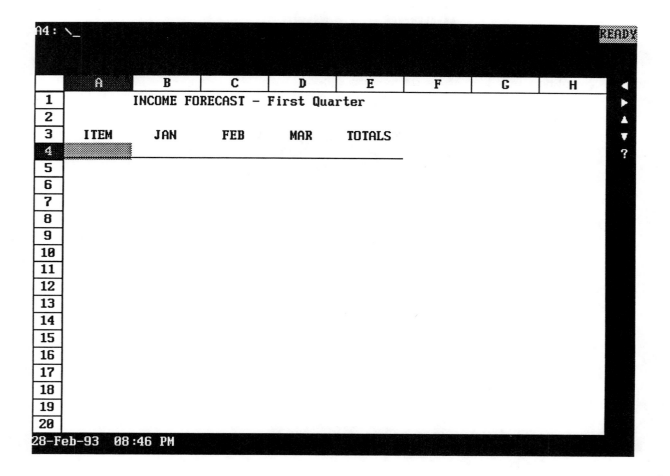

**Figure 3.26** The entry in Cell A4 is copied to Cells B4 through E4

sing the Menu. To increase the width of Column A in our worksheet, follow the steps below.

- Place the cell pointer in **Column A,** access the Menu with the [/] key, and select **Worksheet.**

- Select **Column,** and then **Set-Width.** A prompt for the new width of the column will be displayed.

  **Enter column width (1..240): 9**

  The nine is present because this is the default width. You may alter the width using the **[Left Arrow]** and **[Right Arrow]** keys, or type in a number for the new width.

- Change the width of **Column A** to 14. Press the **[Enter]** key to complete the command.

Now that you have changed the width of Column A, enter the items in **Column A, Rows 5** through **19**. You will use the **[Space Bar]** to indent "Partners," "Associates," and "Paralegals." The initials, names and "Total Income" will be centered. Leave Row 18 blank. Your worksheet should now look like the one in Figure 3.27.

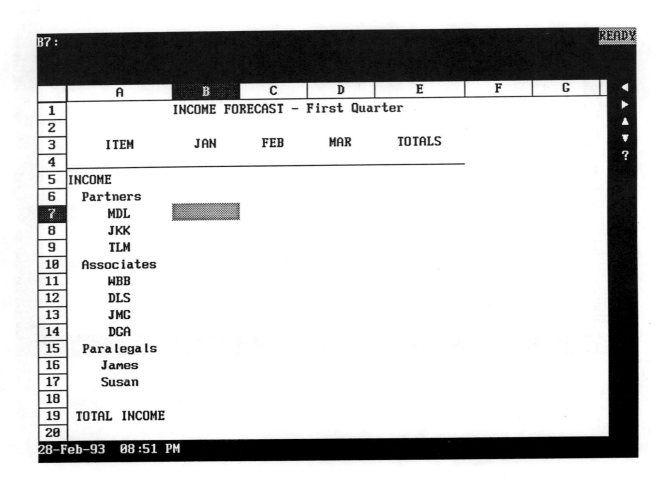

**Figure 3.27** The Income Forecast Worksheet with the items entered in Column A

### 3. Copying a Group of Cells

The next step in the creation of our worksheet will demonstrate the value of the /Copy command. First, enter the income amounts for each attorney and paralegal in the January column. (Remember, you may not use commas when entering a number. We will format these numbers later.) Your worksheet should now look like the one in Figure 3.28.

```
B17: 12800                                                              READY

        │    A    │    B    │  C   │  D   │    E    │  F   │   G   │   ◄
      1 │         INCOME FORECAST - First Quarter                        ►
      2 │                                                                ▲
      3 │   ITEM      JAN      FEB    MAR     TOTALS                      ▼
      4 │ ──────────────────────────────────────────────                ?
      5 │INCOME
      6 │  Partners
      7 │    MDL       40000
      8 │    JKK       32000
      9 │    TLM       28800
     10 │  Associates
     11 │    WBB       28800
     12 │    DLS       24000
     13 │    JMG       24000
     14 │    DGA       22400
     15 │  Paralegals
     16 │    James     12800
     17 │    Susan     12800
     18 │
     19 │TOTAL INCOME
     20 │
28-Feb-93  08:52 PM
```

**Figure 3.28** The Income Forecast Worksheet with the amounts for January entered

Instead of entering the same amounts in the February and March columns, use the **/Copy** command to copy the numbers in January to February and March. When the command prompts you to enter the range to copy, type or highlight B7..B17 and press **[Enter]**. When the command prompts you to enter where to copy, type or highlight **C7..D7** and press **[Enter]**. Your worksheet should now look like the one in Figure 3.29.

READY

|  | A | B | C | D | E | F | G |
|---|---|---|---|---|---|---|---|
| 1 | INCOME FORECAST - First Quarter | | | | | | |
| 2 | | | | | | | |
| 3 | ITEM | JAN | FEB | MAR | TOTALS | | |
| 4 | | | | | | | |
| 5 | INCOME | | | | | | |
| 6 | Partners | | | | | | |
| 7 | MDL | 40000 | 40000 | 40000 | | | |
| 8 | JKK | 32000 | 32000 | 32000 | | | |
| 9 | TLM | 28800 | 28800 | 28800 | | | |
| 10 | Associates | | | | | | |
| 11 | WBB | 28800 | 28800 | 28800 | | | |
| 12 | DLS | 24000 | 24000 | 24000 | | | |
| 13 | JMC | 24000 | 24000 | 24000 | | | |
| 14 | DGA | 22400 | 22400 | 22400 | | | |
| 15 | Paralegals | | | | | | |
| 16 | James | 12800 | 12800 | 12800 | | | |
| 17 | Susan | 12800 | 12800 | 12800 | | | |
| 18 | | | | | | | |
| 19 | TOTAL INCOME | | | | | | |
| 20 | | | | | | | |

28-Feb-93   08:54 PM

**Figure 3.29** The Income Forecast Worksheet after the amounts in the January
column have been copied to the February and March columns

### 4. Entering and Copying Formulas

Entering the formulas in Column E is the next step in the creation of the spreadsheet. Enter a *formula* in **Cell E7** that will add **Cells B7**, **C7**, and **D7**. Then, use the **/Copy** command to copy the entry in **Cell E7** to the range **E8..E9**. You could copy **Cell E7** all the way down to **E17**, but it will place zeros in **Cells E10** and **E15**.

> *Lotus 1-2-3 will automatically change the row numbers or column letters in your formulas as you copy them to create the correct formula for each cell.*

After you have copied the formula to the range **E8..E9**, you will execute another **/Copy** command to copy the formula to the range **E11..E14**. Then, you will execute the **/Copy** command again to copy the formula to the range **E16..E17**. Your worksheet should now look like the one in Figure 3.30.

```
E14: [W12] +B14+C14+D14                                                    READY

        ┌──────┬─────────┬─────────┬─────────┬─────────┬─────────┬─────────┐  ◄
        │   A  │    B    │    C    │    D    │    E    │    F    │    G    │  ►
   ┌────┤      INCOME FORECAST - First Quarter                             │  ▲
   │  1 │                                                                  │  ▼
   │  2 │                                                                  │  ?
   │  3 │  ITEM      JAN       FEB       MAR      TOTALS                    │
   │  4 │ ─────────────────────────────────────────────────────           │
   │  5 │INCOME                                                            │
   │  6 │  Partners                                                        │
   │  7 │    MDL      40000     40000     40000    120000                  │
   │  8 │    JKK      32000     32000     32000     96000                  │
   │  9 │    TLM      28800     28800     28800     86400                  │
   │ 10 │  Associates                                                      │
   │ 11 │    WBB      28800     28800     28800     86400                  │
   │ 12 │    DLS      24000     24000     24000     72000                  │
   │ 13 │    JMC      24000     24000     24000     72000                  │
   │ 14 │    DCA      22400     22400     22400     67200                  │
   │ 15 │  Paralegals                                                      │
   │ 16 │    James    12800     12800     12800     38400                  │
   │ 17 │    Susan    12800     12800     12800     38400                  │
   │ 18 │                                                                  │
   │ 19 │ TOTAL INCOME                                                     │
   │ 20 │                                                                  │
   28-Feb-93  08:55 PM
```

**Figure 3.30** The Income Forecast Worksheet with the Row Totals entered

In the event that you copied the formula into Cell E10 or E15, use the **[Delete]** key or **/Range Erase** to erase the cell entry.

## 5. Entering the Column Totals

The next step in the creation of our spreadsheet is to enter the underlines and column totals. First, enter a repeating underline (\_) in **Cell B18**. Then, copy **Cell B18** to the range **C18..E18**.

For the totals of **Columns B** through **E**, we will use an @SUM Function. In **Cell B19**, type an @SUM Function to add the range **B7..B17**. Then, copy **Cell B19** to the range **C19..E19**.

The last step in creating the spreadsheet is to place a double underline in the range **B20..E20**. A double underline can be created with a repeating equals sign (\=). Enter the repeating equals sign in **Cell B20**, and then copy the entry to the range **C20..E20**.

## 6. Formatting the Spreadsheet

To complete our spreadsheet, we will format the income numbers in the **Comma** format and the totals in the **Currency** format. We will use **0** decimal places.

First, format the range **B7..D17** in the **Comma** format with **0** decimal places using **/Range Format , (Comma) 0**. Then, format the range **E7..E19** in the **Currency** format with **0** decimal places using **/Range Format Currency, 0**. The format will not affect Cell **E18**. Repeat this format with range **B19..D19**.

> *If a value cell entry becomes too large for its cell, it will appear in exponential form or asterisks will fill the cell. When you increase the width of the cell sufficiently, the value will appear.*

## 7. Inserting a Column or Row [/Worksheet Insert]

To demonstrate how to insert a column or row into a worksheet, you will be added as an attorney or paralegal in our spreadsheet. Inserting a row is accomplished with the /Worksheet Insert Row command. To insert a column, you would use /Worksheet Insert Column. Rows are inserted directly above the position of the cell pointer when the Menu is accessed. Columns are inserted to the left of the cell pointer. To insert a row, follow the steps below.

- Move the cell pointer to the row of the spreadsheet directly below the place where you would like your row to appear.

- Access the Menu with the [/] key and select **Worksheet**. Select **Insert**, and then **Row**. Lotus 1-2-3 will prompt you to:

    **Enter row insert range:**

    If you wish to insert only one row above the cell pointer, press **[Enter]** to complete the command. If you wish to insert more than one row, move the pointer up or down the number of rows that you desire to insert, and then press the **[Enter]** key to complete the command.

Enter your initials or name and the income amount you would expect to bring into the firm each month. Remember that very large numbers will appear exponentially or be replaced with asterisks until you increase the column width.

Copy a row total formula to your row in Column E. You may need to edit (**[F2]**) your "Total Income" functions to include the addition of another row. Your monthly income numbers will need to be formatted with **/Range Format , (comma) 0.** Your final worksheet should appear similar to the one in Figure 3.31.

```
A16: {H13} [W14] ^Kris                                            READY

         ┌─────────────┬────────┬────────┬────────┬─────────┬────────┬────────┐  ◄
         │      A      │   B    │   C    │   D    │    E    │   F    │   G    │  ►
      1  │        INCOME FORECAST - First Quarter                             │  ▲
      2  │             │        │        │        │         │        │        │  ▼
      3  │    ITEM     │  JAN   │  FEB   │  MAR   │ TOTALS  │        │        │  ?
      4  │─────────────────────────────────────────────────────────          │
      5  │INCOME       │        │        │        │         │        │
      6  │  Partners   │        │        │        │         │        │
      7  │    MDL      │ 40,000 │ 40,000 │ 40,000 │$120,000 │        │
      8  │    JKK      │ 32,000 │ 32,000 │ 32,000 │ $96,000 │        │
      9  │    TLM      │ 28,800 │ 28,800 │ 28,800 │ $86,400 │        │
     10  │  Associates │        │        │        │         │        │
     11  │    WBB      │ 28,800 │ 28,800 │ 28,800 │ $86,400 │        │
     12  │    DLS      │ 24,000 │ 24,000 │ 24,000 │ $72,000 │        │
     13  │    JMG      │ 24,000 │ 24,000 │ 24,000 │ $72,000 │        │
     14  │    DGA      │ 22,400 │ 22,400 │ 22,400 │ $67,200 │        │
     15  │  Paralegals │        │        │        │         │        │
     16  │    Kris     │ 30,000 │ 30,000 │ 30,000 │ $90,000 │        │
     17  │    James    │ 12,800 │ 12,800 │ 12,800 │ $38,400 │        │
     18  │    Susan    │ 12,800 │ 12,800 │ 12,800 │ $38,400 │        │
     19  │─────────────────────────────────────────────────────────          │
     20  │TOTAL INCOME │$255,600│$255,600│$255,600│$766,800 │        │
     21  │=================================================================
28-Feb-93  09:01 PM
```

**Figure 3.31**  The New Income Forecast Worksheet

# E. USING A LOTUS 1-2-3 WINDOW [/WORKSHEET WINDOW]

A Lotus 1-2-3 **Window** splits the worksheet screen into two windows. This feature becomes useful when your worksheet becomes so large that you can no longer see the headings at the top or left side while you are working. If the worksheet in Figure 3.31 had several more rows of data, you would reach a point in entering data at the bottom of the worksheet where you could no longer see the headings at the top of the screen. To keep the headings at the top of the worksheet screen, we can place a Window above Row 5.

A Window can be horizontal or vertical. Placing a Window in the worksheet is accomplished with the /Worksheet Window command. The following steps will create a horizontal Window above Row 5.

- With the cell pointer in Row 5, access the Menu with the [/] key.

- Select **Worksheet**, and then select **Window**.

- Select **Horizontal**.

A horizontal Window will be placed above Row 5. To move from one side of the Window to the other, use the **[F6]** key. Move to the lower half of the screen and use the **[Down Arrow]** key to scroll down in the spreadsheet to see how the headings remain intact.

To clear the Window, select **/Worksheet Window Clear**.

## F. PRINTING A WORKSHEET [/PRINT PRINTER]

Printing a worksheet is accomplished with the /Print Printer command. Before you execute this command, however, save your worksheet with the **/File Save** command. In the event that the print job causes your computer to freeze, this will prevent you from losing your worksheet. Follow the steps below to print the worksheet.

- Access the Menu with the [/] key and select **Print**. Select **Printer**.

- Select **Range** to specify the range of the spreadsheet to be printed. You may type the range, **A1..E21**, or move to **Cell A1** with the **[Home]** key, anchor the cell pointer with the period and highlight the range. Pressing **[Enter]** returns you to the Print Menu.

- Selecting **Go** will send your spreadsheet to the printer. Lotus 1-2-3 does not always automatically send a command to the printer to eject the page after a range has been printed. This is so that you may print other ranges on the same page. To eject your worksheet from the printer, select **Page** after selecting **Go**.

> *With some network versions of Lotus 1-2-3, you must select Quit, after selecting Page, in order to print the spreadsheet.*

- Selecting **Quit** will return you to the worksheet.

## G. DATABASE FEATURES

Lotus 1-2-3 is equipped with database features that will allow you to sort, query, and perform other actions upon a worksheet. The most helpful database feature is Sort. Enter the worksheet in Figure 3.32 to practice the Sort feature. You will need to increase the width of Column A to 14. The expense items are each indented with two spaces.

```
A9: (F2) [W16] ' Property Tax                                              READY

                A          B        C        D        E        F        G
   1   EXPENSES            JAN      FEB      MARCH    APRIL
   2
   3   Utilities          45       45       45       45
   4   Car Payments       700      700      700      700
   5   Medical            100      100      100      100
   6   Car Repairs                 300
   7   Telephone          35       35       35       35
   8   Clothing           200      200      200      200
   9   Property Tax                         795
  10   Gardener           38       38       38       38
  11   Car Registr.       78
  12   Gasoline           175      175      175      175
  13   Food               400      400      400      400
  14   Cable              21       21       21       21
  15   Mortgage           1,124    1,124    1,124    1,124
  16   City Fees          33       33       33       33
  17   Insurance                            433
  18   ===================================================================
  19   TOTAL EXPENSES     2,949    3,171    4,099    2,871
  20   ===================================================================
02-Apr-93  02:53 PM
```

**Figure 3.32** The Expense Worksheet

To sort the expense items follow the instructions below.

- Access the Menu with the [/] key.

- Select **Data**, select **Sort**.

- Select **Data-Range** to specify the entire body of information to be sorted. This range will include each of the expense items and their monthly amounts. Type in, or highlight, the range **A3..E17**, and press **[Enter]**.

- Select **Primary-Key**. The Primary-Key is the range you wish to sort upon. We will sort by expense item name. Type in, or highlight, the range **A3..A17**, and press **[Enter]**.

- When you are prompted for the sort order, select **A** for ascending, and press **[Enter]**.

- Select **Go** to perform the sort. The completed sort should look like Figure 3.33.

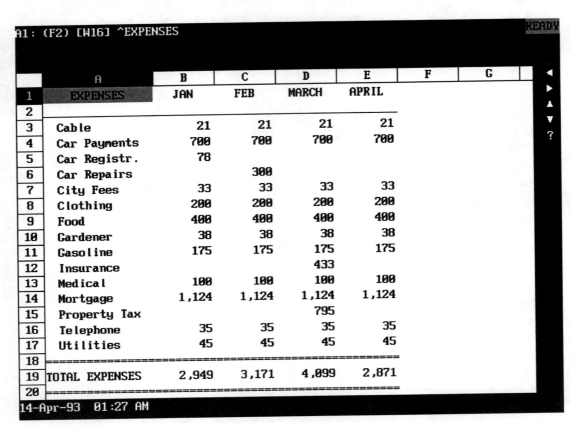

A1: (F2) [W16] ^EXPENSES                                                    READY

| | A | B | C | D | E | F | G |
|---|---|---|---|---|---|---|---|
| 1 | EXPENSES | JAN | FEB | MARCH | APRIL | | |
| 2 | | | | | | | |
| 3 | Cable | 21 | 21 | 21 | 21 | | |
| 4 | Car Payments | 700 | 700 | 700 | 700 | | |
| 5 | Car Registr. | 78 | | | | | |
| 6 | Car Repairs | | 300 | | | | |
| 7 | City Fees | 33 | 33 | 33 | 33 | | |
| 8 | Clothing | 200 | 200 | 200 | 200 | | |
| 9 | Food | 400 | 400 | 400 | 400 | | |
| 10 | Gardener | 38 | 38 | 38 | 38 | | |
| 11 | Gasoline | 175 | 175 | 175 | 175 | | |
| 12 | Insurance | | | 433 | | | |
| 13 | Medical | 100 | 100 | 100 | 100 | | |
| 14 | Mortgage | 1,124 | 1,124 | 1,124 | 1,124 | | |
| 15 | Property Tax | | | 795 | | | |
| 16 | Telephone | 35 | 35 | 35 | 35 | | |
| 17 | Utilities | 45 | 45 | 45 | 45 | | |
| 18 | | | | | | | |
| 19 | TOTAL EXPENSES | 2,949 | 3,171 | 4,099 | 2,871 | | |
| 20 | | | | | | | |

14-Apr-93  01:27 AM

**Figure 3.33** The Sorted Expense Items

## H. GRAPHING

Using the Expense worksheet, we will graph the total expenses for January through April.

- Access the Menu with the [/] key.

- Select **Graph**, select **Type**. There are several types of graphs available. We will select **Bar**.

- You must specify the **X** axis (the bottom of the graph) and at least one data range **A—F** (the left side of the graph). Select **X** and type, or highlight, the range **B1..E1**, then press **[Enter]**. Select **A** and type, or highlight, the range **B19..E19**, then press **[Enter]**.

- To view the graph, select **View**. The graph is shown in Figure 3.34. Press the **[Space Bar]** to return to the Menu. Select **Quit** to return to the worksheet.

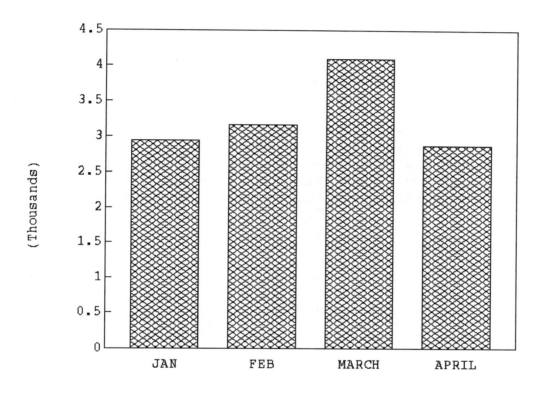

**Figure 3.34** A bar graph created from the totals in the Expense Worksheet

If you wish to print the graph, you must select **Save** from the **/Graph** Menu, give the file a name, press **[Enter]**, and select **Quit**. Then, exit the Lotus 1-2-3 worksheet to the Lotus 1-2-3 Access Menu where **PrintGraph** is located.

# I. RETRIEVING A FILE [/FILE RETRIEVE]

To retrieve a file into a blank worksheet, follow the instructions below.

- Access the Menu with the [/] key.

- Select **File**, select **Retrieve**. The Lotus 1-2-3 worksheet files in the selected default directory will be displayed along with the message:

  **Name of file to retrieve:**

  This message will be followed by the name of the default directory. You may retrieve one of the listed files by highlighting its name and pressing the **[Enter]** key. (You may change the default directory with **/File Directory**.)

- If you would like to view files in a different directory, or on a different disk, press the **[Esc]** key to remove the default drive and directory from the retrieve message. Then, type in the new file location such as **A:**. If you specify a directory, follow the directory name with another backslash, **C:\TEMP\**. Pressing **[Enter]** will bring up Lotus 1-2-3 files located in the drive and/or directory. Highlight the desired file name and press the **[Enter]** key.

# J. EXITING LOTUS 1-2-3

To exit from Lotus 1-2-3, use the **/Quit** command.

- Access the Menu with the [/] key and select **Quit**.
  Lotus 1-2-3 will ask you if you wish to quit. Highlighting **Yes** and pressing the **[Enter]** key will take you to the Lotus 1-2-3 Access Menu, or beep you with a warning message if you have not saved your spreadsheet.

- From the Lotus 1-2-3 Access Menu, select **Exit** to leave the program.

# *Summary*

Lotus 1-2-3 can be used to create many types of spreadsheets. The Lotus 1-2-3 worksheet uses the function keys, mouse, and menus to execute commands. The Command Menus are accessed with the forward slash key [/]. Items from the Menu are selected by highlighting them and pressing **[Enter]**, or by pressing the first character within their name.

There are two types of cell entries in Lotus 1-2-3, Labels and Values. Labels are character entries and numbers that are not intended to be used for mathematical computations (e.g., a telephone number). Labels may be centered, or left or right justified within a cell by preceding the Label with a justification character. All Labels are automatically left justified unless they are preceded with a justification character.

Values are numeric cell entries. These entries consist of numbers, formulas and functions. A formula is any equation placed within a cell. A function is a formula which has been pre-programmed into Lotus 1-2-3. Value cell entries may not be justified. If a Value is preceded by a justification character, Lotus 1-2-3 will think that the entry is a Label and will not perform computations with the entry.

Cell entries may be copied or moved within the Lotus 1-2-3 Worksheet. Column widths may be increased or decreased; and columns or rows may be inserted or deleted. Database actions may be performed within the worksheet, and graphs may be created from the worksheet data. In total, the Lotus 1-2-3 worksheet is a flexible tool for helping to plan and analyze past and future events.

# *Lotus 1-2-3 Command List*

This command list provides a quick reference for the Lotus 1-2-3 commands.

## COPYING CELLS

The copy command allows you to copy a cell entry from one or more cells to one or more other cells. It is accomplished by the following steps:

*/*
**COPY**
**Type or highlight the range of cells you wish to copy and press [Enter].**
**Type or highlight the range of cells where you wish to copy and press [Enter].**

## DELETING A COLUMN OR ROW

This command is similar to the command to insert a column or row. Before you begin this command, place the cell pointer within the column or row to be deleted.

*/*
**WORKSHEET**
**DELETE**
**COLUMN or ROW**
**Highlight the Column(s) or Row(s) to be deleted and press [Enter].**

## ERASING A RANGE

To erase a single cell, or a group of cells, use the **[Delete]** key or the command to erase a range.

**/**
**RANGE**
**ERASE**
**Specify the range to be erased and press [Enter].**


## ERASING THE WORKSHEET

To clear the worksheet so that you may begin a new one, the worksheet must be erased.

**/**
**WORKSHEET**
**ERASE**
**Respond Yes to the prompt.**


## EXITING LOTUS 1-2-3

To exit the program, make sure you have saved your spreadsheet, and follow the steps below.

**/**
**QUIT**
**Respond Yes to the prompt.**
**At the Lotus 1-2-3 Access Menu, select EXIT.**


## FORMATTING CELLS

The Format command allows you to create a uniform appearance for a range of numbers.

**/**
**RANGE**
**FORMAT**
**Select the desired format type.**
**Type or highlight the range to be formatted and press [Enter].**

## INCREASING OR DECREASING THE WIDTH OF A COLUMN

To increase or decrease the width of a column, move the cell pointer to that column and follow these steps:

> **/**
> **WORKSHEET**
> **COLUMN**
> **SET-WIDTH**
> **Use the [Arrow] keys or type the width (number of characters) you desire for this column and press [Enter].**

## INSERTING A COLUMN OR ROW

This command allows you to insert a new column or row within the worksheet. Before you begin this command, you must place the cell pointer in the column to the right of where you want the new column to be placed, or in the row below where you want the new row to be placed.

> **/**
> **WORKSHEET**
> **INSERT**
> **COLUMN or ROW**
> **Move the highlight bar to highlight the number of columns or rows to be inserted and press [Enter].**

## MOVING CELLS

To move a range of cells, use the command below.

> **/**
> **MOVE**
> **Type or highlight the range of cells to be moved and press [Enter].**
> **Move the cell pointer to the row and column where you would like to move the cells and press [Enter].**

## Printing a Worksheet

Follow the commands below to print a worksheet.

**/**
**PRINT**
**PRINTER**
**RANGE**
Type or highlight the range of cells and press [Enter].
**GO**
**PAGE**       This command sends a blank page after your worksheet to flush the worksheet out of the printer. Lotus 1-2-3 may not automatically send a page feed to the printer. This enables you to print more than one range on a single page.

## Retrieving a Worksheet

To retrieve a worksheet, you need to tell Lotus 1-2-3 where the worksheet is located and its name.

**/**
**FILE**
**RETRIEVE**
Specify the location and name of the file and press [Enter].
Use the [Esc] key to remove any unwanted directory or drive designations.

## Saving a Spreadsheet

To save a spreadsheet, you need to access the Save command and specify a location and name for the file.

**/**
**FILE**
**SAVE**
Specify the location and name for the file and press [Enter]. If the file has previously been saved, press [Enter] and respond to the prompts.

## WINDOWS

A Window can be created within the worksheet screen to split the screen into two windows. You can move back and forth between the windows with the **[F6]** key. Begin the command with the cell pointer in the Row below where you wish the Window to appear.

*/*
**WORKSHEET**
**WINDOW**
**Select HORIZONTAL, VERTICAL, or CLEAR (to remove the Window)**

# *Exercise*

## *Part 1*

You have been asked to prepare a federal tax computation worksheet for the Talbot family. An example of the worksheet, with figures supplied by the Talbot's, is shown below.

**TAX COMPUTATION (Fed.) — THE TALBOT FAMILY**

| DESCRIPTION | AMOUNT |
|---|---|
| **INCOME** | |
| Wages, Salaries, Tips, Etc. | 45612 |
| Taxable Interest Income | 756 |
| Dividend Income | 175 |
| Tax Refunds | 632 |
| Other Gains (Losses) | 500 |
| **TOTAL INCOME** | |
| Less Adjustments | 135 |
| **ADJUSTED GROSS INCOME** | |
| ==================================================== | |
| **ITEMIZED DEDUCTIONS** | |
| Paid Taxes | |
| State and Local Taxes | 1010 |
| Other Taxes | 135 |
| **Total Paid Taxes** | |
| **Personal Interest** | 56 |
| **Total Paid Interest** | |
| **Total Misc. Contributions** | 545 |
| **TOTAL ITEMIZED DEDUCTIONS** | |
| ==================================================== | |
| **EXEMPTIONS** | 6000 |
| **TAXABLE INCOME** | |
| ==================================================== | |
| **TAXES OWED BEFORE CREDITS** (20% of Taxable Income) | ============== |

Enter this worksheet into Lotus 1-2-3. The totals of certain items have been left blank for you to enter formulas or functions. Most of these totals are self-explanatory. Taxable income is Adjusted Gross Income less Itemized Deductions and Exemptions. After all values have been entered, format the Amounts in the **Comma** format with **0** decimal places.

Enter your name in Column A, below the last line of your worksheet. Save and print the worksheet.

## *Part 2*

The Talbot's would like to see what effect the purchase of a home would have upon their taxes. Purchasing a home adds deductions for paid real estate taxes and mortgage interest. The Talbot's estimate the following amounts for these items:

| | |
|---|---|
| **Paid Real Estate Taxes** | **1,500** |
| **Mortgage Interest** | **10,400** |

Add these two items to the Deductions portion of the worksheet, adjusting your formulas and functions accordingly.

Save this worksheet under a new file name. Print the worksheet.

# Chapter Index

# CHAPTER 4

# DBASE III PLUS®

---

## *Chapter Preface*

dBase III Plus is a database management system ("DBMS") that allows you to organize a summary of information about particular documents or items for easy retrieval. Databases can be set up in this program for case evidence, in-house forms, client and case records, calendars, library updates and many other pieces of information.

In this chapter, we will create a database for a law firm's list of current cases. We will enter records and perform searches on the database. At the end of the chapter is an exercise in which you will create a database for a sample case.

## A. THE DBASE III PLUS DATABASE

dBase is a summary database program. As was discussed in Chapter 9 of the text, summary databases contain pieces of information about each document or item within the database. They do not contain the full text of documents.

Summary databases are made up of files, fields and records. The example we will be using in this chapter is a law firm's case list database. This database will contain items of information about every case currently handled by the firm.

### 1. Files

A database file is a collection of similar information. The file for our Case List database will be:

**CASELIST**

## 2. Fields

Fields are the structure of a database. They are items of information that will commonly be found in each of the entries in the database. The fields for the Case List database will be information that we want to store about each of the cases.

**Case Name**
**Case Number**
**Client**
**Subject**
**Date Case Filed**
**Responsible Attorney**

## 3. Records

The records of the database are the group of field entries for each case in the Case List database file. A record for the *Smith v. Berry* case is shown below.

| | |
|---|---|
| Case Name | **Smith v. Berry** |
| Case Number | **80023** |
| Client | **Berry, Simon Jr.** |
| Subject | **Breach of Contract** |
| Date Case Filed | **06/24/92** |
| Responsible Attorney | **EMD** |

# B. dBase III Plus File Names, Field Names, and Field Types

There are certain rules that must be followed in creating files and fields in dBase III Plus. These rules are:

## 1. File Names

In order to save your database file, you will need to give it a name. In dBase, *file names may be 1 to 8 characters in length.* They must begin with a letter, and may not contain spaces. The name for our firm's case list database will be:

### CASELIST

> *You do not give your file name a three-character extension. dBase automatically assigns a .DBF extension to all database files.*

## 2. Field Names

When you construct your database, you will give each field a name. *Field names may be 1 to 10 characters in length.* They must begin with a letter, and may not contain spaces or periods. After the first letter, you can use letters, numbers or the underline character. The field names which we have developed for this database have been changed below to meet the dBase field name requirements.

> **CASE_NAME**
> **CASE_NUMBR**
> **CLIENT**
> **SUBJECT**
> **DATE_FILED**
> **RESP_ATTY**

## 3. Field Types

There are five types of fields in dBase III Plus. They are:

**Character**  Anything you can type from your keyboard. A telephone number or address is a character, not a numeric, because it is not used for math.

> **JANUARY  22 Post Road  ============**

**Numeric**  Any number used in a mathematical computation. These numbers will have a fixed number of decimal places.

> **8   9.2   10.365   11.21   12.00**

**Date**  Dates in the form: mm/dd/yy.

> **08/25/92  01/01/45**

**Logical**  Used for data which will be (T)rue or (F)alse, (Y)es or (N)o, or some other two alternative combination.

> **T   F   Y   N**

**Memo**  For lengthy descriptions, dBase creates a separate memo file where you can store memos up to 4K characters in length for each memo field. When entering data in the memo field, you need to get to the memo screen with **[Ctrl]+[Home]**. When you are finished with your entry, you return to the record by pressing **[Ctrl]+[End]**.

Our case list database consists of the following field types:

| | |
|---|---|
| **CASE_NAME** | **Character** |
| **CASE_NUMBR** | **Character** |
| **CLIENT** | **Character** |
| **SUBJECT** | **Memo** |
| **DATE_FILED** | **Date** |
| **RESP_ATTY** | **Character** |

The CASE_NUMBR field is a Character field because the number will not be used in mathematical computations.

## C. ENTERING THE PROGRAM

To enter dBase type **dbase [Enter]** OR select the program name or icon from a menu screen.

When you enter dBase, you will be greeted by a license explanation. After assenting to the licensing agreement by pressing the **[Enter]** key, the dBase III Plus Assistant will be displayed.

## D. WORKING WITH DBASE III PLUS

dBase III Plus offers two ways to work with the program, the Assistant and the Dot Prompt screen.

*The Assistant*: The Assistant, shown in Figure 4.1, contains pull-down menus that help the user formulate commands. It also contains a Menu Bar, a Status Bar, and Navigation and Message Lines.

- The Menu Bar is the top line of menus in the Assistant. Underneath the menu bar are the selections that can be made in each menu. You can move along the Menu Bar using your **[Arrow]** keys to open menus. Menu options which are currently available will be displayed in bold type.

- The Status Bar is the bar at the bottom or the screen. It displays where you are located, the current drive letter, the database name (when one has been created or retrieved), and the menu option number currently highlighted.

- The Navigation and Message Lines are the final two lines below the status bar. The Navigation Line displays information about using the Assistant and seeking help. The Message Line gives information or instructions regarding the highlighted menu selection.

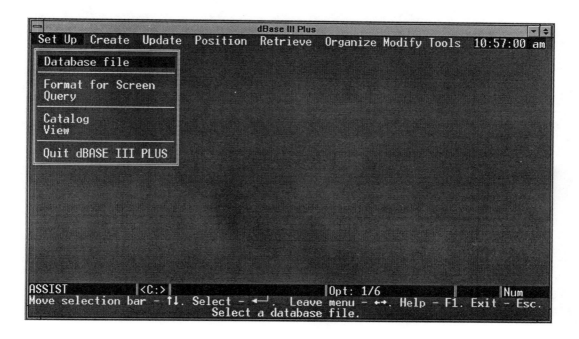

**Figure 4.1** The Assistant

***The Dot Prompt Screen:*** The Dot Prompt screen, shown in Figure 4.2, is a blank screen displaying only a period at the lower left-hand corner. This is the original way that dBase was operated. Some advanced users continue to prefer this method. Using it requires knowledge of the dBase command structure. Press **[Esc]** to view the Dot Prompt screen. Press **[F2]** to return to the Assistant.

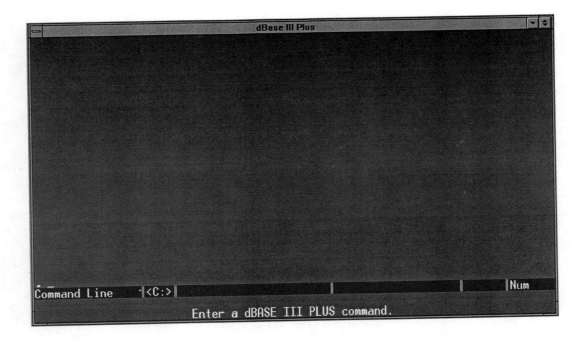

**Figure 4.2** The Dot Prompt Screen

In this chapter we will operate dBase from the Assistant and also demonstrate how to use the Dot Prompt commands.

## E. USING A DATABASE FILE

If you have already created a database file and wish to use it, follow the steps below. If you wish to create a new database file, go on to Section G.

- Open the **Set Up** menu and select **Database file**.

- Select the drive where the file is located.

- Select the file name from those listed.

- Respond **Y** or **N** to the question of whether the file is indexed depending upon the situation.

The name of the database will be placed on the status line.

To close a database file, you can open a new database file or exit the program. dBase handles the saving of the file for you.

## F. CREATING A DATABASE FILE

To create the CASELIST database:

- Open the **Create** menu and select **Database file**.

- Highlight the disk drive letter where the file will be stored and press **[Enter]**. Notice that dBase is building your command above the status bar at what is called the Action Line.

- Enter the name of the database file: **CASELIST** and press **[Enter]**.

dBase will then prompt you for the database fields in the **Create Screen**, shown in Figure 4.3. If you do not wish to see the help information at the top of the Create Screen, press **[F1]**.

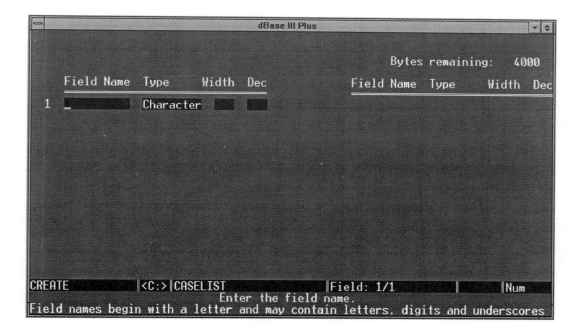

**Figure 4.3** The Create Screen

At this screen, in addition to supplying the names of the fields, we must identify the field type, its width, and the number of decimal places (for numeric fields only). The navigation and message lines will provide you with help as you enter the data.

## 1. Fields

The fields that we will create for this database are:

**CASE_NAME
CASE_NUMBR
CLIENT
SUBJECT
DATE_FILED
RESP_ATTY**

Type the name of the first field and press the **[Enter]** key. You will then need to specify the field type.

## 2. Field Types

For each field, the type of field must be specified so that dBase knows what type of data is to be stored within the field. The field types for our fields are:

| | |
|---|---|
| **CASE_NAME** | **Character** |
| **CASE_NUMBR** | **Character** |
| **CLIENT** | **Character** |
| **SUBJECT** | **Memo** |
| **DATE_FILED** | **Date** |
| **RESP_ATTY** | **Character** |

"Character" is already entered in the field type column. Press the **[Enter]** key to move on to the width column. To switch to another field type, type the first letter of the field type or toggle through the field types with the **[Space Bar]** and press **[Enter]** when the desired field type is displayed.

## 3. Field Widths

The field width column is where you tell dBase the maximum amount of characters you will be entering into the field (1-254). For example, in the CASE_NAME field, we will be entering names like "SDF Corporation v. Terra, Inc." For this name we will need 30 spaces. To be on the safe side, we will make this field 40 spaces long. In the event that we need to enter a longer case name, we can come back to this screen later and increase the field width.

There are some fields that have a pre-set width that is automatically entered when that field type is selected. These fields are:

Logical Fields: Automatic width of 1
Date Fields:    Automatic width of 8
Memo Fields:   Automatic width of 10

> *The width of 10, which is set for Memo Fields, does not mean that there are only 10 spaces available for your memos. You still have 4K of space.*

The widths of our fields will be:

| | | |
|---|---|---|
| **CASE_NAME** | **Character** | **40** |
| **CASE_NUMBR** | **Character** | **10** |
| **CLIENT** | **Character** | **25** |
| **SUBJECT** | **Memo** | **10** |
| **DATE_FILED** | **Date** | **8** |
| **RESP_ATTY** | **Character** | **4** |

## 4. Number of Decimal Places

The Decimal Column only requires an entry when the field type selected is numeric. In this column, you will specify the number of decimal places that the numbers in your database will contain.

## 5. Completing the Database Structure

Pressing the **[Enter]** key after entering the width of the CASE_NAME field takes us to the next line. Enter the remaining fields into the database. The completed structure should look like Figure 4.4.

## 6. Saving the Database Structure

To save the Database Structure, press **[Ctrl]+[End]**. Press **[Enter]** again to confirm the save. You will be asked if you wish to enter records at this time. Press **N** for No. You will return to the Assistant.

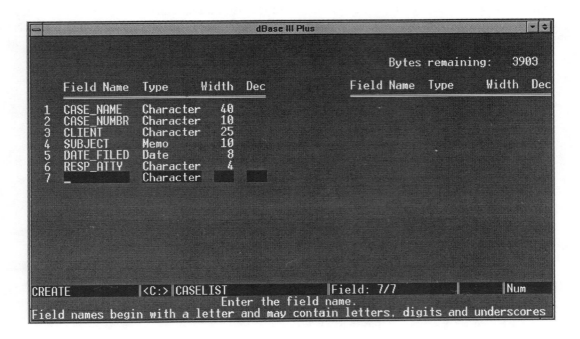

**Figure 4.4** The Completed Database Structure

## G. ENTERING RECORDS

Records may be entered into a database in the **Update** menu with **Append**.

### 1. Appending Records

Appending is adding records to the database. To enter the first records into your database follow the instructions below.

- Open the **Update** menu and select **Append**. The Append screen, shown in Figure 4.5, will be displayed.

At the Append screen enter the five records below. It is important when entering records to do so uniformly. If you make entries in a particular field in ALL CAPS, always make the entries in this manner. When you later search the database, a search for DGL will not find dgl. The Responsible Attorneys in each record will be identified by their initials. The Case Number in Record 4 indicates that this is the first patent we have filed for this corporation; this record is not a court case, and will not have a case number.

When entering data in the SUBJECT fields, type a short memo beginning with the words shown for the SUBJECT fields. See the paragraph below regarding entering data into memo fields. You can move between fields with the [**Enter**] key and the [**Arrow**] keys. You can move between records with [**Page Up**] and [**Page Down**].

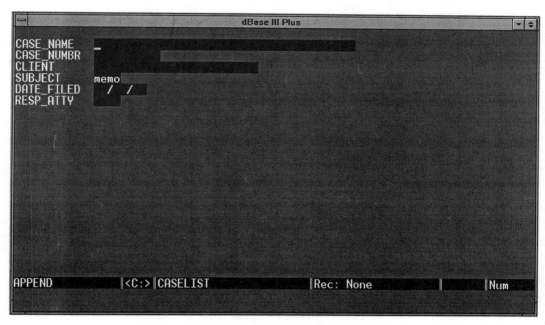

**Figure 4.5** The Append Screen

Entering data into memo fields requires that you move to a screen that will allow you to type up to 4K of data. As you can see in Figure 4.5, when you look at where you enter your records, the SUBJECT field contains the word *memo*. To create your **SUBJECT** for each record, follow the steps below.

- With the cursor in the SUBJECT field, press [**Ctrl**]+[**Home**]. This will take you to a word processor where you may enter the memo.

- Enter a sentence or short paragraph describing the case.

- Return to the Append screen by pressing [**Ctrl**]+[**End**].

Enter these records now.

| | | |
|---|---|---|
| #1 | Case Name | **Smith v. Berry** |
| | Case Number | **80023** |
| | Client | **Berry, Simon Jr.** |
| | Subject | **Breach of contract . . .** |
| | Date Case Filed | **06/24/92** |
| | Responsible Attorney | **EMD** |

| #2 | Case Name | **Simpson v. SDF Corporation** |
| | Case Number | **71176** |
| | Client | **SDF Corporation** |
| | Subject | **Wrongful termination . . .** |
| | Date Case Filed | **04/01/91** |
| | Responsible Attorney | **DGL** |

| #3 | Case Name | **SDF Corporation v. Terra, Inc.** |
| | Case Number | **72587** |
| | Client | **SDF Corporation** |
| | Subject | **Patent infringement . . .** |
| | Date Case Filed | **06/11/91** |
| | Responsible Attorney | **DGL** |

| #4 | Case Name | **SDF Corporation—Earth Eater Patent** |
| | Case Number | **1** |
| | Client | **SDF Corporation** |
| | Subject | **Patent filing . . .** |
| | Date Case Filed | **01/23/92** |
| | Responsible Attorney | **DGL** |

| #5 | Case Name | **Barker v. South Landfill** |
| | Case Number | **76645** |
| | Client | **South Landfill** |
| | Subject | **Injunctive relief . . .** |
| | Date Case Filed | **12/15/91** |
| | Responsible Attorney | **BBK** |

Figure 4.6 shows a record displayed in the Append screen.

## 2. Saving the Records

After entering all five records, press **[Ctrl]+[End]** to save and return to the Assistant.

## 3. Viewing a List of the Records

The **Retrieve** menu will allow you to see a list of your records. To view all of your records:

- Open the **Retrieve** menu and select **List**.

- Select **Execute the command** and press **N** when asked if the output should be directed to the printer.

A list of your records will then appear in an unformatted display as shown in Figure 4.7. Press any key to return to the Assistant.

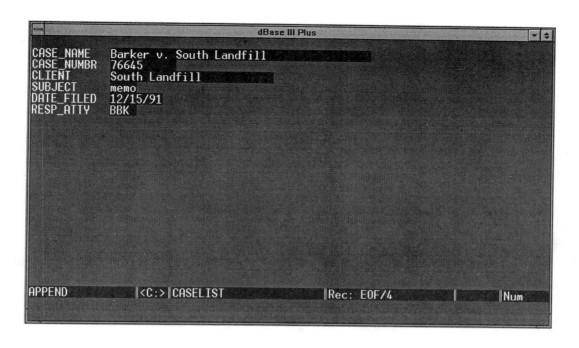

**Figure 4.6** A record displayed in the Append Screen

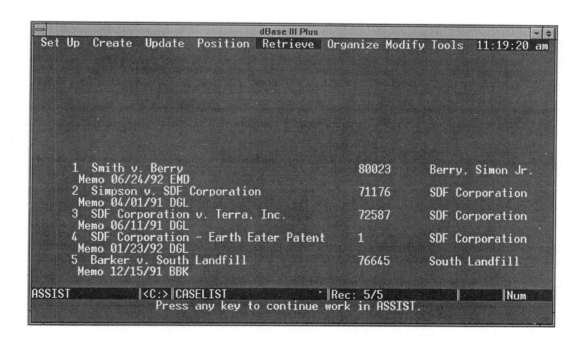

**Figure 4.7** A listing of records

## H. EDITING RECORDS

Editing your records can be performed while you are in **Append**, in the **Edit** screen, or in the **Browse** screen.

### 1. Using Append

In addition to adding new records in the Append screen, you may edit your existing records.

- Open the **Update** menu and select **Append**. A new record will be displayed.

Use the **[Page Up]**, **[Page Down]**, and **[Arrow]** keys to move among the records and fields during your editing. When you are finished, **[Ctrl]+[End]** will save your changes.

### 2. Using Edit

Another way to edit your records is in the Edit screen.

- Open the **Update** menu and select **Edit**.

The current record will be displayed in the Edit screen. (This may be a blank record if you pressed **[Ctrl]+[End]** at a blank record when you were entering the records.) Use the **[Page Up]**, **[Page Down]**, and **[Arrow]** keys to move among the records and fields during your editing. When you are finished, **[Ctrl]+[End]** will save your changes.

### 3. Using Browse

The Browse screen, shown in Figure 4.8, will display a listing of your records in columns. You may edit existing records or add new records at this screen.

- Open the **Update** menu and select **Browse**. The last record will be displayed. Press **[Page Up]** to see all of your records.

You may move between the columns in the Browse Screen with the **[Enter]** and **[Arrow]** keys. The screen can be shifted left or right to view additional columns with **[Ctrl]+[Right Arrow]** and **[Ctrl]+[Left Arrow]**. **[Page Up]** and **[Page Down]** will move you between full screens of records. When browsing through a large database, pressing **[Ctrl]+[Home]** will display and hide selections at the top of the screen to help you move through the database quickly. Try **[Ctrl]+[Home]** and select **Bottom**. This will move you to your last record. To save your changes, exit the Browse screen with **[Ctrl]+[End]**.

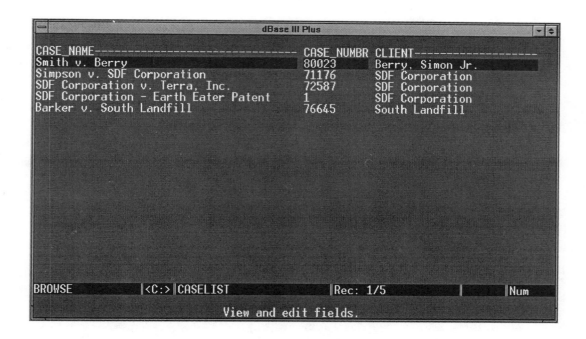

```
┌─                            dBase III Plus                          ▼│▲│
│CASE_NAME───────────────────────────────── CASE_NUMBR CLIENT────────────────│
│Smith v. Berry                             80023      Berry, Simon Jr.       │
│Simpson v. SDF Corporation                 71176      SDF Corporation        │
│SDF Corporation v. Terra, Inc.             72587      SDF Corporation        │
│SDF Corporation - Earth Eater Patent       1          SDF Corporation        │
│Barker v. South Landfill                   76645      South Landfill         │
│                                                                             │
│                                                                             │
│                                                                             │
│                                                                             │
│                                                                             │
│                                                                             │
│                                                                             │
│                                                                             │
│                                                                             │
│BROWSE          │<C:>│CASELIST                  │Rec: 1/5        │    │Num    │
│                           View and edit fields.                             │
└─────────────────────────────────────────────────────────────────────────────
```

**Figure 4.8** The Browse Screen

## I. DELETING RECORDS

Deleting records is a two-step process. First, you must mark the record for deletion, and then you must delete it. The two steps act as a safety measure to prevent accidental deletions. We will mark Record 5 for deletion, but we will not delete it. (If you saved a blank record by mistake, you may mark that record and delete it.)

### 1. Marking a Record for Deletion

To mark a record for deletion:

- Open the **Update** menu and select **Delete**.

┌─────────────────────────────────────────────────────────────────────┐
│   *Be careful not to press [Enter] again as this will select Execute the* │
│ *command and mark the current record for deletion.*                    │
└─────────────────────────────────────────────────────────────────────┘

- Select **Specify scope**.

- Select **Record** and type the number of the record to be deleted (e.g., **5** or **6**). Press **[Enter]**.

- Select **Execute the command** and press any key to return to the Assistant.

The record will not be removed from the file until you pack the records. List the records to see the deletion mark by following the steps below.

- Open the **Retrieve** menu and select **List**.

- Select **Execute the command** and respond **N** to the printer output message.

The listing will show that an asterisk is placed next to the record marked for deletion as shown in Figure 4.9. Press any key to return to the Assistant.

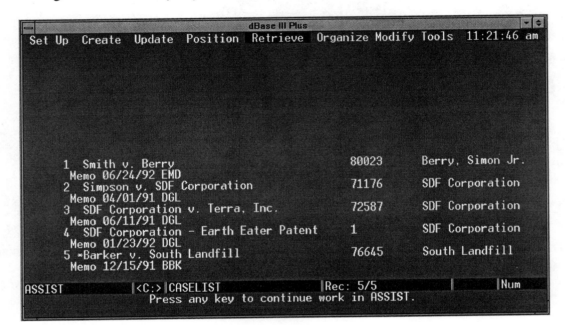

**Figure 4.9** An asterisk indicates a record marked for deletion

When you are in the Browse screen, you may also mark a record for deletion by placing the cursor within the record and pressing **[Ctrl]+[U]**. **[Ctrl]+[U]** will also remove the deletion mark.

## 2. Recalling a Record Marked for Deletion

You may remove a deletion mark in the Update menu by selecting Recall. To remove the deletion mark on Record 5, follow the steps below.

- Open the **Update** menu and select **Recall**.

- Select **Specify Scope**, select **Record**, type **5** and press **[Enter]**.

- Select **Execute the Command** to complete the recall.

### 3. Deleting a Marked Record

Permanently removing the marked record(s) from your database is called packing. To pack (erase) marked records, follow the steps below.

- Open the **Update** menu and select **Pack**.

Press any key to return to the Assistant.

Any records that were marked for deletion are now permanently removed from the database.

## J. CHANGING THE DATABASE STRUCTURE

If you find that you need to add or alter a field in your database, you need to return to the Create Screen and change the database structure. To change the database structure:

- Open the **Modify** menu and select **Database file**.

You will be returned to the Create Screen to make the changes. Press **[Ctrl]+[End]** to save any changes and press **[Enter]** to confirm.

## K. LISTING RECORDS

Listing the records of your database is performed in the Retrieve menu by selecting List. You may list all of your records, list specific records, list specific fields of the records, or list records that meet certain criteria. The list options are shown in Figure 4.10. Listing all of your records is accomplished by simply executing the command.

### 1. Listing Specific Records

You may list a specific record, or group of records, by specifying a scope to list.

- Open the **Retrieve** menu and select **List**.

- Select **Specify scope**. The scope options will be displayed as shown in Figure 4.11.

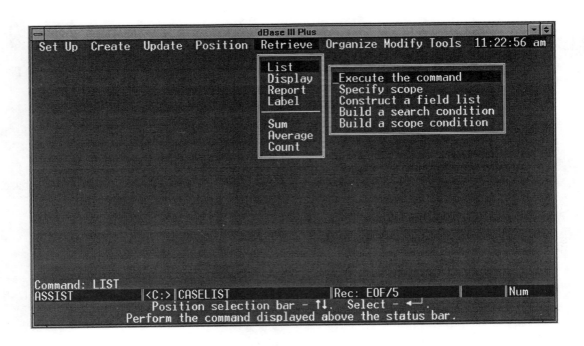

**Figure 4.10** The List Options

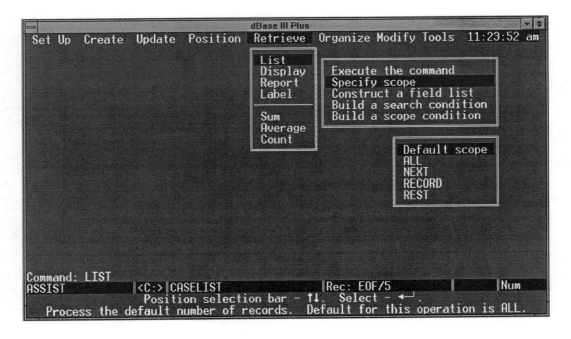

**Figure 4.11** The Scope Options

- You may then select any one of the following:

  **Default scope** to display a list of all of your records.

  **All** to display a list of all of your records.

  **Next** to list the next x number of records in the database. This command will depend upon where you are in your viewing of the records.

  **Record** to list a specific record.

  **Rest** to list from the current record to the end of the file.

- Select **Record** and type **2** to list Record 2.

- Select **Execute the command** to produce the list. Respond **N** when asked whether you wish to send the output to the printer.

Press any key to return to the Assistant.

## 2. Listing Specific Fields

You may wish to limit the fields that are displayed in your list of records. For example, if you only wanted to see a list of case names and the dates they were filed, you could create a list containing these two fields by selecting **Construct a field list** from the **List** selection of the **Retrieve** menu.

- Open the **Retrieve** menu and select **List**.

- Select **Construct a field list**. The fields of your database are displayed as shown in Figure 4.12. You may choose any field that is highlighted by moving to it and pressing the **[Enter]** key.

- For this example, select the **CASE_NAME** and **DATE_FILED** fields. Press the **[Right Arrow]** or **[Left Arrow]** key to leave the field selection. The Action Line at the bottom of the screen will display the selected fields.

- Select **Execute the command** to view the list. Respond **N** when asked whether to direct the output to the printer. The list is shown in Figure 4.13.

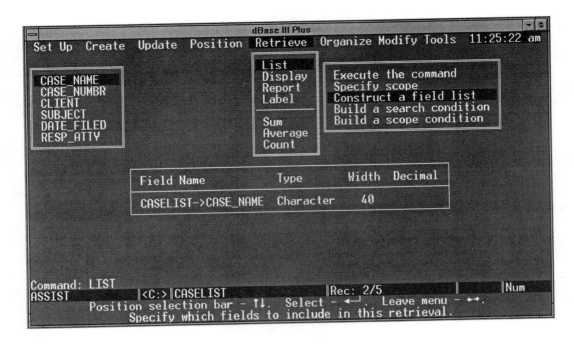

**Figure 4.12** The fields displayed in the Construct a field list option

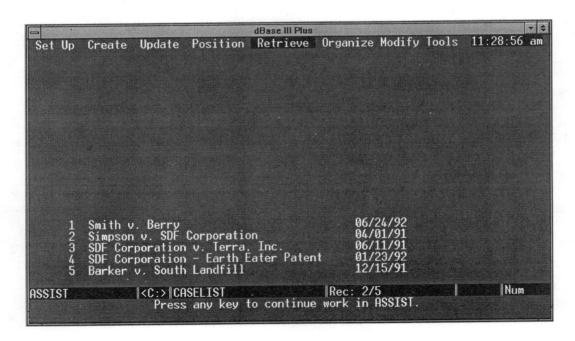

**Figure 4.13** A list containing only selected fields

Press any key to return to the Assistant.

Another way to list specific fields is to create a view file in the **Create** menu by selecting **View**. This allows you to save several different ways of viewing your database. You may use any one of the views by selecting it from **View** in the **Set Up** menu.

### 3. Building a Search Condition

To search for records that meet a specific criteria, you will use the **Build a search condition** option.

- Open the **Retrieve** menu and select **List**.

- Select **Build a search condition**. The fields available for searching are highlighted as shown in Figure 4.14. The SUBJECT field cannot be searched in this option.

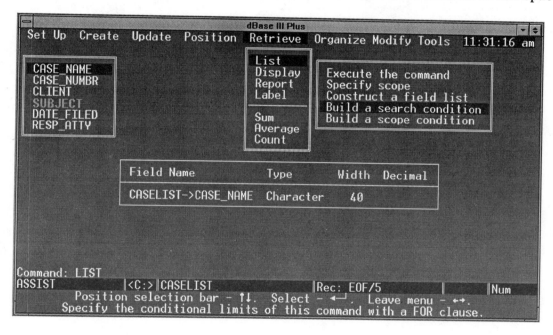

**Figure 4.14** When building a search condition, the fields available for searching are highlighted

- To search for all cases where **DGL** is the responsible attorney, select the **RESP_ATTY** field from the fields displayed. The available relational operators will then be displayed as shown in Figure 4.15.

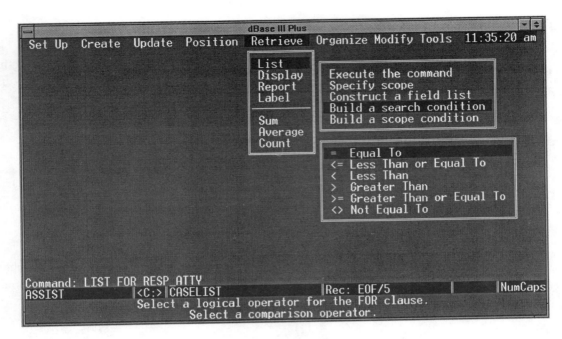

**Figure 4.15**  The display of Relational Operators

- Select the **Equal To** operator and you will be prompted to enter the information for which you are searching.

- Type **DGL** at the displayed prompt as shown in Figure 4.16. Do not use quotation marks; they will be supplied for you. Press **[Enter]**.

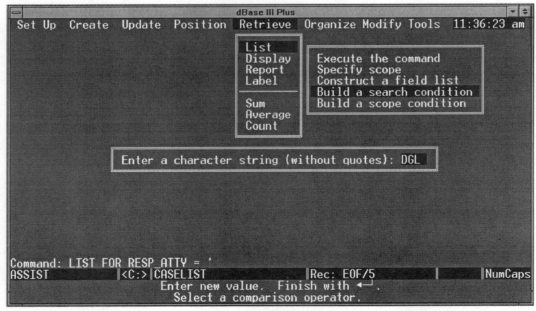

**Figure 4.16**  The attorney's initials for whom we are searching will be entered at this prompt

*dBase III Plus*

- Select **No more conditions**.

- Select **Execute the command** to complete the listing and respond **N** to the printer prompt.

Records 2, 3, and 4, which have DGL as the responsible attorney, will be displayed as shown in Figure 4.17. Press any key to return to the Assistant.

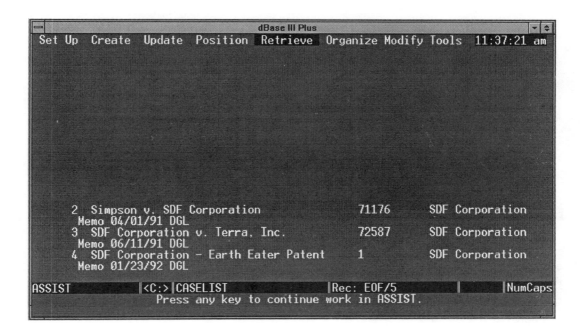

**Figure 4.17** The list of records where DGL is entered in the RESP_ATTY field.

Now, using the same steps, build a search condition using the DATE_FILED field to find all cases filed on or after January 1, 1992 (enter 01/01/92). Use the Greater Than or Equal To operator. Your results should include records 1 and 4 as shown in Figure 4.18.

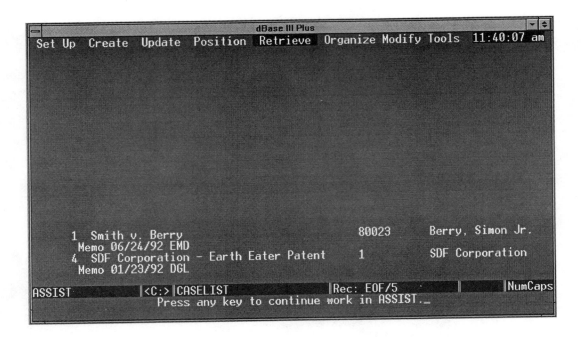

**Figure 4.18** The results of a search for cases filed on or
after January 1, 1992

Press any key to return to the Assistant.

## 4. Building a Search Using Connectors

The **AND** and **OR** connectors are used to combine two or more search conditions. For example, to locate all cases filed on or after January 1, 1992 where DGL is the responsible attorney, we will need to combine searches of the DATE_FILED field and the RESP_ATTY field.

- Open the **Retrieve** menu and select **List**.

- Select **Build a search condition**.

- Select the **DATE_FILED** field.

- Select **Greater Than or Equal To** and enter **01/01/92**.

- Add another search condition by selecting the connector **Combine with .AND.** The connector selections are shown in Figure 4.19.

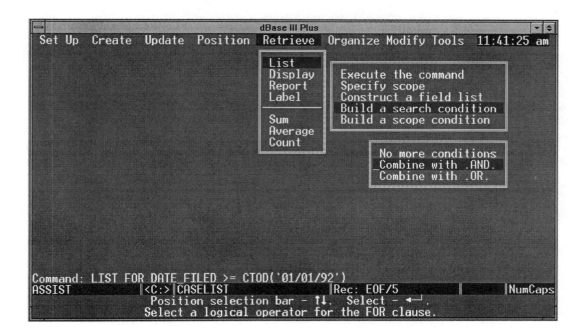

**Figure 4.19**  The Connector Selections

- Select the **RESP_ATTY** field, select **Equal To**, type **DGL**, and press **[Enter]**.

- Select **No more conditions**.

- Select **Execute the command** and respond **N** to the printer prompt.

This search will list Record 4 as shown in Figure 4.20.

Press any key to return to the Assistant and try another search. For this search use the AND connector to find all cases that were filed on or after January 1, 1992, and were filed before June 30, 1992.  The results are displayed in Figure 4.21.

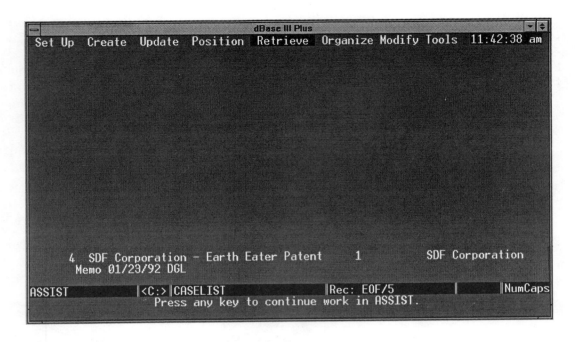

**Figure 4.20** The results of the search for all cases filed on or after January 1, 1992, that have DGL as the responsible attorney

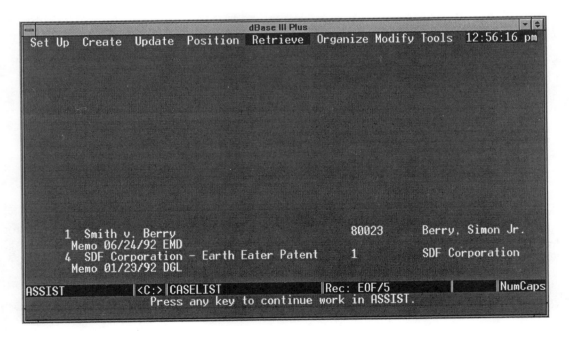

**Figure 4.21** The results of the search for cases filed on or after January 1, 1992, and before June 30, 1992

Press any key to return to the Assistant.

Now we will perform a search using the OR connector. An OR connector takes the results of the first condition and expands them to include the results of the second condition. Perform a search to locate all cases where the responsible attorney is DGL or EMD. The results of the search are displayed in Figure 4.22.

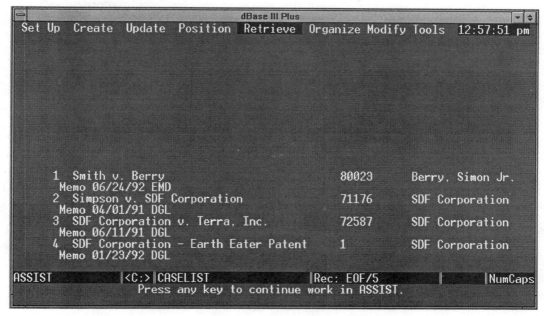

**Figure 4.22** The results of the search for cases where the responsible attorney is DGL or EMD

Press any key to return to the Assistant.

## 5. Listing Records with Display

A good way to list the records in a large database is to use Display in the Retrieve menu. When you use Display, the listing will pause at each full screen of records. To display all of the records, follow the steps below.

- Open the **Retrieve** menu and select **Display**.

- Select **Specify scope**.

- Select **All**.

- Select **Execute the command**.

You may leave the display listing at any time by pressing the **[Esc]** key. Press any key to return to the Assistant.

## L. CREATING A QUERY FILE

Another way to list records that meet a certain criteria is to create a Query file in the Create menu. Several different Query files may be created for the database. Queries that you run frequently should be saved in a query file. For example, for weekly attorney staff meetings, separate lists of cases for each attorney are frequently prepared. Queries could be created and saved that search for each attorney's initials in the **RESP_ATTY** field. The queries for each attorney could be accessed prior to the staff meeting and sent to the printer. Query files can also be used when you wish to work only with records that meet the query criteria. After working with the query file, to return to the full database, you need to place the database file in use again in the Set Up menu. To create DGL's case list query file, we would follow the steps below.

- Open the **Create** menu and select **Query**.

- Specify the drive letter and give the file a name. Call this query file **BYDGL**.

- In the Set Filter menu, select **Field Name,** highlight the field **RESP_ATTY**, and press **[Enter]**.

- Select **Operator**. For this example, select **Matches**.

- Enter a **Constant/Expression**. For this example, enter **"DGL"** (must be in quotes). The Create Query screen should now look like the one in Figure 4.23.

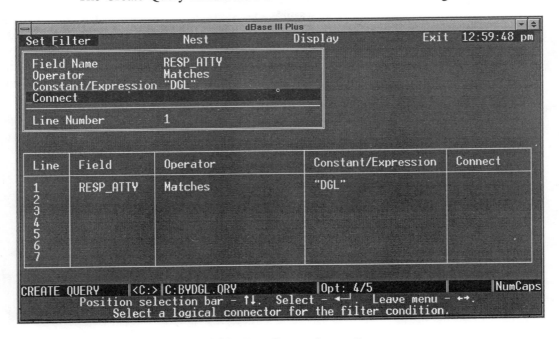

**Figure 4.23**  The Create Query Screen

- Use the **[Right Arrow]** key to move to the **Display** menu and press **[Enter]** to view the results. **[Page Up]** and **[Page Down]** will move through the records found by the query.

- Save the file by opening the **Exit** menu and selecting **Save**.

To use the query file, select **Query** in the **Set Up** menu and choose the drive and file name. To return to viewing your entire database file, select **Database file** from the **Set Up** menu and select the drive and file name.

## M. SORTING AND INDEXING

Most records within a database file have not been entered in any particular order. There are two ways to reorder your records, Sorting and Indexing.

**Sorting** creates a *new database file* with the records rearranged in the order you have specified. Therefore, you will have a file with your records in the order in which they were entered, and another with them in the sorted order. You can sort on any character, numeric, or date field.

**Indexing**, the fastest and most efficient way to reorder, creates an index file that tells dBase how to display your data. Your original database remains intact, and a new database is not created.

### 1. Sorting

To Sort a file it must be in use. If it is in use, its name will be displayed on the Status Bar. We will sort the CASELIST database alphabetically by case name. To perform this sort:

- Open the **Organize** menu and select **Sort**. The database fields will be displayed as shown in Figure 4.24.

- Select **CASE_NAME** by highlighting it and pressing the **[Enter]** key. If you wish to sort on more than one field (i.e., Last_Name, First_Name) you would select a second field at this time. Fields that are not highlighted, like the SUBJECT field, cannot be selected.

- Leave the field choices by pressing the **[Left Arrow]** or **[Right Arrow]** key.

- Select a drive letter and enter a file name. Call this file: **BYNAME**.

dBase will perform the sort. Press any key to return to the Assistant.

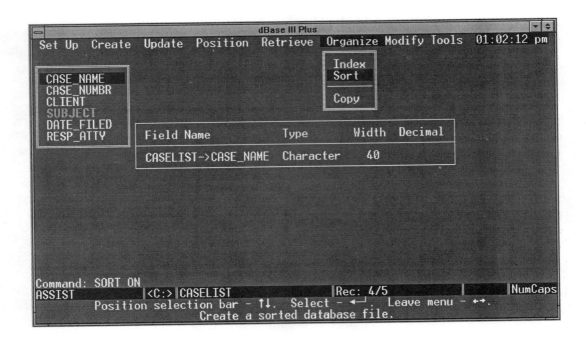

**Figure 4.24** Performing a sort involves selecting the field
upon which to sort

To view the new database you have created called BYNAME:

- Open the **Set Up** menu and select **Database file**.

- Select the appropriate drive letter, select the new database file name **BYNAME**, and respond **N** to the index prompt. The database name will appear on the Status Bar.

- List the database in the **Retrieve** menu.

Place the **CASELIST** database back in use in the **Set Up** menu so that we may continue. Answer **No** at this time to the index prompt.

## 2. Indexing

Indexing is the fastest and most efficient way to reorder your records. You use the original database file and create indexes according to the orders in which you desire to see your records. The selected index file temporarily reorders your records. The records retain their original record number in the index.

The main advantage of an index over a sort is that when you add new records to your database, and it is indexed, the records will automatically be placed in the proper order. If we added a new record to the CASELIST database, we would have to resort it and create an entirely new database to place the records in the correct order.

To create an index on the CASE_NAME field, follow the instructions below.

- Open the **Organize** menu and select **Index**.

- When prompted for the **index key expression,** type the name of the field upon which to index: **CASE_NAME** as shown in Figure 4.25. If you cannot remember the field names, press **[F10]**.

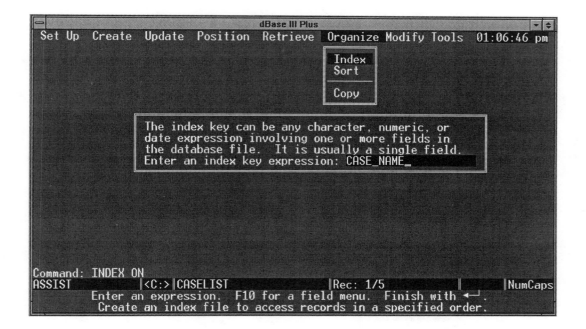

**Figure 4.25** The Index Screen

- Select a drive letter and name the file: **BYNAME**. This name can be the same as the sort file name because dBase places different extensions on the file names.

dBase will create the index. Press any key to return to the Assistant. List the records in the Retrieve menu to view the new order.

You can create several different index files for a single database. When you open a database file in the Set Up menu, you will be asked if it is indexed. Responding **Y** for Yes will display a list of the available indexes for the database. You may choose up to seven indexes to have open at once in your database. The first you select will be the master and will be how the records will be ordered. The reason you would open the others is that changes made in the database file will only be updated in open indexes.

## N. PRINTING A DATABASE

You may print a quick unformatted listing of a database file or search by responding **Y** for Yes when asked if you wish to direct the output of the listing to the printer.

A more formal approach is to create a custom report. We will create for our CASELIST database a custom report that will display the case names and the dates they were filed.

### 1. Creating a Report

- Open the **Create** menu and select **Report**.

- Select a drive letter and name the report file: **CASEREP**.

The Create Report screen will be displayed with its menu options as shown in Figure 4.26. If the help list is displayed, press **[F1]** to remove it.

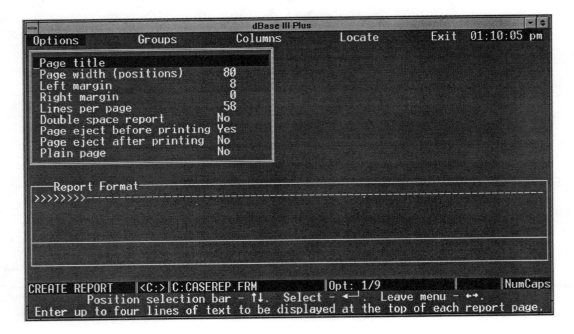

**Figure 4.26** The Create Report Screen

- Create a page title by opening the **Options** menu and selecting **Page title**. Type the title: **MASTER CASE LIST** and press the **[Enter]** key 4 times.

- Open the **Columns** menu and select **Contents** to specify a field to be included in the report. Enter the first field name, **CASE_NAME** and press **[Enter]**. (**[F10]** will display the field names when **Contents** is selected.) Select **Heading** and enter **Case Name** for that column. To move to the next column, press **[Page Down]**. Enter the next column **Contents**, **DATE_FILED**, and enter the heading **Date Filed**. The screen should now appear similar to the one shown in Figure 4.27. Changes to the columns may be made in the **Locate** menu.

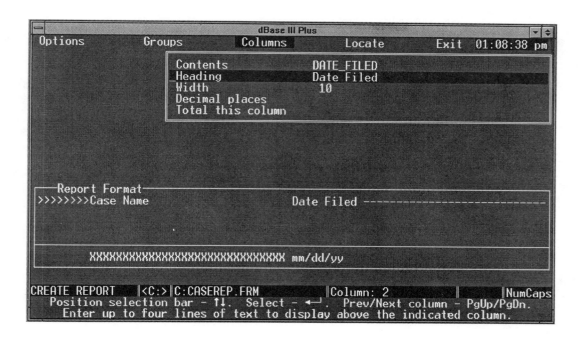

**Figure 4.27** The Column Headings of a report

- Save the report by opening the **Exit** menu and selecting **Save**.

## 2. Running a Report

To run a report such as CASEREP, follow the instructions below.

- Open the **Retrieve** menu and select **Report**.

- Select the drive letter where the report is located.

- Select the report name from the list that appears.

*dBase III Plus*

- Select **Execute the command**.

- Respond **Y** for Yes to the printer question if you wish the output to print. The report should appear similar to the one shown in Figure 4.28.

```
Page No.        1
04/02/93
                                    MASTER CASE LIST

    Case Name                       Date Filed


    Smith v. Berry                  06/24/92
    Simpson v. SDF Corporation      04/01/91
    SDF Corporation v. Terra, Inc.  06/11/91
    SDF Corporation - Earth Eater   01/23/92
    Patent
    Barker v. South Landfill        12/15/91
```

**Figure 4.28** The Printed Report

Press any key to return to the Assistant.


## O. COPYING A DATABASE FILE

You may copy a database file from one disk to another by opening the file and following the steps below.

- Open the **Organize** menu and select **Copy**.

- Select a drive letter where you wish the file to be copied and give it a name.

- Select **Execute the command**.

Press any key to return to the Assistant.


## P. EXITING dBASE

To leave the dBase program, open the **Set Up** menu and select **Quit dBASE III PLUS**. If you accidentally exit to the Dot Prompt, type **quit** to exit. dBase will close and save your databases for you.

# Q. THE DOT PROMPT COMMANDS

The same tasks that we performed in the Assistant can be performed using the Dot Prompt. In fact, when you become more familiar with dBase, you probably will prefer the Dot Prompt. Go to the Dot Prompt from the Assistant by pressing **[Esc]**. The commands are listed here for reference purposes. You can move from the Assistant to the Dot Prompt at any time when you are working with a database to try some of these commands. To return to the Assistant from the Dot Prompt, press **[F2]**.

## 1. Creating a Database File

To create the database file CASELIST:  **CREATE C:CASELIST**.

The same create screen that you see in the Assistant will be displayed. Fields are entered in the same manner and saved with **[Ctrl]+[End]**.

## 2. Using a Database File

To place the CASELIST file in use:  **USE C:CASELIST**.

## 3. Entering Records

Enter records by typing:  **APPEND**.

Save the records with **[Ctrl]+[End]**. View the records with:  **LIST**.

## 4. Editing Records

You can edit records by typing:  **APPEND, EDIT**, or **BROWSE**.  **[Ctrl]+[End]** will save the changes.

## 5. Deleting Records

As in the Assistant, deleting records is a two-step process. You must first mark the record for deletion and then pack the database. To mark a record for deletion type: **DELETE RECORD n** (where **n** is the number of the record). Typing **LIST** will list the records and display the deletion mark (*). If you have many records, use **DISPLAY ALL**. To complete the deletion type: **PACK**. Type **LIST** again to view the results.

## 6. Changing the Database Structure

You may change the structure of your database by typing:

**MODIFY STRUCTURE**

**[Ctrl]+[End]** will save the changes.

You may list the structure of your database by typing:

**LIST STRUCTURE**

You may print a list of the structure by typing:

**LIST STRUCTURE TO PRINTER**

## 7. Listing Records

You may list your records in the following ways:

| | |
|---|---|
| **LIST** | Lists all records |
| **LIST RECORD n** | Lists a specific record number |
| **LIST NEXT n** | Lists the next **n** number of records |
| **LIST REST** | Lists the remaining records |
| **LIST CASE_NAME, CLIENT** | Lists specific fields |
| **LIST FOR RESP_ATTY = "DGL"** | Lists records which meet specific criteria |

**LIST FOR DATE_FILED >= CTOD("01/01/92")**
> Lists for specific criteria in a date field. The required elements are **CTOD("MM/DD/YY")**.

**LIST FOR DATE_FILED >= CTOD("01/01/92") .AND. RESP_ATTY = "DGL"**
> Lists for specific criteria using the AND connector. Note that the connector must be contained in periods.

## 8. Displaying Records

Display is performed in much the same manner as list. However, the listing will pause with each full screen of records. Some examples of its use are:

**DISPLAY ALL**
**DISPLAY RECORD n**
**DISPLAY NEXT n**
**DISPLAY REST**

## 9. Sorting

To perform a sort and create the new sorted file, you use the following command demonstrated with the CASE_NAME field creating a new file named BYCASE:

**SORT ON CASE_NAME TO C:BYCASE**

If you were sorting on more than one field, the field names would be separated by commas.

**SORT ON RESP_ATTY, CASE_NAME TO C:BYATTY**

## 10. Indexing

To index a file, the following command is used:

**INDEX ON CASE_NAME TO C:BYCASE**

If indexing on more than one field, the field names are separated with the + symbol.

**INDEX ON RESP_ATTY + CASE_NAME TO C:BYATTY**

To place a the CASELIST database file in use with the BYATTY index, type:

**USE C:CASELIST INDEX BYATTY**

## 11. Printing

To route lists and other displays to the printer, add the following to the end of the command:

**TO PRINTER**

To create a customized report named CASEREP, you can get to the screen where reports are created by typing:

**CREATE REPORT C:CASEREP**

## 12. Exiting dBase

To exit dBase from the Dot Prompt, type: **QUIT**.

# *Summary*

dBase III Plus is a summary database program that keeps records of data within a file. There are two ways to work with dBase III Plus, from the Assistant and from the Dot Prompt.

When creating a new database, you must designate the fields, the field types, the field widths, and the number of decimal places for the field entries (numeric fields only). After you have created the database, you may enter your records.

Databases may be ordered by sorting or indexing. Sorting creates a new database file with the records sorted in the requested order. Indexing creates an index file that may be used at any time on your database.

You may list all of your records, a portion of the records, or those records that meet certain criteria. This listing can be directed to the printer for an informal report, or using a custom report that you have created.

# *Exercise*

This exercise presents a hypothetical case regarding the Grove Dumpsite. Read the synopsis of the case and review the documents that form part of the evidence for the case. You will create a database for the evidentiary documents, print the database structure, print a report of your records, and perform and print a query.

# THE GROVE DUMPSITE CASE

In 1941, the Department of Defense ordered major oil and gas companies in Southern California to produce high octane aviation fuel for the aircraft being used in World War II, instead of gasoline for automobiles. A by-product of this high octane fuel was a form of hazardous sludge. The oil companies, faced with having to dispose of tons of this sludge, asked the Department of Defense where they should dump it. The Government ordered the oil companies to dispose of the sludge at the Grove Dumpsite, located some 30 miles south of Los Angeles in a rural, undeveloped area. At the end of World War II, the dumpsite was covered over with dirt and forgotten.

In 1980, the once rural area containing the dumpsite had become the affluent neighborhood of Oak Field in Orange County, California. A developer purchased the land around the dumpsite and built several tracts of luxury homes. Prospective purchasers who inquired about the vacant lot adjacent to the homes were told that the next phase of homes would be built there.

In 1982, while playing at the "vacant lot," some children found a mud puddle of oil that appeared to be bubbling up from underground. They told their parents, and the parents started asking questions about the lot. After making inquiries at the City Manager's office, it was learned that the vacant lot was actually the Grove Dumpsite.

The homeowners soon began to wonder what effect the dumpsite was having upon their health. The dumpsite became the suspected cause of every cold, allergy, disease, miscarriage, and birth deformity.

In 1983, the homeowners filed a class action lawsuit in Orange County Superior Court naming each of the dumping oil companies, the developer, and the city and county as defendants. Our firm represents Oyster Oil Company. The database you will be creating will be one of evidentiary documents only.

# THE DOCUMENTS

The following documents have been placed on your desk by the partner in charge of the case.

A letter, dated June 6, 1982, from the Oak Field Homeowners Association ("OFHA") to Jim Dodd, the City Manager of Oak Grove. The letter requests more information about the vacant lot adjacent to the Oak Field development. This letter is located in file number 6002.10.7.

A letter, dated December 8, 1941, from the Department of Defense to Oyster Oil Company mandating that it shift its gasoline production to high octane aviation fuel. This letter is located in file number 6002.10.4.

A letter, dated December 20, 1941, from Oyster Oil Company to the Department of Defense requesting the location of a dumpsite suitable for the dumping of the sludge by-product of the aviation fuel. This letter is located in file 6002.10.4.

A 1980 brochure from Field Developers showing the Oak Field development and outlining the plans for the areas surrounding the current development, including the future development of what we now know as the dumpsite. This brochure is located in file 6002.10.8.

A letter, dated February 3, 1979, from Field Developers to the City Manager of the City of Oak Grove requesting information about the vacant lot adjacent to the proposed Oak Field development. This letter is located in file 6002.10.8.

A report, dated March 23, 1955, prepared by the City Engineer of the City of Oak Grove describing the nature of the Grove Dumpsite and the decision to leave it covered with dirt instead of excavating it and moving the sludge to another site. This report is located in file 6002.10.5.

A report, dated January 15, 1955, from Soil and Plant Labs to the City of Oak Grove, recommending that the sludge be removed from the Grove Dumpsite, and hauled out into the ocean for disposal. This report is located in file 6002.10.5.

The sales contract for the purchase of a Oak Field home, dated July 16, 1980, between Jim and Mary Peters and Field Developers. This contract is located in file 6002.10.9.

## CREATING THE DATABASE

Create a database for these evidentiary documents. To do so, look at the description of the documents and determine the fields you would create for this database, their field type and width.

## ENTERING RECORDS

For each document described, enter a record into your database. Enter your records in a uniform manner (all caps, no caps, or initial caps) so that you will have no trouble searching later.

## PRINTING YOUR DATABASE STRUCTURE

So that your instructor may see the fields that you have created, follow the steps below in the Assistant.

- Open the **Tools** menu and select **List Structure**.

- Respond **Y** to direct the output to the printer and press any key to return to the Assistant.

(From the Dot Prompt you can perform this task by typing **LIST STRUCTURE TO PRINTER.**)

### PRINTING A REPORT OF YOUR DATABASE

After you have entered all of your records, print a list of them by selecting **List** in the **Retrieve** menu and directing the output to the printer. Do not worry if the printout appears unformatted.

### LISTING SPECIFIC RECORDS

Using the List option of the Retrieve menu, build a search condition to locate all records that are a "Report." Direct the output to the printer.

## *Dot Prompt Command List*

This is just a partial list of the Dot Prompt commands available in dBase. A full list of commands can be found by typing **help**.

| | |
|---|---|
| APPEND | To add records to the database file. |
| ASSIST | To go back to the menu from the dot prompt. |
| AVERAGE | Computes the average of specified numeric fields. |
| BROWSE | Allows full screen menu editing of several records. |
| CLEAR | Erases the screen. |
| CLEAR ALL | Closes all open database files. |
| COUNT | Counts the number of records in a database file that meet a specific condition. |

| | |
|---|---|
| CREATE | Lets you establish a new database. |
| DELETE | Marks a record for removal from a file. |
| DELETE FILE | Removes a specific database file from the directory. |
| DIR | Displays the disk directory. |
| DISPLAY | Lists the current record. |
| EDIT | Full-screen editor to change contents of fields and records. |
| ERASE | Deletes a specified file from the directory and catalog. |
| GO/GOTO | Followed by a record number, this command moves you to a specific record. |
| GO BOTTOM | Moves to the last record in the file. |
| GO TOP | Moves to the first record in the file. |
| INDEX | Creates an index file that causes the contents of the database file to be displayed as if rearranged based on the specified field, although the data remains in the original record number order of the file. |
| LIST | Displays the contents of a database file. |
| LOCATE | Searches the database file for the first record which meets a specified criteria. |
| PACK | Permanently removes records marked for deletion. |
| QUIT | Closes all open files and exits dBase. |
| RECALL | Allows records that are marked for deletion to be reinstated. |
| RENAME | Changes the name of a file. An open file cannot be renamed. |
| REPLACE | Replaces the contents of the named field with the desired new contents. Used when the change affects all the records in the database. |
| REPORT FORM | Displays a tabular report form generated with CREATE/MODIFY REPORT. |
| SEEK | Conducts a very rapid record search by seeking the first record in an indexed database file with a key that matches the value of the specified expression. |

| | |
|---|---|
| SKIP | Moves the record pointer in an active database file forward or backward a specified number of records. |
| SORT | Physically reorders records in a database. |
| SUM | Totals expressions involving numeric fields in the active database file. |
| USE | Opens a database file. Also simultaneously closes any active database file currently in use. |

# Chapter Index

# CHAPTER 5

# DBASE IV®

---

# Chapter Preface

dBase IV is a database management system (DBMS) that allows you to organize documents or items of information for easy retrieval. Databases can be set up in this program for case evidence, in-house forms, client and case records, calendars, library updates and many other pieces of information.

In this chapter, we will create a database for a law firm's list of current cases. We will enter records and perform searches on the database. At the end of the chapter is an exercise in which you will create a database for a sample case.

# A. THE dBASE IV DATABASE

dBase is a summary database program. As was discussed in Chapter 9 of the text, summary databases contain pieces of information about each document or item within the database. They do not contain the full text of documents.

Summary databases are made up of files, fields, and records. The example we will be using in this chapter is a law firm's case list database. This database will contain items of information about every case currently handled by the firm.

## 1. Files

A database file is a collection of similar information. The file name for our case list database will be:

**CASELIST**

## 2. Fields

Fields are the structure of a database. They are items of information that will commonly be found in each of the entries in the database. The fields for the law firm case list database will be information that we want to store about each of the cases.

**Case Name**
**Case Number**
**Client**
**Subject**
**Date Case Filed**
**Responsible Attorney**
**Date File Opened**
**Date File Closed**

## 3. Records

The records of the database are the group of field entries for each case to be contained within the case list database file. A record for the *Smith v. Berry* case is shown below.

| | |
|---|---|
| Case Name | **Smith v. Berry** |
| Case Number | **80023** |
| Client | **Berry, Simon Jr.** |
| Subject | **Breach of Contract** |
| Date Case Filed | **06/24/92** |
| Responsible Attorney | **EMD** |
| Date File Opened | **04/19/92** |
| Date File Closed | |

# B. dBASE IV FILE NAMES, FIELD NAMES, AND FIELD TYPES

There are certain rules that must be followed in creating files and fields in dBase IV. These rules are:

## 1. File Names

In order to save your database file, you will need to give it a name. In dBase, file names may be 1 to 8 characters in length. They must begin with a letter, and may not contain spaces. You do not give your file name a three-character extension. dBase automatically assigns a .DBF extension to all database files. The name for our firm's case list database will be:

**CASELIST**

## 2. Field Names

When you construct your database, you will give each field a name. Field names may be 10 characters or less. They must begin with a letter, and may not contain spaces or periods. After the first letter, you can use letters, numbers or the underline character. The field names that we have developed for this database have been changed below to meet the dBase field name requirements.

**CASE_NAME**
**CASE_NUMBR**
**CLIENT**
**SUBJECT**
**DATE_FILED**

**RESP_ATTY**
**DATE_OPEN**
**DATE_CLOSE**

## 3. Field Types

There are six types of fields in dBase IV. The six types of fields are:

**Character**  Anything you can type from your keyboard. A telephone number or address is a character, not a numeric, because it is not used for math.

**JANUARY  22 Post Road  ============**

**Numeric**  Any number used in a mathematical computation. These numbers will have a fixed number of decimal places, and may contain a + or −.

**8.13  9.20  10.36  11.21  12.00**

**Float**  Float is a numeric field that allows you to vary the number of places after the decimal point.

**8.13  9.2  10.356  11.20943**

**Date**  Dates in the form: mm/dd/yy. The forward slashes are entered for you.

**08/25/92  01/01/45**

**Logical**  Used for data that will be (T)rue or (F)alse, (Y)es or (N)o, or some other either/or combination.

**T  F  Y  N**

**Memo**  For lengthy descriptions, dBase creates a separate memo file where you can store memos up to 64K characters in length. When entering data in the memo field, you need to get to the memo screen with **[Ctrl]+[Home]** or **[F9] (Zoom)**. When you are finished with your entry, you return to the database edit screen through the **Exit Menu** or by pressing **[Ctrl]+[End]**.

Our case list database consists of the following field types:

| | |
|---|---|
| **CASE_NAME** | **Character** |
| **CASE_NUMBR** | **Character** |
| **CLIENT** | **Character** |
| **SUBJECT** | **Memo** |
| **DATE_FILED** | **Date** |
| **RESP_ATTY** | **Character** |
| **DATE_OPEN** | **Date** |
| **DATE_CLOSE** | **Date** |

The CASE_NUMBR field is a character field because the number will not be used in mathematical computations.

## C. ENTERING THE PROGRAM

To enter dBase type **dbase [Enter]** OR select the program name or icon from a menu screen.

When you enter dBase, you will be greeted by a dBase program graphic and a license explanation. After assenting to the license agreement the dBase IV Control Center will be displayed.

## D. WORKING WITH dBASE IV

dBase IV offers two ways to work with the program, the Control Center and the Dot Prompt.

The Control Center is a menu panel that helps the user formulate commands. It is shown in Figure 5.1.

The Dot Prompt is a blank screen displaying only a period at the lower left-hand corner. This is the original way that dBase was operated, and requires knowledge of the dBase command structure. Many advanced users continue to prefer this method. The Dot Prompt screen is shown in Figure 5.2.

---

*Occasionally you will find yourself at the Dot Prompt. Whether you have gone there on purpose, or really do not know how you got there, you may return to the Control Center by pressing [F2], or exit the program by typing "**quit.**"*

---

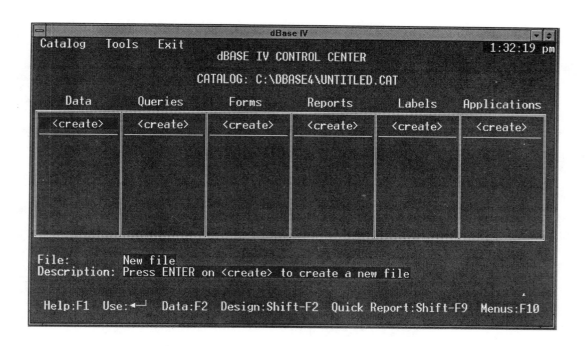

**Figure 5.1** The dBase IV Control Center

**Figure 5.2** The dBase IV Dot Prompt Screen

In this workbook, we will operate dBase from the Control Center. Use of the Dot Prompt commands is explained in Chapter 4 on dBase III Plus. These commands are the same in both programs.

*dBase IV*

# E. THE CONTROL CENTER

Figure 5.1 shows the dBase IV Control Center. The Control Center contains file panels, a catalog identifier, and pull-down menus. At the bottom of the screen is a list of special keys that can be used with the program.

## 1. The File Panels

The Control Center contains six file panels. Each file panel will contain the names of files created in that panel. The file panels are as follows:

| | |
|---|---|
| **Data** | Lists the names of your database files. |
| **Queries** | Lists the names of the query files that contain the results of database searches. |
| **Forms** | Lists the names of files containing customized input forms. |
| **Reports** | Lists the names of files containing report formats you have designed. |
| **Labels** | Lists all files containing label formats for mailing and other types of labels. |
| **Applications** | Lists the names of all files that contain custom dBase programs and applications. |

To create a new file in any one of the six File Panels, highlight **<create>** in the desired panel and press **[Enter]**.

## 2. The Catalog Identifier

Catalogs are where dBase IV stores its database files. The dBase catalogs function in a manner similar to directories. When a file is created, it will be put into the current catalog. The catalog identifier displays the current catalog.

## 3. The Pull-Down Menus

The Control Center contains Pull-Down Menus at the top of the screen that will assist you in performing many dBase functions. You may access these menus by pressing the **[F10]** key, or by holding down the **[Alt]** key and pressing the first letter of the menu option name. For example, [Alt]+[E] will open the **Exit Menu** as shown in Figure 5.3. The **[Esc]** key will back you out of a menu selection.

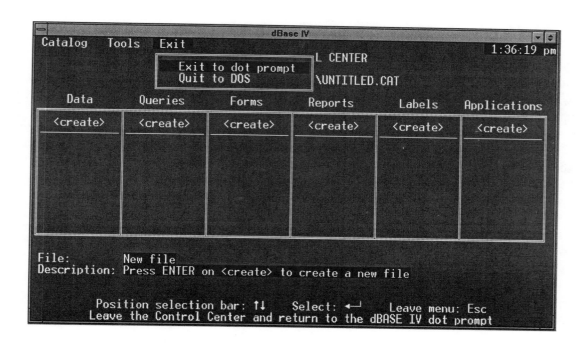

**Figure 5.3** The Exit Menu is opened using the [F10] key or [Alt]+[E]

## 4. The Special Keys

dBase's special keys are found on the **navigation line** at the bottom of the screen. Some of these special keys are listed below.

**F1**      **Help.**

**F2**      **Data.** This key takes you to your database Edit and Browse screens.

**Shift-F2**      **Design.** From the Control Center, this key takes you to the Database Design screen. The Database Design screen is used to create and alter your field structure. From the Browse and Edit Screens, this key will take you to the Query Design screen.

**Shift-F9**      **Quick Report.** This key allows you to print a quick report of your database.

**F10**      **Menus.** This key takes you to the Menu Bar at the top of the screen.

**ESC**      **Escape.** This key allows you to move back one database screen.

## F. CATALOGS

Catalogs are where your database files will be stored. dBase lets you create separate catalogs for storing different types of databases. Personal databases, databases for a single client, in-house databases, and so forth, can all be stored in separate catalogs.

The catalog identifier at the Control Center displays the disk drive, directory location, and name of the current catalog in use. This is where your files will be stored unless you change catalogs. The common default catalog is the UNTITLED catalog. You may save your database files in this catalog if you wish.

If you wish to store your database files on a diskette, you will want to create a catalog on the diskette in which to store the files.

If you have your database files in a catalog other than the current catalog, or in a catalog present on a diskette, you will need to change the current catalog in order to use the database files present there.

To create a new catalog, or to change the current catalog, follow the steps below.

- Open the **Catalog Menu** using **[F10]** or **[Alt]+[C]**

- Select **Use a different catalog**. A **create** option and a list of the catalog selections is displayed at the right side of the screen. If your catalog is listed, highlight the name and press the **[Enter]** key.

- To create a new catalog, or to change to an existing catalog on a disk in a drive other than the one listed in the catalog identifier, you will need to select **<create>**. After you have selected **<create>** you will be prompted for a catalog name. Type the appropriate disk drive letter followed by a catalog file name. Catalog names may be 1 to 8 characters and may not contain spaces or punctuation. The underline character is acceptable. An example of a catalog created on a diskette in the A: drive would be: **A:DBFILES**. If you have a catalog present on the diskette and are using **<create>** to change to that catalog, you will type the drive letter followed by the catalog name as shown in the previous example. This does not damage your database files stored in the catalog.

Occasionally, a database file will have been stored to a disk without being placed in a catalog. To add such a file to the current catalog:

- Open the **Catalog** menu and select **Add file to catalog**.

- If you need to change the drive letter for the file location, highlight the displayed drive letter and press **[Enter]**. Possible drive selections will be displayed. Highlight the appropriate drive letter and press **[Enter]**.

- Highlight the file name and press [**Enter**].

As you create files, they will automatically be saved onto the current catalog.

## G. CREATING A DATABASE FILE

To create the CASELIST database select **<create>** in the **data panel**. dBase will take you to the Database Design screen where you will create your database structure. The Database Design screen is shown in Figure 5.4.

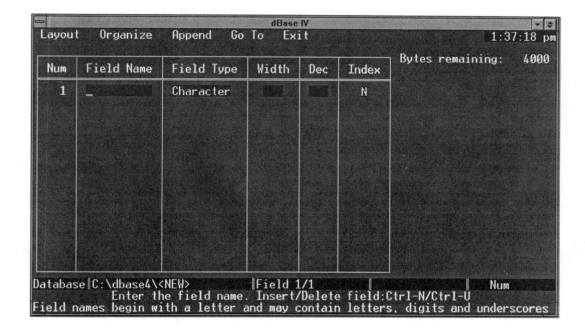

**Figure 5.4** The Database Design Screen

In addition to supplying the names for the database fields, you must identify the field types, their widths, the number of decimal places for numeric fields, and indicate whether you wish to create an index upon individual fields.

## 1. Fields

The fields that we will create for this database are:

**CASE_NAME**
**CASE_NUMBR**
**CLIENT**
**SUBJECT**
**DATE_FILED**
**RESP_ATTY**
**DATE_OPEN**
**DATE_CLOSE**

Type the name of the first field and press the **[Enter]** key. You will then be prompted for the field type.

## 2. Field Type

For each field, the type of field must be specified so that dBase knows what type of data is to be stored within the field. The field types for our fields are:

| | |
|---|---|
| **CASE_NAME** | **Character** |
| **CASE_NUMBR** | **Character** |
| **CLIENT** | **Character** |
| **SUBJECT** | **Memo** |
| **DATE_FILED** | **Date** |
| **RESP_ATTY** | **Character** |
| **DATE_OPEN** | **Date** |
| **DATE_CLOSE** | **Date** |

"Character" is already entered in the field type column as shown in Figure 5.5. Press the **[Enter]** key if this is the type of field you want. To switch to another field type, type the first letter of the field type or toggle through the field types with the **[Space Bar]** and press **[Enter]** when the desired field type is displayed.

## 3. Field Width

The field width column is where you tell dBase the maximum amount of characters you will be entering into the field. For example, in the CASE_NAME field, we will be entering names like "SDF Corporation v. Terra, Inc." For this name we will need 30 spaces. To be on the safe side, we will make this field 40 spaces long. In the event that we need to enter a longer case name, we can come back to this screen and increase the field width. Type **40** and press the **[Enter]** key.

The widths of our fields will be:

| | | |
|---|---|---|
| **CASE_NAME** | **Character** | **40** |
| **CASE_NUMBR** | **Character** | **10** |
| **CLIENT** | **Character** | **25** |
| **SUBJECT** | **Memo** | **10** |
| **DATE_FILED** | **Date** | **8** |
| **RESP_ATTY** | **Character** | **4** |
| **DATE_OPEN** | **Date** | **8** |
| **DATE_CLOSE** | **Date** | **8** |

There are some fields that have a pre-set width that is automatically entered when that field type is selected. These fields are:

Logical Fields: Automatic width of 1
Date Fields:    Automatic width of 8
Memo Fields:   Automatic width of 10

*The width of 10, which is set for Memo Fields, does not mean that there are only 10 spaces available for your memos. You still have 64K of space.*

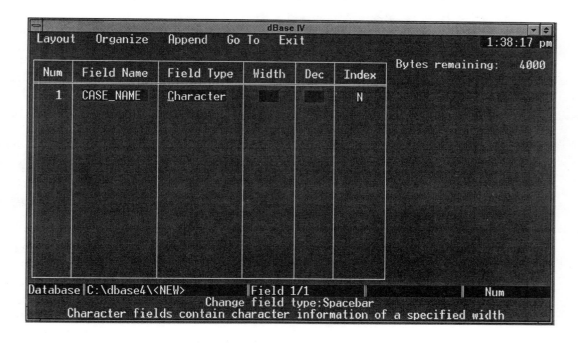

**Figure 5.5** The Field Type may be selected by pressing the first letter of the Field Type or by using the [Space Bar] to toggle to the desired type and pressing [Enter]

## 4. Number of Decimal Places

The Decimal Column only requires an entry when the field type selected is Numeric. In this column, you will specify the number of decimal places that the numbers in the field will contain.

## 5. Index Creation

dBase IV offers the option of creating an index upon a field at the time the field is created. An index is a file that will sort your database upon that field. For example, an index on the CASE_NAME field will order the records alphabetically by case name. We will respond **Y** for yes in the CASE_NAME field to create an index sorting by the names of the cases. Indexes may be created on more than one field. You may also create indexes later through a menu selection.

Enter the fields for the CASELIST database into the Database Design screen.

| | | | |
|---|---|---|---|
| **CASE_NAME** | **Character** | **40** | **Y** |
| **CASE_NUMBR** | **Character** | **10** | **N** |
| **CLIENT** | **Character** | **25** | **N** |
| **SUBJECT** | **Memo** | **10** | **N** |
| **DATE_FILED** | **Date** | **8** | **N** |
| **RESP_ATTY** | **Character** | **4** | **N** |
| **DATE_OPEN** | **Date** | **8** | **N** |
| **DATE_CLOSE** | **Date** | **8** | **N** |

The completed structure should look like Figure 5.6.

## 6. Saving the Database Structure

To save the Database Structure, press **[Ctrl]+[End]**, or with the highlight bar on the blank row beneath your last field, press the **[Enter]** key. You will be prompted for the location and name of the file as shown in Figure 5.7. Type the appropriate drive letter and the file name **CASELIST** and press **[Enter]** (e.g., A: CASELIST).

The file will be placed in the current catalog, and you will be asked if you wish to enter records at this time. Select **No** at this time to return to the Control Center.

As you can see in Figure 5.8, the name of your database file is placed above the line in the Data Panel. This means that the file is in use. To close the file, you can highlight its name and press the **[Enter]** key. Select **Close file** from the menu that appears. A closed file is placed below the line as shown in Figure 5.9.

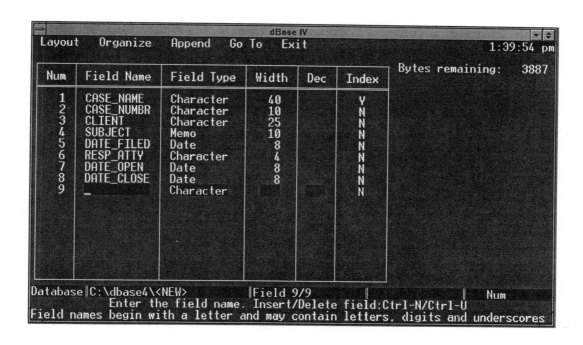

**Figure 5.6** The Completed Database Structure

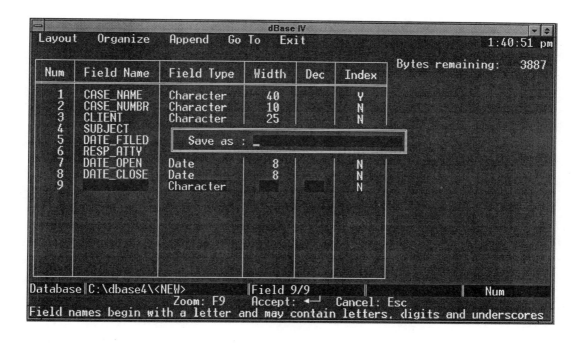

**Figure 5.7** Pressing the [Enter] key at a blank row prompts you for the name of the file

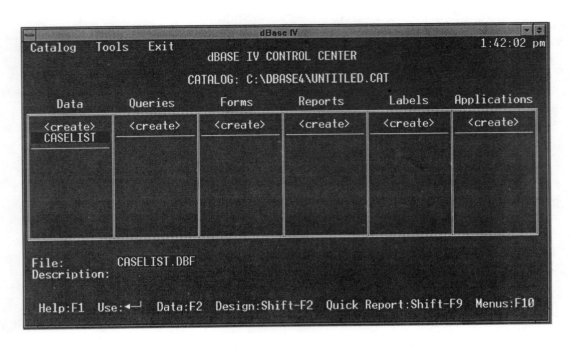

**Figure 5.8** The CASELIST database file is in use when its name appears above the line in the Data Panel

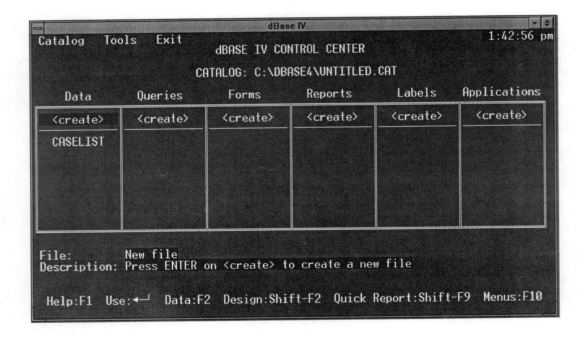

**Figure 5.9** A file is closed when its name appears below the line within a panel

To place the file in use again, highlight the file name and press **[Enter]**. A screen similar to the Close File screen appears. Select **Use file** to place the file name above the line in the Data Panel.

> *When you exit dBase correctly through the **Exit Menu**, or by typing **quit** at the Dot Prompt, dBase automatically saves your databases. It is not necessary to close your files before you exit.*

# H. ENTERING RECORDS

Records may be entered into a database from the **Database Edit screen** or the **Browse screen**.

## 1. The Database Edit Screen

To enter the first records into your database, make sure that the database file is in use and move to the Edit screen by pressing the **[F2]** (Data) key. The Edit screen displays one record

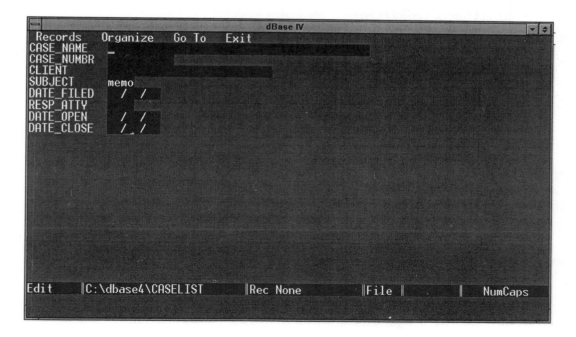

**Figure 5.10** The Database Edit Screen

## 2. Entering the Records

At the Edit screen enter the five records listed below. You can move between fields with the **[Enter]** key and the **[Arrow]** keys. You can move between records with **[Page Up]** and **[Page Down]**.

In the memo field SUBJECT, type a short memo beginning with the words shown for the SUBJECT fields. Entering data into memo fields requires that you move to a screen which will allow you to type up to 64K of data. As you can see in Figure 5.10, when you look at where you enter your records, the **SUBJECT** field contains the word *memo*. To create the SUBJECT field for each record, follow the steps below.

- With the highlight bar in the memo field, press the **[F9]** (**Zoom**) key or **[Ctrl]+[Home]** to get to the Memo Creation screen.

- Enter a sentence or short paragraph describing the record.

- Return to the Edit screen by pressing **[Ctrl]+[End]**, or leave through the **Exit Menu**.

After data has been entered into a memo field, the word *Memo* will appear in capital letters. This lets you know that there is an entry in the memo field. After data has been entered into a memo field, you may look at the data again at any time with the **[F9]** key, and then leave the memo by again pressing the **[F9]** key. However, if you make any changes, you will want to leave with **[Ctrl]+[End]** or through the **Exit Menu**.

The responsible attorneys in each record are identified by their initials. This is a customary practice in the law office.

The Case Number in Record 4 indicates that this is the first patent we have filed for this corporation. This record is not a court case, and will not have a case number.

A completed record is shown in Figure 5.11.


| #1 | Case Name | **Smith v. Berry** |
|----|-----------|--------------------|
|    | Case Number | **80023** |
|    | Client | **Berry, Simon Jr.** |
|    | Subject | **Breach of contract . . .** |
|    | Date Case Filed | **06/24/92** |
|    | Responsible Attorney | **EMD** |
|    | Date File Opened | **04/19/92** |
|    | Date File Closed | |

| #2 | Case Name | **Simpson v. SDF Corporation** |
|---|---|---|
| | Case Number | **71176** |
| | Client | **SDF Corporation** |
| | Subject | **Wrongful termination . . .** |
| | Date Case Filed | **04/01/91** |
| | Responsible Attorney | **DGL** |
| | Date File Opened | **08/25/90** |
| | Date File Closed | |

| #3 | Case Name | **SDF Corporation v. Terra, Inc.** |
|---|---|---|
| | Case Number | **72587** |
| | Client | **SDF Corporation** |
| | Subject | **Patent infringement . . .** |
| | Date Case Filed | **06/11/91** |
| | Responsible Attorney | **DGL** |
| | Date File Opened | **11/08/90** |
| | Date File Closed | |

| #4 | Case Name | **SDF Corporation—Earth Grinder Patent** |
|---|---|---|
| | Case Number | **1** |
| | Client | **SDF Corporation** |
| | Subject | **Patent filing . . .** |
| | Date Case Filed | **01/23/92** |
| | Responsible Attorney | **DGL** |
| | Date File Opened | **10/12/91** |
| | Date File Closed | **01/01/93** |

| #5 | Case Name | **Barker v. South Landfill** |
|---|---|---|
| | Case Number | **76645** |
| | Client | **South Landfill** |
| | Subject | **Injunctive relief . . .** |
| | Date Case Filed | **12/15/91** |
| | Responsible Attorney | **BBK** |
| | Date File Opened | **11/30/91** |
| | Date File Closed | **06/20/92** |

## 3. The Browse Screen

An alternative to the Edit screen is the Browse screen shown in Figure 5.12. This screen displays multiple records in column form. You may move to the Browse screen from the Edit screen (after you have entered at least one record) by pressing the **[F2]** key.

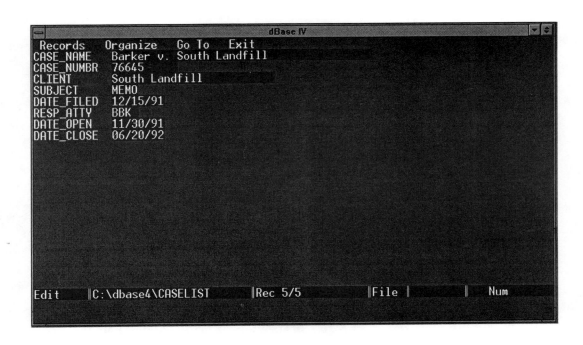

```
┌────────────────────────── dBase IV ──────────────────────────┐▼│⬍│
│─                                                              │  │
│  Records    Organize    Go To    Exit                         │
│ CASE_NAME    Barker v. South Landfill                         │
│ CASE_NUMBR   76645                                            │
│ CLIENT       South Landfill                                   │
│ SUBJECT      MEMO                                             │
│ DATE_FILED   12/15/91                                         │
│ RESP_ATTY    BBK                                              │
│ DATE_OPEN    11/30/91                                         │
│ DATE_CLOSE   06/20/92                                         │
│                                                               │
│                                                               │
│                                                               │
│                                                               │
│                                                               │
│                                                               │
│                                                               │
│                                                               │
│                                                               │
│ Edit    ‖C:\dbase4\CASELIST        ‖Rec 5/5        ‖File ‖    ‖   Num │
│                                                               │
└───────────────────────────────────────────────────────────────┘
```

**Figure 5.11** A record displayed in the Edit screen

```
┌────────────────────────── dBase IV ──────────────────────────┐▼│⬍│
│─                                                              │  │
│  Records    Organize    Fields    Go To    Exit               │
│┌────────────────────────────────────┬───────────┬───────────┐│
││ CASE_NAME                          │ CASE_NUMBR │ CLIENT    ││
│├────────────────────────────────────┼───────────┼───────────┤│
││ Smith v. Berry                     │ 80023     │ Berry, Simon Jr.  ││
││ Simpson v. SDF Corporation         │ 71176     │ SDF Corporation   ││
││ SDF Corporation v. Terra, Inc.     │ 72587     │ SDF Corporation   ││
││ SDF Corporation - Earth Grinder Patent │ 1     │ SDF Corporation   ││
││ Barker v. South Landfill           │ 76645     │ South Landfill    ││
││                                    │           │           ││
│└────────────────────────────────────┴───────────┴───────────┘│
│ Browse   ‖C:\dbase4\CASELIST     ‖Rec 1/5       ‖File ‖    ‖   Num   Ins │
│                                                               │
└───────────────────────────────────────────────────────────────┘
```

**Figure 5.12** The records displayed in the Browse screen

The [Tab] and [Shift]+[Tab] keys will move the highlight bar between the fields. The [F2] key will toggle you back and forth between the Edit and Browse screens. You may enter and edit records in either screen.

## 4. Saving the Records

To save the database records, press [Ctrl]+[End] or return to the Control Center through the Exit Menu, ([Alt]+[E]), and select **Exit**.

## 5. Looking at the Records

From the Control Center the records of a database may be viewed at any time by highlighting the database name and pressing the [F2] key. Once in the Edit or Browse screens, the [F2] key will toggle back and forth between them. To return to the **Control Center**, you may press the [Esc] key if you have not altered any records. If you have altered the records, exit through the Exit Menu.

# I. DELETING RECORDS

Deleting records is a two-step process. First, you must mark the record for deletion, and then you must delete it. The two steps act as a safety measure to prevent accidental deletions.

It is easiest to delete records from the Browse screen. To get to the Browse screen from the Control Center, press the [F2] key once or twice.

## 1. Marking a Record

To mark a record for deletion, highlight the record to be deleted in the Browse screen, and follow the steps below.

- Access the Records menu using the **[F10]** key or **[ALT]+[R]**.

- Select **Mark the record for deletion**. The Status Bar will indicate that this record is marked for deletion.

> *You can also remove the deletion mark in the Records Menu.*

## 2. Deleting the Record

Permanently removing the marked record(s) from your database is called packing. You pack (erase) the marked records by following the steps below.

- Access the **Organize Menu**.

- Select **Erase Marked Records**. dBase will ask you if you are sure you wish to delete this record. Normally you will say "yes," but if you are following along with this chapter, say "no" so that you may keep all of the records.

- To remove the deletion mark from the marked record, open the **Records Menu** and select **Clear deletion mark**.

Return to the **Control Center** through the **Exit Menu**.


## J. CHANGING THE DATABASE DESIGN

If you find that you need to add or alter a field in your database, you need to change the database design. To change the database design, you must return to the Database Design screen where we entered the field specifics of the database.

From the Control Center, move to the database design screen by pressing **[Shift]+[F2]** (Design). The **Organize Menu** is automatically opened. You do not need to use this menu, so press the **[Esc]** key to back out of it. We will change the width of the CASE_NAME field to **45**.

Using the **[Arrow]** keys and the **[Tab]** and **[Shift]+[Tab]**, you can move around in this screen and make any necessary changes. Move to the width column of the CASE_NAME field, type in the new width, and press **[Enter]**.

Save this change by exiting through the **Exit Menu** and selecting **Save Changes and Exit**. Answer **Yes** at the prompt.


## K. SEARCHING THE DATABASE

A search within a database is called a query. Queries are instructions to dBase requesting records that fit certain criteria. For example, we could request a list of all cases in our CASELIST database where DGL is the responsible attorney.

dBase IV uses a query design method called QBE or "Query By Example."

To develop a query, the database file you are querying must be in use (above the line) in the Data panel. With the database in use, move the highlight bar to the **Queries panel** and select **<create>**. dBase will take you to the **Query Design screen** shown in Figure 5.13.

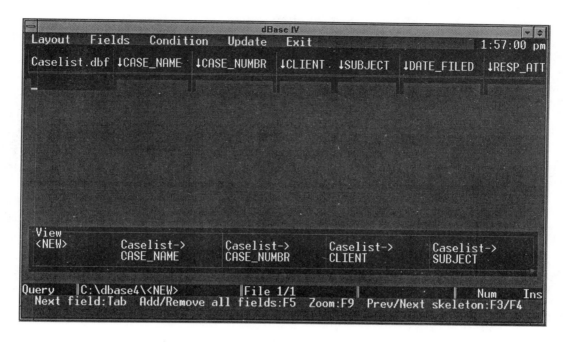

**Figure 5.13** The Query Design Screen

### 1. The File Skeleton and View Skeleton

The top of the **Query Design screen** is called the **file skeleton**. The bottom of the screen is called the **view skeleton**.

The **file skeleton** is where you request particular items from the database. The **view skeleton** is where you can limit the fields that are displayed in the query results. For example, if you wanted to see a list of case names and the dates they were filed, you could select only these two fields for viewing by eliminating the other fields from the view skeleton.

The **[F3]** and **[F4]** keys will move you back and forth between the file and view skeletons.

### 2. Query By Example (QBE)

The file skeleton is used to search for items within your database. Each of the database fields are displayed in the file skeleton. To perform a query, use the **[Tab]** and **[Shift]+[Tab]** keys to move to the field column (field box) in which you desire to search.

The **field box** is where you enter a search condition for a particular field. There are different rules for how you enter a query into a field box depending on the type of field you are querying.

Character
: Items to be searched for within a Character field must be enclosed within quotation marks.

**"DGL"**

dBase will search for an entry in the queried field exactly as it is typed within the quotation marks. For example, **"dgl"** will not find **"DGL."** This is why it is important that the persons entering records into the database enter them in a uniform manner (e.g., all caps, no caps, or initial caps).

Numeric
: Numbers to be searched for within a Numeric field do not require quotation marks or any other qualification.

**153**

Float
: Float fields are searched in the same manner as Numeric fields.

**176.453**

Date
: When searching a Date field, the date must be enclosed within curly braces "{ }."

**{12/05/78}**

Logical
: Logical fields may only contain **T** or **F**, **Y** or **N**, or some other either/or combination. Searches for any one of these letters within a Logical field requires that the letter appear between two periods.

**.T.**

Memo
: Searches may be performed on Memo fields using a **condition box** and the **$** (containing) operator.

**$ "Construction defect"**

The following search will demonstrate a search within a Character field. Perform the search upon the CASELIST database.

**SEARCH #1: All cases where DGL is the responsible attorney.**

To search for **DGL** in the **Responsible Attorney** field:

- Tab to the **RESP_ATTY** field.

- Type **"DGL"** and press **[Enter]**. The entry will look like the one in Figure 5.14.

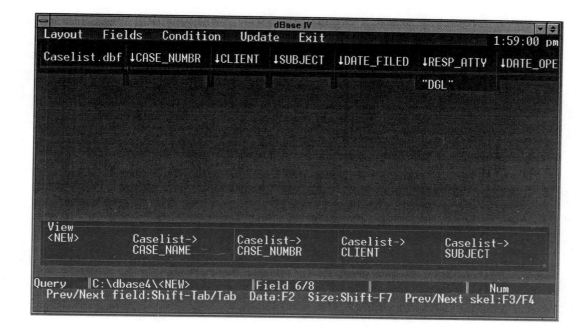

**Figure 5.14** Entering a query in the RESP_ATTY field

- Press the **[F2]** (Data) key to process the query.

The results of your query will appear in the Edit or Browse screen depending upon the screen in which you last viewed your records. The **[F2]** key will take you to the Browse screen if you are in the Edit screen. The **[Tab]** and **[Shift]+[Tab]** keys will move you between the field columns. The results viewed in the Browse screen should look like Figure 5.15. When you are finished viewing the records, return to the query design screen by pressing **[Shift]+[F2]** (Design).

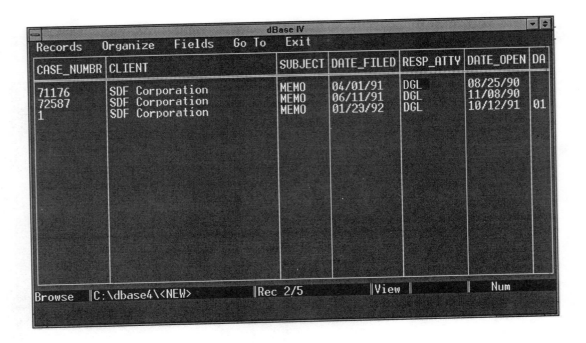

**Figure 5.15** The results of the query search for DGL with the RESP_ATTY field

## 3. Using Relational Operators

The relational operators used in dBase IV are:

| | |
|---|---|
| = | **Equals** |
| > | **Greater than** |
| < | **Less than** |
| >= | **Greater than or equal to** |
| <= | **Less than or equal to** |
| <> or # | **Not equal to** |
| $ | **Containing** |
| Like | **Word search using wildcard characters** |
| Sounds Like | **Search for words with similar sounds** |

We will perform the following search using a relational operator.

**SEARCH #2: All cases filed on or after January 1, 1992.**

To look within our database for all of the cases that have been filed since the beginning of 1992, we will use the greater than or equal to operator (>=) in the **DATE_FILED** field box.

- Remove "DGL" from the **RESP_ATTY** field box by pressing **[Ctrl]+[Y]**.
- Use **[Shift]+[Tab]** to move back to the **DATE_FILED** field.

- In the **DATE_FILED** field type **>={01/01/92}** and press the **[Enter]** key. Your entry should look like the one shown in Figure 5.16.

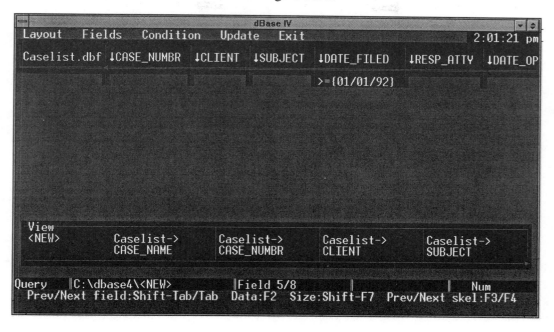

**Figure 5.16** A Date Search

- Press the **[F2]** (**Data**) key to process the query. The query results are shown in Figure 5.17.

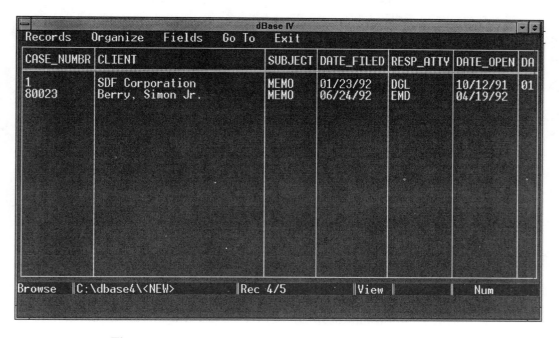

**Figure 5.17** The query results in the Browse screen

- Return to the Query Design screen by pressing **[Shift]+[F2]**.

## 4. Combining Searches Using Connectors

The **AND** and **OR** Connectors are represented in Query By Example by constructing AND queries along the same row, and placing OR queries in separate rows. When AND queries are within the same field box, the entries are separated by commas.

> **SEARCH #3: All cases filed on or after January 1, 1992, where the responsible attorney is DGL.**

To search for all cases filed after 01/01/92 where the Responsible Attorney is DGL, we would construct an **AND** query as follows:

- Leave the previous query as constructed in the **DATE_FILED** field.

- Tab to the **RESP_ATTY** field, and in the first row type **"DGL"** and press the **[Enter]** key. Your query should look like the one in Figure 5.18.

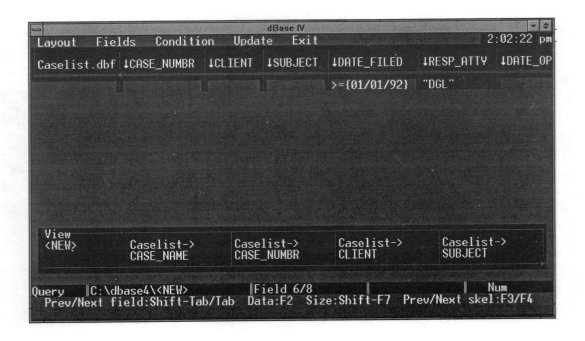

**Figure 5.18** A search using the Connector AND is constructed with the conditions in the same row

- Press the **[F2]** (**Data**) key to process the query. The query results are shown in Figure 5.19.

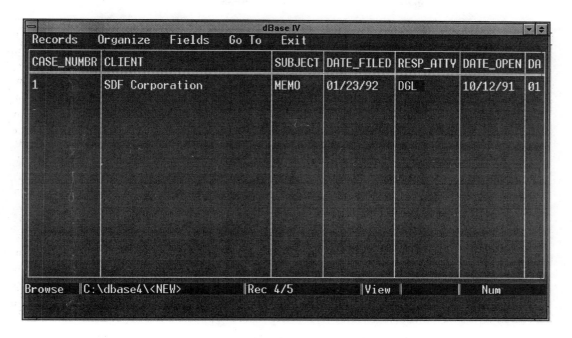

**Figure 5.19**  The Query Results

- Return to the Query Design screen with **[Shift]+[F2]** (Design).

Constructing a query with the AND connector in the same field box is demonstrated in Search #4.

**SEARCH #4:  All cases filed on or after January 1, 1992, and on or before June 30, 1992.**

If we wish to see all the cases filed on or after January 1, 1992, and on or before June 30, 1992, a comma is used to indicate **AND** within the **DATE_FILED** field box.

- Remove the entry in the **RESP_ATTY** field with **[Ctrl]+[Y]**.

- Move to the **DATE_FILED** field and add a **comma** after **>={01/01/92}**. Without spacing, add **<={06/30/92}** and press the **[Enter]** key. Your query should look like the one shown in Figure 5.20.

- Press the **[F2]** (Data) key to process the query. The query results are shown in Figure 5.21.

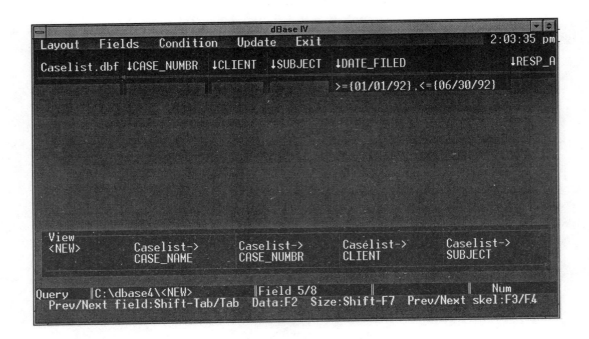

**Figure 5.20** To use the AND connector within a field box, the query conditions are separated with a comma

| CASE_NUMBR | CLIENT | SUBJECT | DATE_FILED | RESP_ATTY | DATE_OPEN | DA |
|---|---|---|---|---|---|---|
| 1 | SDF Corporation | MEMO | 01/23/92 | DGL | 10/12/91 | 01 |
| 80023 | Berry, Simon Jr. | MEMO | 06/24/92 | EMD | 04/19/92 | |

Browse ‖C:\dbase4\<NEW> ‖Rec 4/5 ‖View‖ ‖ Num

**Figure 5.21** The Query Results

- Return to the Query Design screen with **[Shift]+[F2]** (Design).

A query using the OR connector is demonstrated in Search #5.

**SEARCH #5: All cases where the responsible attorney is DGL OR EMD.**

To construct a query using OR, the entries are placed in separate rows. For example, if we wish to see all cases where the responsible attorney is **DGL** or **EMD** we follow the steps below.

- Remove the entry in the **DATE_FILED** field box with **[Ctrl]+[Y]**.

- Move to the **RESP_ATTY** field and type **"EMD"**; press the **[Down Arrow]** key and type **"DGL"** in the row below **"EMD"**; then, press the **[Enter]** key. The query should look like the one in Figure 5.22.

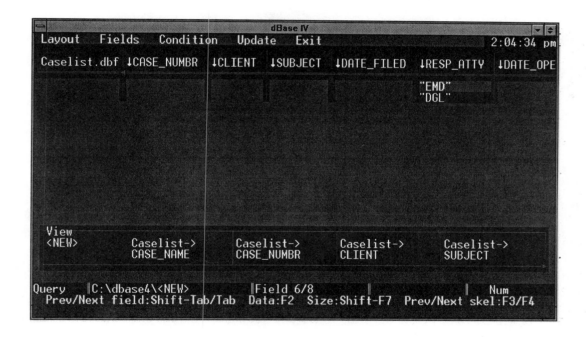

**Figure 5.22** The OR Connector is used by placing query conditions in separate rows

- Press the **[F2]** (Data) key to process the query. The query results are shown in Figure 5.23.

- Return to the Query Design screen with **[Shift]+[F2]** (Design).

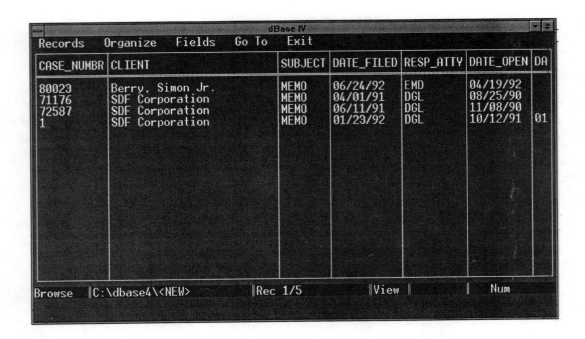

**Figure 5.23**  The Query Results

## 5.  Querying a Memo Field

Since a memo field may contain up to 64K of data, a query is performed using a condition box and the $ (containing) operator.

> **SEARCH #6:  All records that contain the words "Breach of contract" within the SUBJECT field.**

Follow the steps below to create a query searching for the words **"Breach of contract"** within the **SUBJECT field.**

- Remove the entries from the **RESP_ATTY** field box with **[Ctrl]+[Y].**

- Access the **Condition Menu** with **[Alt]+[C]** and select **Add condition box**. A condition box will appear in the lower right-hand corner of the screen as shown in Figure 5.24.

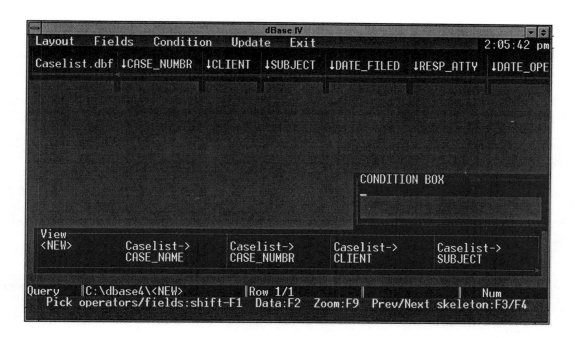

**Figure 5.24** A Condition Box

- In the condition box, the query of the **SUBJECT** field is formulated by typing the text to be located, followed by the **$** (containing) operator, and then the name of the field ("Breach of contract"$SUBJECT). Press **[Enter]** to check the syntax of the query. The query entered in the condition box is shown in Figure 5.25.

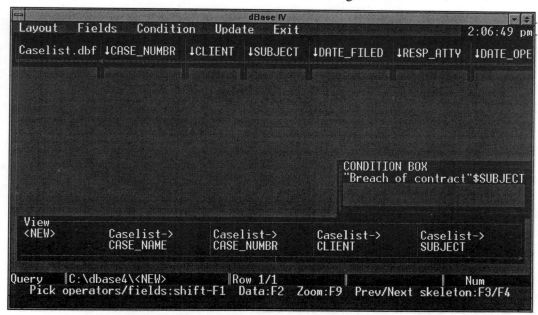

**Figure 5.25** A query of the memo field, SUBJECT, using a condition box and the containing operator ($)

- Press **[F2]** to process the query. The query results are shown in Figure 5.26.

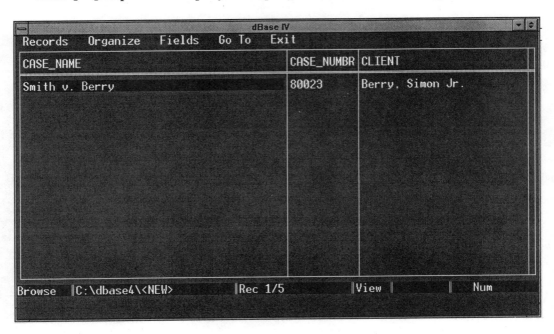

**Figure 5.26** The Query Results

- Tabbing to the memo field (SUBJECT), in the search results, and pressing **[F9]** will display the contents of the memo as shown in Figure 5.27. You may leave the memo by pressing **[F9]** again.

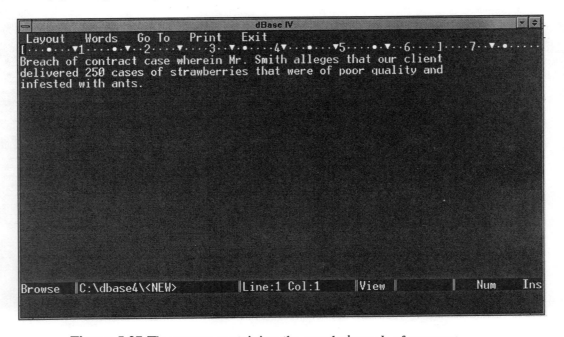

**Figure 5.27** The memo containing the words *breach of contract*

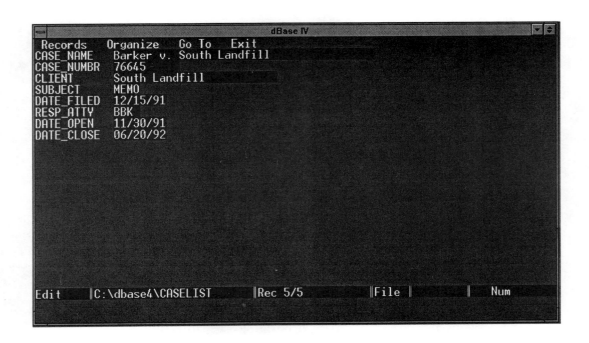

**Figure 5.11** A record displayed in the Edit screen

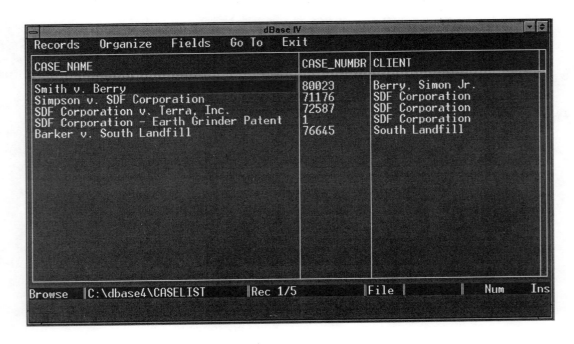

**Figure 5.12** The records displayed in the Browse screen

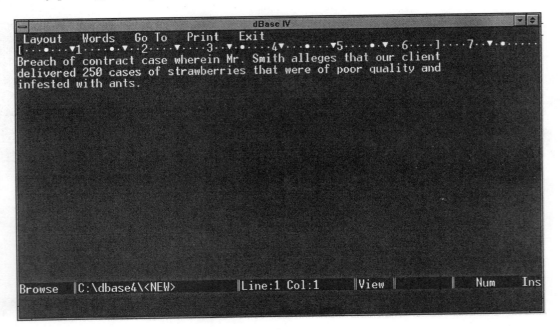

- Return to the Query Design screen with **[Shift]+[F2]** (Design).

- Remove the condition box by accessing the **Condition menu** and selecting **Delete condition box.**

The containing operator may also be used within a field box.

**SEARCH #7: Locate all cases where SDF Corporation is a party.**

We will conduct this search using the containing operator ($) to search for **"SDF"** within the **CASE_NAME** field.

- In the **CASE_NAME** field box, enter **$"SDF"** as shown in Figure 5.28 and press **[Enter]**.

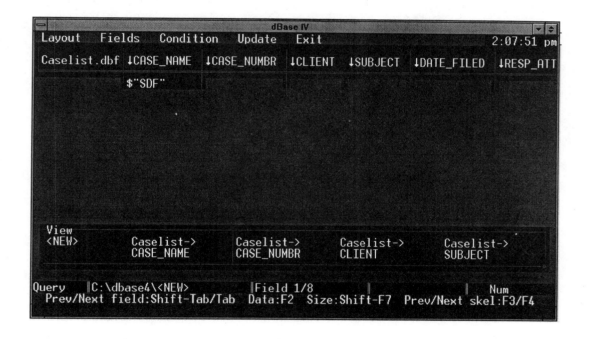

**Figure 5.28** A search using the containing operator within a field box

- Press **[F2]** to process the query. The query results are shown in Figure 5.29.

- Press **[Shift]+[F2]** to return to the Query Design screen and use **[Ctrl]+[Y]** to erase the field entry in the **CASE_NAME** field.

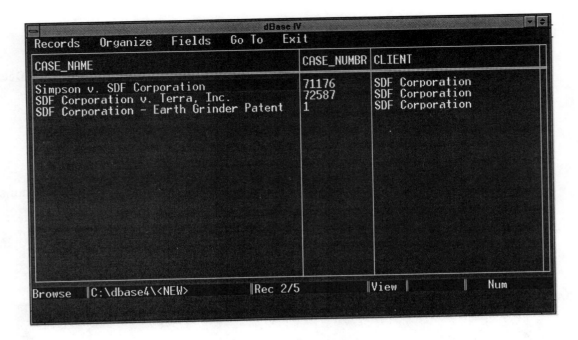

**Figure 5.29** The results containing SDF in the CASE_NAME field

## 6. View Queries

The lower half of the Query Design screen, the view skeleton, is used to limit the fields that will be displayed in the query results. For example, we might want to see a list of all of the firm's cases and their responsible attorneys. For this query, we will want to view all of the records, but only the **CASE_NAME** and **RESP_ATTY** fields.

To remove unwanted fields from the view skeleton, use the **[Tab]** and **[Shift]+[Tab]** keys *in the file skeleton* to move to the field names to be removed. Press the **[F5]** key to remove them from the view skeleton. If you remove the wrong field, highlight the field name again and press **[F5]**. This will put the field back. You may remove or replace all of the fields by moving to the Caselist.dbf box and pressing **[F5]**.

For our view query example, follow the steps below.

- Move to the **Caselist.dbf** box and press **[F5]**. This will remove all of the fields from the view skeleton.

- Move to the **CASE_NAME** field and press **[F5].**

- Move to the **RESP_ATTY** field and press **[F5]**.

Your view skeleton should now contain only the **CASE_NAME** and **RESP_ATTY** fields as shown in Figure 5.30.

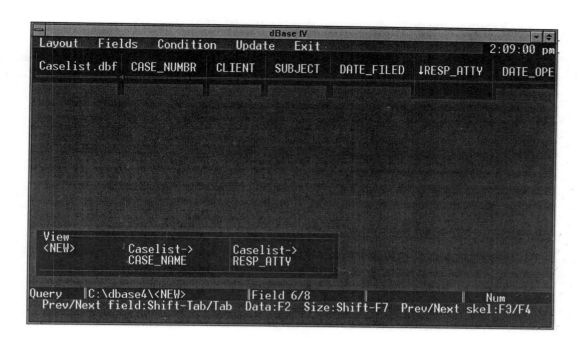

**Figure 5.30**  A View Query

- Process the query by pressing the **[F2]** key. The query results are shown in Figure 5.31.

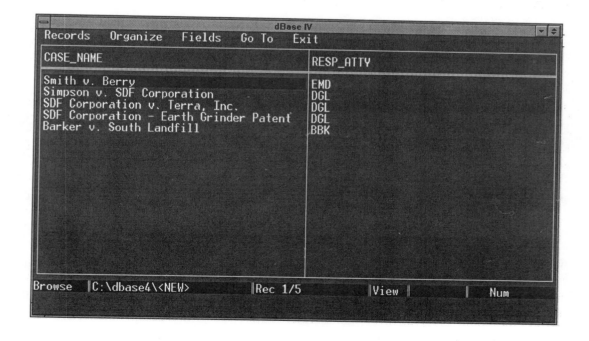

**Figure 5.31**  The Query Results

- Return to the query design screen using **[Shift]+[F2]** (Design).

Exit the query design screen through the **Exit Menu** using **[Alt]+[E]**, select **Abandon changes and exit**, and respond **yes** when asked if you are sure. You will return to the Control Center.

---

> *If you wanted to save a query file, you would select **Save changes and exit** from this **Exit Menu**.*

---

## L. SORTING AND INDEXING

Most records within a database file have not been entered in any particular order. There are two ways to reorder your records, **Sorting** and **Indexing**.

**Sorting** creates a *new database file* with the records rearranged in the order you have specified. Therefore, you will have a database file with your records in the order in which they were entered, and another with the records in the sorted order.

**Indexing** is the fastest and most efficient way to reorder. Indexing creates an index file that tells dBase how to order the data in your database file. The original database remains intact. You may have up to 47 different indexes for each database.

### 1. Sorting

To Sort a file, highlight the file name in the Data Panel of the Control Center and press **[Shift]+[F2]** (Design). At the **Database Design screen**, the **Organize Menu** will automatically be opened for you. Select **Sort Database on Field List** and you will reach the **Sort Box** shown in Figure 5.32.

To create a new database, with the CASELIST records ordered alphabetically by the name of the case, we will sort the database on the **CASE_NAME** field. The steps below will accomplish the Sort and save our new sorted database as **CASES**.

- Enter the field name to sort upon, **CASE_NAME**, in the field order column and press **[Enter]**.

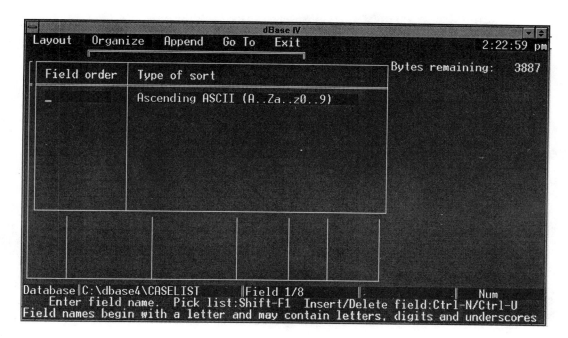

**Figure 5.32** The Sort Box

---

> *If you cannot remember the exact name of your field, [Shift]+[F1] will give you a list of your fields and allow you to highlight your field name and select it with the [Enter] key.*

---

- In the **Type of Sort Box**, toggle the four available ordering options with the **[Space Bar]** until you reach **Ascending Dictionary**, and press **[Enter]**. Your screen should now look like the one in Figure 5.33.

- If you wanted to sort on further criteria, (e.g., if you had a LAST_NAME field and a FIRST_NAME field) you could add another field name on the next line.

  We do not wish to sort on any other fields, so press the **[Enter]** key at the blank second line and you will be prompted for a database name for the sorted file. Save the sorted file as **CASES** (or A:CASES or B:CASES). dBase will then prompt for a description of the file. You can enter one if you wish and/or press **[Enter]** to return to the database design screen.

- **Exit** to the **Control Center** through the **Exit Menu** selecting **Save changes and exit**. Press **[Enter]** to confirm the exit.

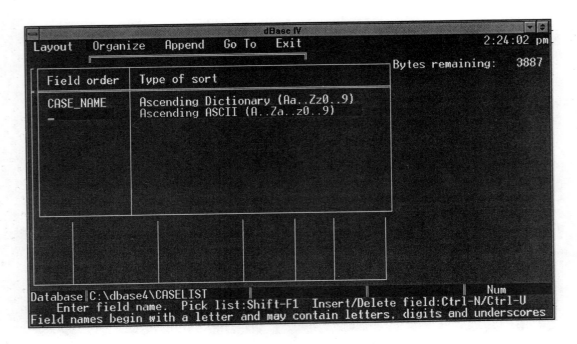

**Figure 5.33** A sort on the CASE_NAME field

The new database file is placed in the data panel as shown in Figure 5.34. The CASELIST database has the records in the original order. The CASES database has the records ordered by the name of the case.

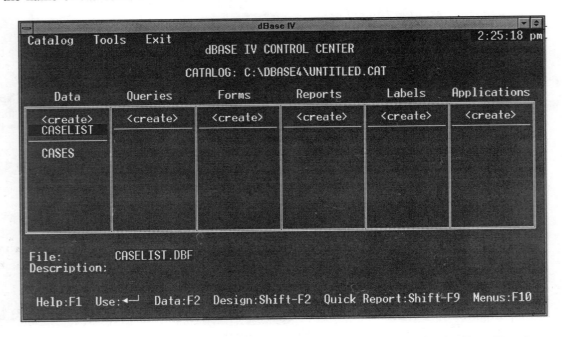

**Figure 5.34** The new database, CASES, is placed below the line in the Data Panel

To see the sorted records in the CASES database, highlight **CASES**, press the **[Enter]** key twice to place it in use, and press **[F2]**. The records will be displayed in the Browse or Edit screen. To toggle between the screens use **[F2]**. The records in the Browse screen are shown in Figure 5.35.

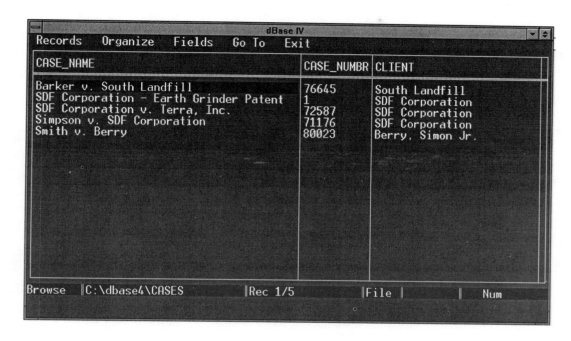

**Figure 5.35** The records within the sorted database, CASES

**Exit** to the **Control Center** through the **Exit Menu** and place the CASELIST database back in use by highlighting it and pressing the **[Enter]** key twice.

## 2. Indexing

Indexing is the fastest and most efficient way to reorder your records. You use the original database file and create indexes according to ways you desire to see your records. The selected index file temporarily reorders your records. The records retain their original record number.

You can create indexes at the time you design the database by typing a **Y** in the Index Column, or you can create an index manually. You may create up to 47 indexes on a single database, and you can index query files as well as database files.

The main advantage of an index over a sort is that when you add new records to your database, and it is indexed, the records will automatically be placed in the proper order. If we added a new record to the sorted CASES database, we would have to resort it, and create an entirely new database to place the record in the correct order.

We created an automatic index on the **CASE_NAME** field when we created the CASELIST database. The steps below will create a new index which can order the records by the date filed.

- From the **Control Center**, highlight the database name (**CASELIST**) and press **[Shift]+[F2]** (Design).

- In the **Organize Menu, Create new index** is highlighted. Press **[Enter]** to select this option. The Index Box shown in Figure 5.36 will appear. To make entries into the items in the Index Box, you need to move to an item and press **[Enter]** to open it to receive the entry.

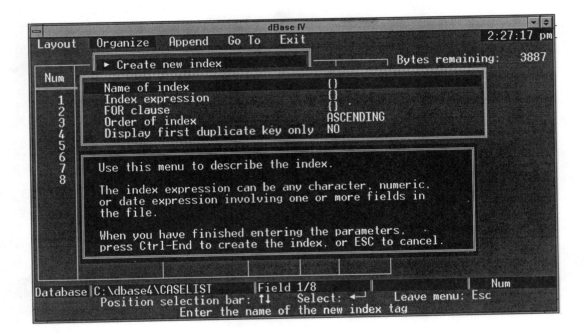

**Figure 5.36** The Index Box

- With the **Name of index** box highlighted, press **[Enter]** to open it to receive data. We will name this Index File **BYDATE** since we will be ordering the records upon the Date Field. Type **BYDATE** and press **[Enter]**.

- Open the **Index expression** box by highlighting it and pressing **[Enter]**. This is where you place the name of the field you wish to index upon. Assuming that we cannot remember the name of our Date Field, press **[Shift]+[F1]** (Pick) to see a list of the fields as shown in Figure 5.37.

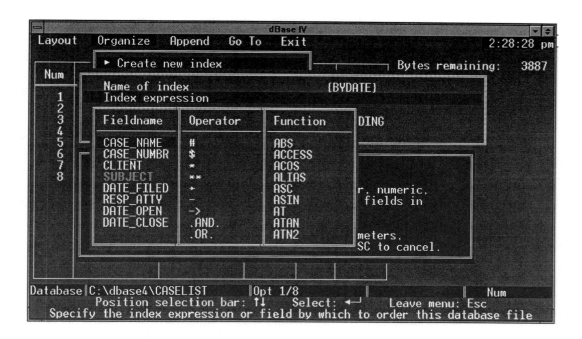

**Figure 5.37** The pick list of field names

- Highlight the name of the date filed field in the pick list, **DATE_FILED**, and press **[Enter]**. Press **[Enter]** again to complete the entry.

We are creating a simple index, so we have entered all that is needed. The screen should look like the one in Figure 5.38.

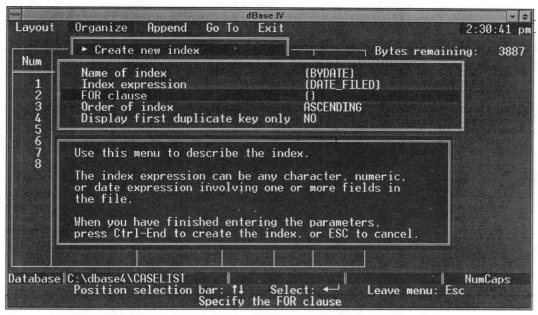

**Figure 5.38** The creation of an index upon the DATE_FILED field

- To complete the index creation, press **[Ctrl]+[End]**. You will be returned to the Database Design screen.

- Exit to the Control Center through the Exit Menu with **[Alt]+[E]**. Select **Save changes and Exit**, and press the **[Enter]** key to confirm.

To see the records as they are now indexed by date, make sure the CASELIST database name is highlighted and press **[F2]**. Look at the DATE_FILED field and you will see that the cases are now ordered by the date filed. After looking at your records, press the **[Esc]** key to return to the Control Center.

To change to another index, move to the Database Design screen, from the Control Center, by pressing **[Shift]+[F2]**. The **Organize Menu** is automatically opened. Select **Order records by index**. The indexes that have been created for this database will appear at the right of the screen. Natural Order is the order in which the records were entered. Any index may be selected by highlighting its name and pressing **[Enter]**. Highlight the **CASE_NAME** index as shown in Figure 5.39 and press **[Enter]**. You will be returned to the database design screen. You may press **[F2]** at the Database Design screen to see the new order of your database.

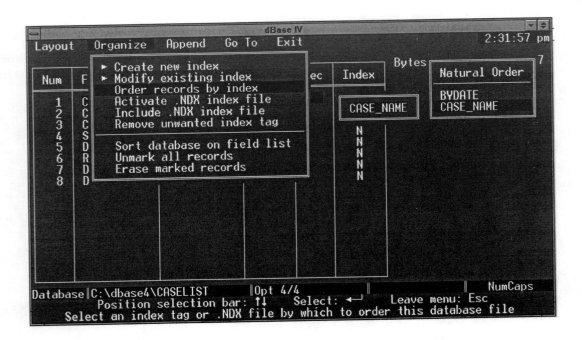

**Figure 5.39** The indexes for the CASELIST database

Return to the Control Center through the Exit Menu, selecting Exit.

## M. PRINTING A DATABASE

You may print the contents of a database file or a query file using a Quick Report option, or by creating a Report.

### 1. Quick Report

To receive a quick printout of your database, or the results of a query, you can use **[Shift]+[F9]** (Quick Report). The results of a Quick Report may be unformatted and difficult to read.

To perform a Quick Report from the Control Center, highlight the database or query file name, press **[Shift]+[F9]** and select **Begin printing**. Be patient, it can take more than a few moments for dBase to process the report.

### 2. Creating a Report

For a simple report that will display your data in a readable fashion, create a report in the **Reports Panel** of the Control Center using the **Quick Layouts** option. To create a Report on a database file, the database file name must be above the line in the Data Panel. For a Report on a query, the query file name must be above the line in the query panel.

The following steps will create the report.

- From the **Control Center**, move the highlight bar to the **Reports Panel**, highlight **<create>**, and press **[Enter]**.

- The **Layout Menu** is automatically opened and **Quick layouts** is highlighted. Select **Quick layouts**.

- At the sub-menu of **Quick layouts**, select **Form layout**. The screen shown in Figure 5.40 will appear. Each field name is accompanied by a field length containing an indication of the type of data contained within the field. As you get more experienced with dBase IV, you can try altering the field names and lengths, and adding headings, in the report.

- To print the report, access the **Print Menu** with **[Alt]+[P]** and select **Begin printing**. Your report will appear similar to the one shown in Figure 5.41.

- Exit to the Control Center through the **Exit Menu** with **[Alt]+[E].** You may save the report form and give it a name or select **Abandon changes and exit** and confirm with a **Y** for yes.

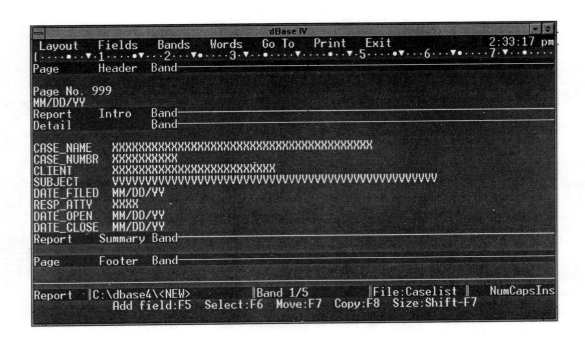

**Figure 5.40** The Form Layout Design

## N. EXITING DBASE

To leave the dBase program, access the **Exit Menu** with **[Alt]+[E]** and select **Quit to DOS**. If you accidentally exit to the Dot Prompt, type **quit** to exit.

CASE_NAME    Barker v. South Landfill
CASE_NUMBR   76645
CLIENT       South Landfill
SUBJECT      Injuctive relief sought by Howard Barker, and
             other nearby residents, against our client to
             prevent the disposing of hazardous waste at the
             landfill.

DATE_FILED   12/15/91
RESP_ATTY    BBK
DATE_OPEN    11/30/91
DATE_CLOSE   06/20/92

CASE_NAME    SDF Corporation - Earth Grinder Patent
CASE_NUMBR   1
CLIENT       SDF Corporation
SUBJECT      Patent filing for the "Earth Grinder" automatic
             mulcher.
DATE_FILED   01/23/92
RESP_ATTY    DGL
DATE_OPEN    10/12/91
DATE_CLOSE   01/01/93

CASE_NAME    SDF Corporation v. Terra, Inc.
CASE_NUMBR   72587
CLIENT       SDF Corporation
SUBJECT      Patent infringement action in which our client is
             suing Terra, Inc. for marketing their product
             "Earth Muncher" that is much too similar to our
             client's product "Ground Muncher."

DATE_FILED   06/11/91
RESP_ATTY    DGL
DATE_OPEN    11/08/90
DATE_CLOSE    /  /

CASE_NAME    Simpson v. SDF Corporation
CASE_NUMBR   71176
CLIENT       SDF Corporation
SUBJECT      Wrongful termination suit filed by Harold Simpson
             alleging that Mr. Smith was terminated based upon
             a faulty drug test.

DATE_FILED   04/01/91
RESP_ATTY    DGL
DATE_OPEN    08/25/90
DATE_CLOSE    /  /

CASE_NAME    Smith v. Berry
CASE_NUMBR   80023
CLIENT       Berry, Simon Jr.
SUBJECT      Breach of contract case wherein Mr. Smith alleges
             that our client delivered 250 cases of
             strawberries that were of poor quality and
             infested with ants.

DATE_FILED   06/24/92
RESP_ATTY    EMD
DATE_OPEN    04/19/92
DATE_CLOSE    /  /

**Figure 5.41**  A report created with the Form Layout

# Summary

dBase is a summary database program that keeps records of data within a file. There are two ways to work with dBase, from the Control Center and from the Dot Prompt. The beginning user should use the Control Center.

The Control Center consists of a menu bar, a catalog identifier, a list of special keys, and six data panels. The data panels display the files that have been created. A file can be put in use by highlighting the file name and pressing the **[Enter]** key twice to place it above the line in the file panel. The data within the file can be viewed by pressing the **[F2]** key.

There are two screens in which you may view your data, the Edit screen and the Browse screen. The Edit screen displays one record at a time. The Browse screen displays multiple records at once. The **[F2]** key toggles between these two screens. To return to the Control Center, press the **[Esc]** key, or exit through the menu if you have made changes.

When creating a new database, you must designate the fields, the field types, their widths, the number of decimal places (numeric fields only), and whether you would like an index created upon the field. After you have created the database, you may enter your records.

Databases may be ordered by sorting or indexing. Sorting creates a new database file with the records sorted in the requested order. Indexing creates an index file that may be used at any time on your database. You may have up to 47 separate index files for a single database.

To search for records within a database, you develop a query in the Query Design screen. The Query Design screen is divided into two parts, the file skeleton and the view skeleton. The file skeleton is where you place your search conditions. The view skeleton lets you select particular fields to be displayed in your query results.

A database or query may be printed using the **[Shift]+[F9]** quick report key, or by creating a report in the Reports Panel of the Control Center.

# Exercise

This exercise presents a hypothetical case regarding the Grove Dumpsite. Read the synopsis of the case and review the documents that form part of the evidence for the case. You will create a database for the evidentiary documents, print the database structure, print a report of your records, and perform and print a query.

# THE GROVE DUMPSITE CASE

In 1941, the Department of Defense ordered major oil and gas companies in Southern California to produce high octane aviation fuel for the aircraft being used in World War II, instead of gasoline for automobiles. A by-product of this high octane fuel was a form of hazardous sludge. The oil companies, faced with having to dispose of tons of this sludge, asked the Department of Defense where they should dump it. The Government ordered the oil companies to dispose of the sludge at the Grove Dumpsite, located some 30 miles south of Los Angeles in a rural, undeveloped area. At the end of World War II, the dumpsite was covered over with dirt and forgotten.

In 1980, the once rural area containing the dumpsite had become the affluent neighborhood of Oak Field in Orange County, California. A developer purchased the land around the dumpsite and built several tracts of luxury homes. Prospective purchasers who inquired about the vacant lot adjacent to the homes were told that the next phase of homes would be built there.

In 1982, while playing at the "vacant lot," some children found a mud puddle of oil which appeared to be bubbling up from underground. They told their parents, and the parents started asking questions about the lot. After making inquiries at the City Manager's office, it was learned that the vacant lot was actually the Grove Dumpsite.

The homeowners soon began to wonder what effect the dumpsite was having upon their health. The dumpsite became the suspected cause of every cold, allergy, disease, miscarriage, and birth deformity.

In 1983, the homeowners filed a class action lawsuit in Orange County Superior Court naming each of the dumping oil companies, the developer, and the city and county as defendants. Our firm represents Oyster Oil Company. The database you will be creating will be one of evidentiary documents only.

## THE DOCUMENTS

The following documents have been placed on your desk by the partner in charge of the case.

A letter, dated June 6, 1982, from the Oak Field Homeowners Association ("OFHA") to Jim Dodd, the City Manager of Oak Grove. The letter requests more information about the vacant lot adjacent to the Oak Field development. This letter is located in file number 6002.10.7.

A letter, dated December 8, 1941, from the Department of Defense to Oyster Oil Company mandating that it shift its gasoline production to high octane aviation fuel. This letter is located in file number 6002.10.4.

A letter, dated December 20, 1941, from Oyster Oil Company to the Department of Defense requesting the location of a dumpsite suitable for the dumping of the sludge by-product of the aviation fuel. This letter is located in file 6002.10.4.

A 1980 brochure from Field Developers showing the Oak Field development and outlining the plans for the areas surrounding the current development, including the future development of what we now know as the dumpsite. This brochure is located in file 6002.10.8.

A letter, dated February 3, 1979, from Field Developers to the City Manager of the City of Oak Grove requesting information about the vacant lot adjacent to the proposed Oak Field development. This letter is located in file 6002.10.8.

A report, dated March 23, 1955, prepared by the City Engineer of the City of Oak Grove describing the nature of the Grove Dumpsite and the decision to leave it covered with dirt instead of excavating it and moving the sludge to another site. This report is located in file 6002.10.5.

A report, dated January 15, 1955, from Soil and Plant Labs to the City of Oak Grove, recommending that the sludge be removed from the Grove Dumpsite, and hauled out into the ocean for disposal. This report is located in file 6002.10.5.

The sales contract for the purchase of a Oak Field home, dated July 16, 1980, between Jim and Mary Peters and Field Developers. This contract is located in file 6002.10.9.


## CREATING THE DATABASE


Create a database for these evidentiary documents. To do so, look at the description of the documents and determine the fields you would create for this database, their field type, length and whether you would like to create an index upon the field.


## ENTERING RECORDS


For each document described, enter a record into your database. Enter your records in a uniform manner (all caps, no caps, or initial caps) so that you will have no trouble searching later.


## PRINTING YOUR DATABASE STRUCTURE


So that your instructor may see the fields which you have created, follow the steps below from the **Control Center**.

1. Highlight your database name in the **Data Panel** and press **[Shift]+[F2]**.

2. Move to the **Layout Menu** with the **[Left Arrow]** key and select **Print database structure**.

3. Select **Begin printing** to print your field list. After printing, press the **[Esc]** key and answer **yes** when asked if you wish to abandon the operation. You will return to the **Control Center**.


## PRINTING A REPORT OF YOUR DATABASE

After you have entered all of your records, move to the **Reports Panel** and create a report using the **Quick Layouts, Form Layout** report. Send the Report to the printer. Exit to the Control Center.


## PERFORMING AND PRINTING A QUERY

Perform a query that will locate all records that are a "Report." Save the query file through the **Save changes and exit** option of the **Exit Menu** at the Query Design screen. You may give the query file any name you wish up to 8 characters.

Print this query file by placing the query file name above the line in the Query Panel, and printing another **Form Layout** report from the **Reports Panel**.

# Chapter Index

# CHAPTER 6

# LEXIS®

## *Chapter Preface*

This chapter will acquaint you with the LEXIS legal research database. This database contains the full-text of materials found in law libraries, standard libraries, and governmental agencies. The chapter will walk you through LEXIS and allow you to follow along on a LEXIS terminal if you have one available. For further training, you may contact Mead Data Central for a training location in your area. Training on LEXIS is usually free and is available to anyone who makes an appointment.

## A. THE LEXIS DATABASE

LEXIS is the computer assisted legal research database operated by Mead Data Central ("Mead Data"). The LEXIS database is stored on mainframe computers located in Ohio, and is accessed through the telephone lines with a computer or terminal.

The commands in LEXIS are executed by pressing a labeled key, a function key, or by transmitting a dot command. LEXIS will often ask you to transmit a command. Transmitting a command means typing the command, and then pressing the **[Enter]** key.

The labeled keys are present on keyboards supplied by Mead Data. They have the LEXIS commands printed on the appropriate keys.

The function keys on standard PC keyboards can perform the same functions as the labeled keys on the LEXIS keyboard. A function key template is provided when you subscribe to LEXIS.

*LEXIS*

A dot command is a two-letter command beginning with a period, such as **.so** for "sign off." Dot commands may be used from any type of keyboard.

In this chapter, both the labeled key name and the dot command will be given for each action described. If you are using the function keys, you can locate the given labeled key name on your template.

## B. ENTERING LEXIS

You will enter LEXIS by selecting a menu option on your computer's screen, or by typing a command. The LEXIS software connects your computer to LEXIS through your computer's modem and the telephone lines. The connection takes a few moments. When the connection is completed, the LEXIS Welcome Screen appears and prompts for your personal identification number (password) as shown in Figure 6.1.

```
WELCOME TO LEXIS AND NEXIS.
LEXIS and NEXIS will be available until  2:00 A.M. Eastern Time.

Please type your personal identification number (7 characters) and press the
TRANSMIT key.
 Press Alt-H for Help or Alt-Q to Quit.
```

**Figure 6.1** The LEXIS Welcome Screen

### 1. Personal Identification Number

The personal identification number requested at the LEXIS Welcome Screen is supplied to subscribers by Mead Data. You will find this number on your LEXIS card. After entering the personal identification number, you are greeted by the LEXIS Bulletin Board, shown in Figure 6.2, which displays information about the database.

### 2. The Research Identifier

At the Bulletin Board screen, LEXIS prompts for the entry of a research identifier at the upper left-hand corner of the screen. A research identifier identifies the client and matter for which the research is being performed. When your office receives a billing statement from LEXIS, the time attributable to each research identifier will be noted on the bill. If you are using an educational password, you may be required to enter the name of the instructor and class for which you are performing the research. The research identifier may be 1 to 32 characters in length.

When you are in LEXIS, and want to begin research for a different client or project, you may change the research identifier at any time by transmitting **c**. LEXIS will prompt for a new research identifier and take you to the LEXIS Library to begin a new research session.

```
1...5...10...15...20...25...30..
```

```
For Rosty's Tax Simplification Bill + Report, HR 13, TRANSMIT:fedtax;tnt;.ns;
headline(93-547 or 93-592).Check in MDEAFR;ALLNEWS for news on Saddam Hussein,
Palestinian deportees, or Mid-East peace talks (see Debut message 5). ALLOWN,
new super group file in the ASSETS lib. combines local real estate ownership
records from 352 counties and deed transfer data from 129 counties nationwide.
```

```
ONLY LEXIS DELIVERS ... the competitive edge for your COURSE WORK
and JOB SEARCH with legal, news, financial and medical sources.

Use of your educational LEXIS ID is governed by the terms in the
"Statement of Terms and Responsibility for Access to the
Educational LEXIS/NEXIS/MEDIS Services".

You may use up to 32 characters to identify the purpose of your research.

For further explanation, press the H key (for HELP) and then the TRANSMIT key.
 Press Alt-H for Help or Alt-Q to Quit.
```

**Figure 6.2** The LEXIS Bulletin Board

## C. LEAVING LEXIS (.SO)

You may leave LEXIS at any time by pressing the **[SIGN OFF]** key or by transmitting **.so**.

## D. THE LEXIS LIBRARY

The LEXIS Library, shown in Figure 6.3, is the main screen which displays the categories of materials available in the LEXIS database. This is the first screen that you encounter after entering your research identifier.

This screen, and the one on the following page, displays the names of the Libraries available in LEXIS. Each Library contains individual databases that LEXIS refers to as Files. You will perform your actual research in the LEXIS Files.

You may move to the next page in the Library screen by pressing the **[NEXT PAGE]** key or by transmitting **.np**.

The individual State Libraries are listed on the second page of the Library screen as shown in Figure 6.4.

Please TRANSMIT the NAME (only one) of the library you want to search.
- For more information about a library, TRANSMIT its page (PG) number.
- To see a list of additional libraries, press the NEXT PAGE key.

| NAME | PG | NAME | PG | NAME | PG | NAME | PG | NAME | PG | NAME | PG | NAME | PG |
|------|----|------|----|------|----|------|----|------|----|------|----|------|----|
| - - - - - - L E X I S - U S - - - - - - - - - - | | | | | | | | PUBLIC | | FINANCIAL | | --NEXIS-- | |
| GENFED | 1 | CODES | 1 | LEGIS | 1 | STATES | 1 | CITES | 6 | RECORDS | | COMPNY | 15 | NEXIS | 13 |
| MEGA | 1 | | | | | | | | | ASSETS | 6 | MERGER | 15 | BACKGR | 13 |
| | | | | MILTRY | 4 | CORP | 2 | LAWREV | 6 | DOCKET | 6 | NAARS | 15 | BANKS | 14 |
| ADMRTY | 2 | FEDCOM | 3 | PATENT | 4 | EMPLOY | 2 | MARHUB | 6 | INCORP | 6 | | | CMPCOM | 13 |
| BANKNG | 2 | FEDSEC | 3 | PENBEN | 4 | HEALTH | 3 | LEXREF | 6 | LIENS | 6 | --INT'L-- | | CONSUM | 13 |
| BKRTCY | 2 | FEDTAX | 3 | PUBCON | 4 | INSRLW | 3 | ABA | 6 | VERDCT | 9 | WORLD | 16 | ENRGY | 14 |
| COPYRT | 2 | IMMIG | 3 | PUBHW | 4 | MEDMAL | 3 | BNA | 6 | --MEDIS-- | | ASIAPC | 16 | ENTERT | 13 |
| ENERGY | 2 | INTLAW | 3 | REALTY | 4 | PRLIAB | 4 | TAXRIA | 6 | GENMED | 12 | EUROPE | 16 | INSURE | 13 |
| ENVIRN | 2 | ITRADE | 3 | TRADE | 5 | STENV | 4 | TAXANA | 6 | MEDEX | 12 | MDEAFR | 16 | LEGNEW | 14 |
| ESTATE | 2 | LABOR | 3 | TRDMRK | 5 | STSEC | 4 | ALR | 6 | MEDLNE | 12 | NSAMER | 16 | MARKET | 14 |
| ETHICS | 2 | LEXPAT | 3 | TRANS | 5 | STTAX | 4 | -ASSISTS- | | | | CANADA | 16 | PEOPLE | 14 |
| FAMILY | 2 | M&A | 4 | CAREER | 6 | UCC | 5 | PRACT | 12 | POLITICAL | | | | SPORTS | 13 |
| FEDSEN | 3 | MSTORT | 5 | | | UTILTY | 5 | GUIDE | 12 | CMPGN | 14 | | | TRAN | 14 |
| | | | | | | | | | | EXEC | 14 | | | | |

AC for AUTO-CITE    LXE (LEXSEE) to retrieve a case/document by cite
 SHEP for SHEPARD'S LXT (LEXSTAT) to retrieve a statute by cite
Press Alt-H for Help or Alt-Q to Quit.

**Figure 6.3** The LEXIS Library

Please TRANSMIT the NAME (only one) of the library you want to search.
- For more information about a library, TRANSMIT its page (PG) number.
- To see a list of additional libraries, press the PREV PAGE key.

| NAME | PG | NAME | PG | NAME | PG | NAME | PG | NAME | PG | NAME | PG | NAME | PG |
|------|----|------|----|------|----|------|----|------|----|------|----|------|----|
| - - - - - - - L E X I S - U S - - - - - - - - - | | | | | | | | | | LEXIS-UK | | LEXIS-CW | LEXIS-FR |
| ALA | 7 | GA | 7 | MD | 7 | NJ | 8 | TENN | 8 | ENGGEN | 10 | COMCAS | 10 | INTNAT | 11 |
| ALAS | 7 | HAW | 7 | MASS | 7 | NM | 8 | TEX | 8 | UKTAX | 10 | AUST | 10 | LOIREG | 11 |
| ARIZ | 7 | IDA | 7 | MICH | 7 | NY | 8 | UTAH | 8 | SCOT | 10 | NZ | 10 | PRESSE | 11 |
| ARK | 7 | ILL | 7 | MINN | 7 | NC | 8 | VT | 9 | UKJNL | 10 | | | PRIVE | 11 |
| CAL | 7 | IND | 7 | MISS | 8 | ND | 8 | VI | 9 | NILAW | 10 | | | PUBLIC | 11 |
| COLO | 7 | IOWA | 7 | MO | 8 | OHIO | 8 | VA | 9 | | | EC-LAW | | REVUES | 11 |
| CONN | 7 | KAN | 7 | MONT | 8 | ORE | 8 | WASH | 9 | | | EURCOM | 10 | | |
| DEL | 7 | KY | 7 | NEB | 8 | OKLA | 8 | WVA | 9 | | | | | | |
| DC | 7 | LA | 7 | NEV | 8 | PA | 8 | WISC | 9 | | | LEXIS-IR | | | |
| FLA | 7 | MAINE | 7 | NH | 8 | PR | 8 | WYO | 9 | | | IRELND | 10 | | |
| | | | | | | RI | 8 | | 8 | | | | | | |
| | | | | | | SC | 8 | | | | | | | | |
| | | | | | | SD | 8 | | | | | | | | |

Press Alt-H for Help or Alt-Q to Quit.

**Figure 6.4** The Second Page of the Library Screen

# E. Selecting a Library and File

To begin your research in LEXIS, you must select the Library containing the category of materials you desire to research. A list of all publications contained within LEXIS, and the Library(ies) and File(s) in which each is contained, is provided to you in booklet form by Mead Data.

## 1. Selecting a Library

To select a Library, type the name of the Library, and press the **[Enter]** key.

To see further information about a library, type the page number corresponding to that Library, and press the **[Enter]** key. Pressing the **[Enter]** key again will return you to the Library screen.

---

### State Libraries

*There are two ways to search within state materials. You may select the library for the state, such as the **CAL** Library, or you can search the **CAL** File within the **STATES** Library. The **STATES** Library contains a database File for each state. An individual state library contains database Files for a variety of caselaw and other materials such as limited partnership and corporation information. Either Library may be used when searching for state caselaw. For example, Georgia Cases may be searched in the **STATES** Library, **GA** File, or within the **GA** Library and a selected caselaw File.*

*The advantage to searching in the **STATES** Library is that you may search in more than one state file at a time by separating the file names with commas. For example, a search can be simultaneously run in the **California** and **Georgia** Files of this library by transmitting **CAL,GA***

*The advantage to searching in the **GA** Library over the **STATES** Library, **GA** File, is that you may limit your search to specific caselaw Files. In the **STATES** Library the **GA** File groups all Georgia decisions together. In the **GA** Library, you may select different Files for Supreme Court Decisions, Appellate Court Decisions, Attorney General Opinions, or other Files which contain a combination of court decisions.*

---

In this chapter, we will be doing research in Georgia caselaw using the Georgia Library. At the screen shown in Figure 6.4, we may select the Georgia Library by transmitting: **GA.**

## 2. Selecting a File

Figure 6.5 shows the Files contained within the Georgia Library.

```
Please TRANSMIT the abbreviated NAME of the file you want to search. To see a
description of a file, type its page number and press the TRANSMIT key.
                                  FILES -- PAGE 1 of 1
   NAME   PG DESCRIP                    NAME   PG DESCRIP

- - - - - - - - - - - - - - - G E O R G I A - - - - - - - - - - - - - - - -
   GA     1 Sup. Ct.        1937 to 12/92  CODE    2 Official Code of Georgia Ann
   APP    1 App. Ct.        1945 to 10/92  CONST   2 Georgia Constitution
   GATAX  1 Sec. of State Rules & Regs.    ALS     2 Advance Legislative Service
   GASEC  1 Comm of Sec     1/73 to  8/92  GACODE  2 CODE and CONST Files
   GAENV  1 Bd of Natural Resources        GATRCK  3 Tracking of pending bills
                            1975 to 12/92  GARGTR  3 Tracking of regulations
   AG     1 AG Ops          1/76 to 11/92  GASOS   1 GAINC and GALTP files
   CASES  1 GA, APP, GATAX, GASEC & GAENV  GAINC   1 Georgia Corporation Info.
   AGCASE 1 GA, APP, GATAX, GASEC, GAENV,  GALTP   1 Georgia Ltd Partnership Info
            & AG files
   STCTS  1 All State Courts              EMORY   1 Emory Law Journal
                                          GALREV  1 Georgia Law Review
                                          GAPROP  3 Real property records
                                          GAOWN   3 GAPROP plus Deed transfers


Press Alt-H for Help or Alt-Q to Quit.
```

**Figure 6.5** The Files Contained Within the Georgia Library

Files are the databases in which you will actually perform your research. The CASES File within the GA Library contains the Supreme and Appellate Court case opinions. This is the File that we will use for our research. To select this File, transmit **CASES**.

After the File has been selected, you are prompted to enter your Search at a screen similar to the one shown in Figure 6.6.

```
Please type your search request then press the TRANSMIT key.
What you transmit will be Search Level 1.

For further explanation, press the H key (for HELP) and then the TRANSMIT key.
 Press Alt-H for Help or Alt-Q to Quit.
```

**Figure 6.6** The Search Request Screen

## F. Developing a Search

The most important task in computerized legal research is developing the search. A search is a request to LEXIS to find certain words, phrases, or characters within documents contained in the File being searched. A good search yields results that are relevant to the issue being researched. A poorly designed search may find too many or too few cases, or cases that are irrelevant to the research issue.

It is important to design your search *before* you access LEXIS. A good search takes time to think through, and time is money when you are connected to LEXIS. Mead Data provides a form, similar to the one shown in Figure 6.7, to assist in developing your search.

There are three steps in developing a search:

1. Identifying the issue to research.

2. Choosing the appropriate library and file.

3. Drafting the search.

### 1. Identifying the Issue to Research

The issue to be researched is the point for which you are seeking support, rebuttal or an answer. The issue which we will use for our example is:

**In Georgia, is a parent liable for a minor's negligent operation of the parent's vehicle, when the minor has not been given permission to operate the vehicle?**

### 2. Choosing the Appropriate Library and File

Choosing the appropriate Library and File involves the selection of the type of materials needed to support, rebut, or answer the issue. We have chosen the GA Library and the CASES File to search for Supreme and Appellate Court cases which answer the question posed by our issue.

**1.** Define your FACT SITUATION or ISSUE — write out the FACTS or ISSUE in a sentence or two.

_____

_____

_____

**2.** List the LIBRARIES and FILES that contain the primary, secondary and law related materials you will search.

**Library:** _____      **File:** _____

_____      _____

_____      _____

## WORDS

**3.** Look back at your issue and circle the facts or sub-issues to explore. Consider the language the author would use and list the words that would express these ideas. Use ∗ and ! where appropriate.

**Issues to Explore**                          **Words and Alternative Expressions**

_____      _____

_____      _____

_____      _____

## SEARCH REQUEST

**4.** Link your search words with connectors (**OR, W/n, AND**) and arrange your search request in levels. It is usually wise to search just one idea at each level. Decide which issue is really central to your research and transmit that level first.

**Level 1:** _____

**Level 2:** _____

**Level 3:** _____

**5.** Look at some of the documents found in your Level 1 search. Do you need to add any additional search words? Modify by transmitting the letter _m_, then enter the next idea as Level 2.

Do you need to change the search itself? Transmit 1m, 2m, etc. (the number of the level you wish to modify, plus m for modify). Then move the cursor to insert or delete words.

Use the FOCUS™ feature to pinpoint specific words you wish to view in your retrieved documents.

Browse through the documents using the KWIC™ display format. Then review those of particular interest in FULL or print or store to disk to review later.

For assistance in developing a search request, feel free to call Customer Service at **800-543-6862** or your Mead Data Central, Inc. account executive.

**Figure 6.7** LEXIS's Search Development Form

## 3. Drafting the Search

In drafting a search in a full-text database, such as LEXIS, key words, alternatives, universal characters, and connectors are used.

### a. *Key Words (Search Terms)*

Key words, sometimes referred to as "search terms," are words which are likely to be found in documents relevant to the issue. Some key words for our issue are shown below.

### KEY WORDS

parent
liable
minor
operation
vehicle

### b. *Alternatives*

The next step in developing the search is to think of alternatives for the key words. Alternatives are words that may have been used in the documents in place of the key words. For example, an alternative for *parent* is *guardian*. An alternative for *liable* is *liability*. Our key words and some possible alternatives are shown below.

| KEY WORDS | ALTERNATIVES |
|---|---|
| parent | **guardian** |
| liable | **liability** |
| minor | |
| operation | **operate, operating** |
| vehicle | **automobile** |

### c. *The Universal Characters*

When the key words and alternatives have common spellings, such as *liable* and *liability*, LEXIS's universal characters, (!) and (*) may be used to simplify the search.

The exclamation point is used for words with a *common root*. For example, *liable* and *liability* have the common root *liab*. Using the exclamation point following this root, *liab!*, will locate all words with this root.

The asterisk is used to replace a *single character* any place in a word. For example, *dr\*nk* will locate *drink, drunk,* and *drank.*

Our search will utilize the exclamation point to cover some of the key words and their alternatives.

## KEY WORDS AND ALTERNATIVES WITH UNIVERSAL CHARACTERS

parent     guardian
liab!
minor
operat!
vehicle     auto!

---

### *PLURALS AND PUNCTUATION*

*LEXIS automatically searches for the plurals of most words. Irregular plurals, such as children for child, however, are not automatically found. Also, the plurals of words ending in "us" or "is" are not automatically found.*

*Punctuation is very important in a LEXIS search. The following symbols are recognized as spaces by LEXIS:*

(
)
-
?
&
$
+
. *Unless within a number or an abbreviation.*
, *(comma) Unless within a number.*
: *Unless within a number.*

*The following symbols are not recognized as spaces by LEXIS:*

;
' *(apostrophe)*
§

*LEXIS converts the symbol for a paragraph, ¶, into the letter **p**. Therefore, use **p10** to pick up all references to ¶10.*

---

d. *Connectors*

To finish developing the search, the key words and alternatives must be connected. For example, if you are searching for cases that contain the words *parent* and *liability*, you will connect the two words with the **AND** connector:

**parent AND liab!**

If you are searching for the word *parent* or *guardian* within the same document as *liability*, you will connect *parent* and *guardian* with the OR connector, and connect these two words to *liability* with the AND connector. Parentheses may be used to make sure that LEXIS processes the search as you have planned.

**(parent OR guardian) AND liab!**


## THE LEXIS CONNECTORS

| | |
|---|---|
| **or** | Retrieves documents containing *either* the word before *or* the word after the connector. |
| **and** | Retrieves documents containing *both* the word before *and* word after the connector. |
| **and not** | Excludes documents from the search results which contain the word or phrase found after the connector. |
| **pre/n** | Retrieves documents in which the word before the connector *precedes* the word after the connector by **n** number of words. |
| **w/n** | Retrieves documents in which the word before the connector is *within* **n** words of the word after the connector. |
| **not w/n** | Retrieves documents in which the word before the connector is included within the document. It excludes documents in which the word before the connector is *within* **n** words of the word after the connector. |
| **w/seg** | Retrieves documents in which the word before the connector is found *within the same segment* as the word after the connector. Segments are parts of documents. For example, cases have segments, among others, for the majority and dissenting opinions. |
| **not w/seg** | Retrieves documents in which the word before the connector is included within the document. However, it *excludes documents* in which the word before the connector is found *within the same segment* as the word after the connector. |

" "          Retrieves documents in which a word or phrase is present in the exact pattern in which it appears within the quotation marks.


Incorporating the expanders and connectors, we will draft our search. LEXIS refers to search requests in Levels. When formulating the search, you will want to begin with a broad search in Level 1. After seeing the cases that are retrieved from the File with the Level 1 search, you may modify the search in Level 2. LEXIS does not charge for modifying a search (other than the time charge). However, you *are* charged when you begin a new search.

The Search Development Form for our **Level 1** search is shown in Figure 6.8. Our Level 1 search will be:

**(parent or guardian w/10 liab! w/50 minor w/50 operat! w/50 vehicle or auto!)**

Note that the connector **w/10** is used between *parent or guardian* and *liab!*. These two terms will likely be found in close proximity to one another. It can be assumed that **w/10** will find words within the same sentence, and that **w/50** will find words within the same paragraph. LEXIS will begin our search by locating all cases in which the key words OR their alternatives are found. It will then take those cases and keep only the ones in which *parent* or *guardian* is found *within 10 words* of *liab!*. Finally, it will take the remaining decisions and limit them further to only those which contain the conditions set forth with the **w/50** connector.

---

### *CONNECTOR PRIORITY*

*LEXIS uses a connector priority for processing a search. The order of processing is shown below.*

> *or*
> *w/n, pre/n, not w/n*
> *w/seg*
> *not w/seg*
> *and*
> *and not*

*If there is more than one w/n connector used in a search, LEXIS will process the smaller number first.*

---

**1.** Define your FACT SITUATION or ISSUE — write out the FACTS or ISSUE in a sentence or two.

*In Georgia, is a parent liable for a minor's negligent operation of the parent's vehicle, when the minor has not been given permission to operate the vehicle?*

**2.** List the LIBRARIES and FILES that contain the primary, secondary and law related materials you will search.

Library: *GA*　　　　　　　　　　　　　　　File: *CASES*

## WORDS

**3.** Look back at your issue and circle the facts or sub-issues to explore. Consider the language the author would use and list the words that would express these ideas. Use * and ! where appropriate.

**Issues to Explore**

*parent, liable, minor, operation, vehicle*

**Words and Alternative Expressions**

*Parent　　　guardian*
*liabl!*
*minor*
*operat!*
*vehicle　　　auto!*

## SEARCH REQUEST

**4.** Link your search words with connectors (**OR, W/n, AND**) and arrange your search request in levels. It is usually wise to search just one idea at each level. Decide which issue is really central to your research and transmit that level first.

Level 1: *(parent or guardian w/10 liab! w/50 minor w/50*
Level 2: *operat! w/50 vehicle or auto!)*
Level 3: _____

**5.** Look at some of the documents found in your Level 1 search. Do you need to add any additional search words? Modify by transmitting the letter *m*, then enter the next idea as Level 2.

Do you need to change the search itself? Transmit 1m, 2m, etc. (the number of the level you wish to modify, plus m for modify). Then move the cursor to insert or delete words.

Use the FOCUS™ feature to pinpoint specific words you wish to view in your retrieved documents.

Browse through the documents using the KWIC™ display format. Then review those of particular interest in FULL or print or store to disk to review later.

For assistance in developing a search request, feel free to call Customer Service at **800-543-6862** or your Mead Data Central, Inc. account executive.

**Figure 6.8**  The Search Development Form for the Level 1 Search

The search is entered into LEXIS as shown in Figure 6.9.

```
(parent or guardian w/10 liab! w/50 minor w/50 operat! w/50 vehicle or auto!)
```

```
Please type your search request then press the TRANSMIT key.
What you transmit will be Search Level 1.

For further explanation, press the H key (for HELP) and then the TRANSMIT key.
 Press Alt-H for Help or Alt-Q to Quit.
```

**Figure 6.9** The search is entered into LEXIS at the Search Request screen

## G. THE SEARCH RESULTS

After processing the search, LEXIS displays a screen showing the number of cases found by the search (see Figure 6.10).

From this screen, you may view the search results in different ways by pressing the following keys, or by transmitting their corresponding dot commands.

| | |
|---|---|
| [KWIC] | .kw |
| [VAR KWIC] | .vk |
| [FULL] | .fu |
| [CITE] | .ci |
| [SEGMTS] | .se |

The display formats which correspond to these commands are explained below. To change from one format to another, press the new key or transmit the new dot command. Move through each of these commands to see how they differ.

```
(PARENT OR GUARDIAN W/10 LIAB! W/50 MINOR W/50 OPERAT! W/50 VEHICLE OR AUTO!)
```

```
Your search request has found 7 CASES through Level 1.
To DISPLAY these CASES press either the KWIC, FULL, CITE or SEGMTS key.
To MODIFY your search request, press the M key (for MODFY) and then the TRANSMIT
key.

For further explanation, press the H key (for HELP) and then the TRANSMIT key.
 Press Alt-H for Help or Alt-Q to Quit.
```

**Figure 6.10**  After processing the search, LEXIS displays this screen indicating
the number of documents satisfying the search conditions

## 1. KWIC (.kw)

The KWIC ("Key Words In Context") command moves to the first instance of your search
terms in the found documents, and displays the search terms surrounded by 25 words (see
Figure 6.11). The search terms will be highlighted on the screen. Pressing the **[NEXT PAGE]**
key, or transmitting **.np**, will take you to the next instance of your search terms or the first page
of the next document.

## 2. VAR KWIC (.vk)

The VAR KWIC command is similar to the KWIC command, except that it displays 50
words on either side of the search terms. Pressing the **[NEXT PAGE]** key, or transmitting **.np**,
will take you to the next instance of your search terms or the first page of the next document.

## 3. FULL (.fu)

The FULL command displays the full text of each document. Pressing the **[NEXT PAGE]**
key, or transmitting **.np**, will take you to the next page of the document or to the first page of
the next document.

The theory of the doctrine, as held by this court and courts of other jurisdictions, is well expressed in Hubert v. Harpe, 181 a. 168, 172, supra, quoted approvingly in Dunn v. Caylor, 218 Ga. 256, 258, supra, as follows: "A father is under no legal obligation to furnish an automobile for the comfort and pleasure of his child, whether minor or adult; and if he does so, it is a voluntary act on his part. In every such case the question is whether the father has expressly or impliedly made the furnishing of an automobile for such purpose a part of his business, so that one operating the vehicle for that purpose with his consent, express or implied, may be considered as his agent or servant. A child, whether minor or adult, may occupy the position of a servant or agent of his parent, and for his [or her] acts as such the parent may be liable under the principles governing the relation of master and servant or of principal and agent." This court, in Evans v. Caldwell, 184 Ga. 203, 204, supra, makes the observation that: "The application of the law of master and servant or of principal and ...

Press Alt-H for Help or Alt-Q to Quit.

**Figure 6.11** The KWIC key, or transmitting .kw, displays the search terms and surrounds them with 25 words

## 4. CITE (.ci)

The CITE command displays the citations of the documents found by the search as shown in Figure 6.12.

## 5. SEGMENT (.se)

The SEGMENT command allows you to select a specific segment of the documents to view. For example, you may wish to view only the **Opinion** segment of each case as you browse through the search results. Pressing the [SEGMTS] key, or transmitting .se, will display the segments available for the materials in the chosen File (see Figure 6.13). To view one or more segments, you transmit the name(s) of the segments.

Transmit **OPINIONBY** to view the portion of each case stating the name of the justice who authored the majority opinion. Use the [NEXT DOC] key to move through the cases. Return to FULL, KWIC, or VAR KWIC by pressing the appropriate key or transmitting a dot command.

LEVEL 1 - 7 CASES

1. STEWART v. STEPHENS, No. 25065, Supreme Court of Georgia, 225 Ga. 185; 166 S.E.2d 890,    March 10, 1969, Argued,    March 20, 1969, Decided

2. DUNN et al. v. CAYLOR, No. 21728, Supreme Court of Georgia, 218 Ga. 256; 127 S.E.2d 367,    July 10, 1962, Argued,    September 6, 1962, Decided

3. CABRAL v. WHITE et al., No. 73043, Court of Appeals of Georgia, 181 Ga. App. 816; 354 S.E.2d 162,    January 23, 1987, Decided, Rehearing Denied February 18, 1987.

4. CALHOUN v. EAVES, No. 42317, Court of Appeals of Georgia, 114 Ga. App. 756; 152 S.E.2d 805,    September 7, 1966, Argued,    November 8, 1966, Decided, Rehearing Denied December 7, 1966.  Certiorari Applied For.

5. STANSELL v. FOWLER, by Next Friend, et al., No. 41732, Court of Appeals of Georgia, 113 Ga. App. 377; 147 S.E.2d 793,    January 6, 1966, Argued,    March 1, 1966, Decided, Rehearing Denied March 23, 1966.  Certiorari Applied For.

6. Yancey v. Munda, No. 35999, Court of Appeals of Georgia, 93 Ga. App. 230; 91 S.E.2d 204,    January 20, 1956, Decided

7. WHITLOCK et al. v. MICHAEL, No. 32425, Court of Appeals of Georgia, 79 Ga. App. 316; 53 S.E.2d 587,    May 21, 1949, Decided

Press Alt-H for Help or Alt-Q to Quit.

**Figure 6.12** The [Cite] key, or transmitting .ci, displays the citations of the documents found by a search.

```
Please transmit, separated by commas, the segment(s) you want displayed.

NAME              NUMBER            COURT             CITE
DATE              NOTICE            HISTORY           DISPOSITION
HEADNOTES         SYLLABUS          COUNSEL           JUDGES
OPINIONBY         OPINION          CONCURBY          CONCUR
DISSENTBY         DISSENT           OPINIONS          WRITTENBY
AGENCY            REQUESTBY         DIVISION          CHAPTER
RULE              TEXT              AUTHORITY         SIGNATORIES

For further explanation, press the H key (for HELP) and then the TRANSMIT key.
  Press Alt-H for Help or Alt-Q to Quit.
```

**Figure 6.13** The Segments Available in the Georgia Library, CASES File

# H. MOVING WITHIN THE SEARCH RESULTS

The special keys and corresponding dot commands that assist you in moving through your search results are:

| | |
|---|---|
| **[FIRST PAGE]** | **.fp** |
| **[NEXT PAGE]** | **.np** |
| **[PREV PAGE]** | **.pp** |
| **[FIRST DOC]** | **.fd** |
| **[NEXT DOC]** | **.nd** |
| **[PREV DOC]** | **.pd** |

These commands are explained below. Use each of them to see how they work with the search results.

## 1. First Page (.fp)

Displays the First Page of a document. This command is accessed with the **[FIRST PAGE]** key or by transmitting **.fp**.

## 2. Next Page (.np)

Displays the Next Page in a document. This command is accessed with the **[NEXT PAGE]** key or by transmitting **.np**. To move ahead **x** number of pages, type the number of pages and press the **[NEXT PAGE]** key, or type **.np** followed by the number (without a space; e.g., .np10). When viewing the search results in the KWIC format, the Next Page command will take you to the next instance of your search conditions.

## 3. Previous Page (.pp)

Displays the Previous Page in a document. This command is accessed with the **[PREV PAGE]** key or by transmitting **.pp**. To move backwards **x** number of pages, type the number of pages and press the **[PREV PAGE]** key, or type **.pp** followed by the number (without a space; e.g., **.pp10**).

## 4. First Document (.fd)

Displays the First Document in the search results. This command is accessed with the **[FIRST DOC]** key or by transmitting **.fd**.

## 5. Next Document (.nd)

Displays the Next Document in the search results. This command is accessed with the **[NEXT DOC]** key or by transmitting **.nd**. To move ahead **x** number of documents, type the number of documents and press the **[NEXT DOC]** key, or type **.nd** followed by the number (without a space; e.g., **.nd10**).

## 6. Previous Document (.pd)

Displays the Previous Document in the search results. This command is accessed with the **[PREV DOC]** key or by transmitting .pd. To move backwards **x** number of documents, type the number of documents and press the **[PREV DOC]** key, or type **.pd** followed by the number (without a space; e.g., **.pd10**).

## 7. Moving to a Specific Document

You may move to a Specific Document in your search results by transmitting the number of the document.

# I. ON-LINE INFORMATION

On-line information is available for Help with LEXIS, the elapsed Time of the current research session, the terms of the current Search Request, and the number of LEXIS Pages for a document being viewed. This information, and the commands that access the information, is explained below. Experiment with each to see how they work. Note that these commands are not dot commands.

## 1. Help (h)

On-line Help may be obtained by transmitting **h** at any time. Pressing the **[Enter]** key or the key designated on the screen will return you to your research.

## 2. Time (t)

The elapsed Time of the current research session may be obtained by transmitting **t** at any time. Pressing the **[Enter]** key or the key designated on the screen will return you to your research.

## 3. Displaying the Search Request (r)

The current Search Request may be displayed by transmitting **r**. Pressing the **[Enter]** key or the key designated on the screen will return you to your research.

## 4. Number of Pages (p)

The number of LEXIS screens, for the selected viewing format, can be seen for the current document by transmitting **p**. Pressing the **[Enter]** key or the key designated on the screen will return you to your research.

# J. CITE CHECKING

## 1. Shepard's® Citations and Auto-Cite®

Cite checking in LEXIS is a valuable tool. Transmitting a single command will display all of the available citations. This is an advantage over performing the task manually. We will cite check one of the cases in our search results. In reviewing the results of our query, the sixth case, *Yancey v. Munda* comes very close to responding to the question contained within our issue (see Figure 6.14).

The validity of this case may be checked using Shepard's® Citations, Auto-Cite®, and/or LEXIS as a Citator.

Shepard's Citations and Auto-Cite are the two main citation services offered in LEXIS.

- Shepard's Citations provides, for a particular case, a list of all parallel cases (the citations for the particular case in different reporters), and all cases which cite the particular case in their opinions.

- Auto-Cite provides a list of parallel cases, a direct history of the case, and a list of the cases that negatively affect the precedential value of the case. A direct history provides a list of lower court decisions for a case, and any subsequent decisions involving the same parties and case facts. Cases that negatively affect the precedential value of a case criticize or overrule the case.

## 2. LEXIS as a Citator

Using LEXIS as a citator provides an update to Shepard's Citations. To use LEXIS as a citator, you run an actual search through the LEXIS database to find all citations to a particular case. This search will pick up any new citations that have not yet made it into Shepard's.

## 3. Accessing Shepard's® Citations and Auto-Cite®

There are three ways to access Shepard's Citations and Auto-Cite:

a) *While viewing a case on the screen*, you may check the citations for that case by transmitting the citation service's two-letter identification.

> **sh**　**Shepard's Citations**
> **ac**　**Auto-Cite**

b) *From any LEXIS screen*, after the client screen, you may check a particular case citation by transmitting the two-letter identifier for the citation service followed by the case citation.

> **sh 93 Ga. App 230**
> **ac 93 Ga. App 230**

c) *Either citation service may also be accessed* through the Select Service menu shown in Figure 6.15. This menu is accessed by pressing the **[SELECT SERV]** key, or by transmitting **.ss**. After you have chosen one of the services, LEXIS will prompt you to enter the case citation.

Yancey v. Munda

No. 35999

Court of Appeals of Georgia

93 Ga. App. 230; 91 S.E.2d 204

January 20, 1956, Decided

PRIOR HISTORY:

Action for damages. Before Judge Stephens. Laurens Superior Court. October 20, 1955.

DISPOSITION: Judgment reversed.

COUNSEL: W. W. Larsen, W. W. Larsen, Jr., for plaintiff in error.

Nelson & Nelson, contra.

JUDGES: Carlisle, J. Gardner, P.J., and Townsend, J., concur.

OPINIONBY: CARLISLE

OPINION:  [*230]  [**205]

1. A father is not liable for a tort, with which he is in no way connected, committed by one of his minor children, which he did not ratify, and from which he did not derive any benefit, merely because of the relationship of parent and child. Chastain v. Johns, 120 Ga. 977 (48 S.E. 343, 66 L.R.A. 958); Griffin v. Russell, 144 Ga. 275 (87 S.E. 10, L.R.A. 1916 F 216, Ann. Cas. 1917 D 994); Hubert v. Harpe, 181 Ga. 168 (182 S.E. 167).

2. However, under an application of the "family-purpose doctrine," if a father or a mother, owning a motor vehicle, and keeping it to be used for the comfort and pleasure of the family, should authorize a minor child to drive the vehicle for the comfort and pleasure of the family, the owner of the vehicle would be liable for the negligence of the minor child operating the vehicle for such purpose. Griffin v. Russell, supra. Cohen v. Whiteman, 75 Ga. App. 286 (43 S.E. 2d 184); Durden v. Maddox, 73 Ga. App. 491 (37 S.E. 2d 219); Hirsh v. Andrews, 81 Ga. App. 655 (59 S.E. 2d 552); Grahl v. McMath, 59 Ga. App. 247 (200 S.E. 342).

3. A father or mother is under no legal duty to furnish a motor vehicle for the comfort and pleasure of his or her family. Durden v. Maddox, supra.

4. To hold a parent liable under the family-purpose doctrine for the negligence of a minor child in operating a motor vehicle owned by the parent it must be made to appear that the parent owning the vehicle kept the vehicle for the comfort and pleasure of the family and expressly or impliedly made it available to the minor child for such purpose. Hirsh v. Andrews, supra.

5. Where, in an action for damages brought against a father for a tort committed by his minor son when the son negligently drove the father's [*231] truck into the plaintiff's automobile, the only allegations contained in the petition which in any way connect the father with the tort of his son is that the defendant father owned the motor vehicle driven by his minor son and that the minor son was driving the vehicle for his (the minor son's) pleasure, the petition is subject to general demurrer in the absence of any allegation that the father kept the motor vehicle for the comfort and pleasure of his family and had either expressly or impliedly authorized its use by his minor son. The trial court, consequently, in the present case, erred in overruling the general demurrer where those essential elements were not alleged in the petition.
Press Alt-H for Help or Alt-Q to Quit.

**Figure 6.14** *Yancey v. Munda*

```
Please transmit the NAME (only one) of the service that you want to use. If you
transmit the NAME of a service that is indicated as inappropriate (I) or
unavailable (U), further information will be provided.
```

```
NAME   CITATION SERVICES                NAME   FREE SERVICES
AC     AUTO-CITE Citation Service       CAI    Computer Assisted
       to verify a citation.                   Instructions.
SHEP   SHEPARD'S Citation Service       TUTOR  LEXIS/NEXIS TUTORIALS
       to list citing references               to assist searching.
       to a case citation.              DEBUT  What is new in LEXIS
LEXSEE LEXSEE Citation Service                 and NEXIS.
       to see the full text of a
       case, as identified by its              ECLIPSE SERVICES
       citation.                        SAV    Save a search for
LXSTAT LXSTAT Citation Service                 automatic updates.
       to see the full text            REC    RECALL a previously      I
       of a code section, as                  saved ECLIPSE search.
       identified by its citation
```

```
If you have changed your mind and do not want to select a service, press the
EXIT SERV key.
  Press Alt-H for Help or Alt-Q to Quit.
```

**Figure 6.15** The Select Service Menu

To return to your research from either of these services, press the **[RESUME LEXIS]** key or transmit **resume lexis**.

Move to the *Yancey v. Munda* case in your search results. Then, access Shepard's Citations by transmitting **sh**. The Shepard's Citations for *Yancey v. Munda* are shown in Figure 6.16.

```
          (c) 1993 McGraw-Hill, Inc. - DOCUMENT 1 (OF 1)

CITATIONS TO: 93 Ga.App. 230
SERIES: SHEPARD'S GEORGIA CITATIONS
DIVISION: GEORGIA APPEALS REPORTS
COVERAGE: First Shepard's Volume Through 12/92 Supplement.
```

| NUMBER | ANALYSIS | CITING REFERENCE | SYLLABUS/HEADNOTE |
|--------|----------|------------------|-------------------|
| 1 | parallel citation | (91 S.E.2d 204) | |
| 2 | | 106 Ga.App. 95 | 1 |
| 3 | | 113 Ga.App. 378 | 4 |
| 4 | | 117 Ga.App. 241 | 1 |
| -- | | 8 Ga.St.B.J. 327 | |
| -- | | 8 MercerL.Rev. 72 | |
| -- | | 8 MercerL.Rev. 175 | |

```
--------------------------------------------------------------------------
To see the text of a citing case, press the citing reference NUMBER and then
the TRANSMIT key.
For further explanation, press the H key (for HELP) and then the TRANSMIT key.
  Press Alt-H for Help or Alt-Q to Quit.
```

**Figure 6.16** Shepard's Citations for *Yancey v. Munda*

Any of the cases listed in the citation service may be viewed by typing the number corresponding to the case. When you are finished viewing a case, press the **[RESUME SHEP]** key or transmit **resume sh** to return to Shepard's Citations. To return to your research, press the **[RESUME LEXIS]** key or transmit **resume lexis**.

To check Auto-Cite for this case, transmit **ac** from Shepard's Citations or the case. If you enter the Auto-Cite service and select a case to be viewed, you return to Auto-Cite by pressing the **[RESUME AC]** key or transmitting **resume ac**. You may return to your research with the **[RESUME LEXIS]** key or by transmitting **resume lexis**. Auto-Cite did not contain any references to this case (see Figure 6.17).

When you use LEXIS as a citator you will search for a case name, such as *Yancey v. Munda*, using the **w/n** connector between the parties' names. For example: **Yancey w/6 Munda**. This will pick up cases that cite to *Yancey v. Munda* and alternative citations such as *Thomas Yancey v. George Munda*.

You can also search for the case citation, 93 Ga. App. 230. A good search is one which utilizes the **pre/n** connector between the volume and page numbers. This is due to the fact that not all cases will use the same abbreviation for the case reporter in their text. For example, 93 pre/5 230 will locate all cases that contain the number 93 preceding the number 230 by as many as five words. When cases have more than one citation, like *Yancey v. Munda*, it is important to use both citations in your search. For example, 93 pre/5 230 OR 91 pre/5 204 will locate references to the Georgia Appellate Reports citation and the South Eastern Reports citation.

```
Auto-Cite (R) Citation Service, (c) 1993 Lawyers Cooperative Publishing

93 GA. APP. 230:                                        Screen 1 of 1

CITATION YOU ENTERED:

Yancey v. Munda, 93 Ga. App. 230, 91 S.E.2d 204 (1956)



-----------------------------------------------------------------------------
To check another citation, type it and press the TRANSMIT key.
Alternate presentation formats are available.
For further explanation, press the H key (for HELP) and then the TRANSMIT key.
To return to LEXIS, press the EXIT SERV key.
 Press Alt-H for Help or Alt-Q to Quit.
```

**Figure 6.17** Auto-Cite for *Yancey v. Munda*

## K. MODIFYING A SEARCH

As previously discussed, a LEXIS search is performed in Levels. The first Level should be a broad search. If too many documents are located, the search may then be modified in subsequent Levels. It is better to modify a search, rather than run an entire new search, because LEXIS assesses a charge for each new search. There is no additional charge for modifying a search.

Our first search located only 7 cases. We will need to expand our search to locate more cases. To modify a search, transmit **m**. The current search request is displayed on the screen along with a message to begin the modification with a connector as shown in Figure 6.18. The connectors commonly used here are AND, W/n, and OR. The AND and W/n connectors will narrow your search. The OR connector will expand your search.

```
Your search request is:
 (PARENT OR GUARDIAN W/10 LIAB! W/50 MINOR W/50 OPERAT! W/50 VEHICLE OR AUTO!)

Number of CASES found with your search request through:
    LEVEL   1...      7

Please transmit the modification to your search request (Level 2).
REMEMBER to start your modification with a CONNECTOR.

For further explanation, press the H key (for HELP) and then the TRANSMIT key.
    Press Alt-H for Help or Alt-Q to Quit.
```

**Figure 6.18** The Search Modification Screen

### 1. Adding a Second Level

In reviewing the results of our Level 1 search, we observed that the phrase "family purpose doctrine" is used throughout these cases. We will add this phrase in the second Level by typing:

### or "family purpose doctrine"

The phrase is enclosed in quotation marks because we want the search to locate this exact phrase (see Figure 6.19).

Pressing the **[Enter]** key begins the search. This search retrieves 125 cases as shown in Figure 6.20.

### 2. Adding a Third Level

The results of our search through Level 2 need to be narrowed in order to find relevant cases. To narrow the search, we will add a third level by transmitting **m**. If you have not moved from the last modification screen, your last entry will appear near the top of the screen. This time we will choose to *limit* the cases to only those which contain the phrase "not liable."

Remember, our issue is questioning whether a parent is liable for the negligence of a minor when the minor did not have permission to operate the vehicle. In particular, we are looking for cases in which the parent has been held not liable for the negligence of the minor.

```
or "family purpose doctrine"
```

```
Your search request is:
 (PARENT OR GUARDIAN W/10 LIAB! W/50 MINOR W/50 OPERAT! W/50 VEHICLE OR AUTO!)

Number of CASES found with your search request through:
   LEVEL   1...        7

Please transmit the modification to your search request (Level 2).
REMEMBER to start your modification with a CONNECTOR.

For further explanation, press the H key (for HELP) and then the TRANSMIT key.
 Press Alt-H for Help or Alt-Q to Quit.
```

**Figure 6.19** The search is expanded in Level 2 with the OR connector.

```
OR "FAMILY PURPOSE DOCTRINE"
```

```
Your search request has found 125 CASES through Level 2.
To DISPLAY these CASES press either the KWIC, FULL, CITE or SEGMTS key.
To MODIFY your search request, press the M key (for MODFY) and then the TRANSMIT
key.

For further explanation, press the H key (for HELP) and then the TRANSMIT key.
 Press Alt-H for Help or Alt-Q to Quit.
```

**Figure 6.20** The modification of the search locates 125 cases.

To narrow our search, we will begin with the AND connector and type the search:

**and "not liable"**

The Level 3 search is shown in Figure 6.21.

```
and "not liable"
```

```
Your search request is:
 (PARENT OR GUARDIAN W/10 LIAB! W/50 MINOR W/50 OPERAT! W/50 VEHICLE OR AUTO!)
 OR "FAMILY PURPOSE DOCTRINE"

Number of CASES found with your search request through:
    LEVEL   1...      7 LEVEL   2...    125

Please transmit the modification to your search request (Level 3).
REMEMBER to start your modification with a CONNECTOR.

For further explanation, press the H key (for HELP) and then the TRANSMIT key.
    Press Alt-H for Help or Alt-Q to Quit.
```

**Figure 6.21**  A search narrowing the results with the AND connector
is added in Level 3.

Pressing the **[Enter]** key begins the search. Our search, through Level 3, has located 33 cases. This is a manageable number.

### 3.  Editing the Search Levels

You may edit the search conditions in Level 2 or later by typing **m** followed by the level number (e.g., m2). The search conditions for that level appear on the screen for modifications, and all levels subsequent to that level are erased. This is called "Back-modifying" and *does* result in a new search charge from LEXIS.

### 4. Viewing Different Levels of the Search Results

The search we have conducted consists of three levels.

**Level 1**     **(parent or guardian) w/10 liab! w/50 minor w/50 operat! w/50 (vehicle or auto!)**

**Level 2**     **or "family purpose doctrine"**

**Level 3**     **and "not liable"**

To view the search results of any of these levels, type the level number and press the **[DIF LEVEL]** key, or transmit **.dln**, where **n** represents the level number. Move to Level 2 by typing **.dl2**.

## L. SEARCHING WITHIN YOUR SEARCH RESULTS (FOCUS)

Occasionally, after executing a search and observing your search results, you will want to search for a specific word, phrase or condition within the search results. The Focus command will allow you to focus in on these terms, which need not have been in your original query. The **Focus** command is accessed by pressing the **[FOCUS]** key, or by transmitting **.fo**.

Within the 125 cases found with the search through Level 2, we can use the Focus command instead of adding the third level to our search. Accessing **Focus** brings up the screen shown in Figure 6.22.

```
(PARENT OR GUARDIAN W/10 LIAB! W/50 MINOR W/50 OPERAT! W/50 VEHICLE OR AUTO!) OR
"FAMILY PURPOSE DOCTRINE"




Please type your FOCUS search request and then press the TRANSMIT key.


The above request is the one you last used before selecting FOCUS.
You can edit and use this request with your FOCUS search request.
For editing instructions, press the E key (for EDIT) and then the TRANSMIT key.

To return to your previous search, press the TRANSMIT key.

For further explanation, press the H key (for HELP) and then the TRANSMIT key.
 Press Alt-H for Help or Alt-Q to Quit.
```

**Figure 6.22** The Focus Screen

We will focus in on cases within our search results which contain the phrase "not liable" by typing the phrase within quotation marks at this screen as shown in Figure 6.23.

```
"not liable"

(PARENT OR GUARDIAN W/10 LIAB! W/50 MINOR W/50 OPERAT! W/50 VEHICLE OR AUTO!) OR
"FAMILY PURPOSE DOCTRINE"




Please type your FOCUS search request and then press the TRANSMIT key.


The above request is the one you last used before selecting FOCUS.
You can edit and use this request with your FOCUS search request.
For editing instructions, press the E key (for EDIT) and then the TRANSMIT key.

To return to your previous search, press the TRANSMIT key.

For further explanation, press the H key (for HELP) and then the TRANSMIT key.
  Press Alt-H for Help or Alt-Q to Quit.
```

**Figure 6.23**  Typing "not liable" at the Focus screen will locate all documents within the search results which contain this phrase

After pressing **[Enter]**, LEXIS informs us that it has found 33 cases that satisfy the Focus request (see Figure 6.24). This is the same result that we obtained with the Level 3 search.

```
"NOT LIABLE"




33 of 125 CASES satisfy your FOCUS search request.
To display these 33 CASES, press any format key (e.g. FULL).

To display FOCUS terms in the CASE you were viewing,
press the TRANSMIT key.

To exit FOCUS and return to the CASE you were viewing, transmit EXIT.

For further explanation, press the H key (for HELP) and then the TRANSMIT key.
  Press Alt-H for Help or Alt-Q to Quit.
```

**Figure 6.24**  The Focus search locates 33 cases that satisfy our conditions

*LEXIS*

The [KWIC] key will take you through the cases, displaying the portion of the focus cases where the phrase "not liable" is found (see Figure 6.25). You may exit **Focus** by pressing the [EXIT FOCUS] key or by transmitting .ef.

```
            236 Ga. 271, *274; 223 S.E.2d 678, **680
                                                                FOCUS
    Myrick v. Alexander, 101 Ga. App. 1 (112 SE2d 697) (1960), and Myrick v.
Sievers, 104 Ga. ...

    ... [*276] [**681]    assumed possession and control of the car over the son's
protests and objections (i.e., the driver was a trespasser).  The court
correctly held that, under those facts, the car was not being used as a family
purpose car and so the owner was  not liable.

    In Pritchett v. Williams, supra, the owner's minor son let a third party
drive the car for the purpose of obtaining cigarettes for the son, but the son
was not in the car at the ...

    ... [*276] [**681]    car when the collision occurred during the course of
that errand.  A majority of the Court of Appeals held that where the facts do
not show that the owner has authorized the family member to authorize a third
person to drive the car, the owner is  not liable  under the family car doctrine
for injuries caused by the negligent operation of the car by such third person
outside the presence and control of the family member.  Because it is
unnecessary for us to decide in this case the questions ...


  Press Alt-H for Help or Alt-Q to Quit.
```

**Figure 6.25** The KWIC command will display the portions of the found documents which contain the Focus condition.


## M. Beginning a New Search

After you have completed a search, you may wish to begin a new search in the same Library and File, change the File, or change the Library.


### 1. New Search (.ns)

You may begin a new search in the same Library and File by pressing the [NEW SEARCH] key or by transmitting .ns. Your previous search is erased and a blank search entry screen is displayed. Use this command now to see the results.


### 2. Changing the File (.cf)

You may change the LEXIS File by pressing the [CHG FILE] key or by transmitting .cf. This command returns you to the menu of files for the current Library. After you have selected a new file, the search screen appears with your previous search displayed. You may type a new search, edit your previous search, or press the [Enter] key to run your previous search in the new file. Use this command from the new search screen to move back to the GA Library to see available files.

### 3. Changing the Library (.cl)

You may change Libraries by pressing the **[CHG LIBRARY]** key or by transmitting **.cl**. This command returns you to the LEXIS Library so that you may select the new Library. After you have selected a new Library, and a File within that Library, the search screen appears with your previous search displayed. You may type a new search, edit your previous search, or press the **[Enter]** key to run your previous search. Use this command to move back to the Library Screen.

## N. FINDING MATERIALS WHEN YOU KNOW THE CITATION (LEXSEE AND LEXSTAT)

There is a quick way to locate a particular document or statute in LEXIS. When you know the citation of a document, you may immediately retrieve that document using LEXSEE. When you know the statute number of a particular statute, you may retrieve it using LEXSTAT. Either of these two services may be accessed at any point in your research, after the client screen. While viewing search results, you may use LEXSEE or LEXSTAT, even if the document or statute for which you are searching is within a different library or file.

### 1. Accessing LEXSEE and LEXSTAT

LEXSEE and LEXSTAT can be accessed by typing the service name followed by the citation or code section for which you are searching.

**LEXSEE 93 ga. app. 230**

**LEXSTAT ca civ 43.6**

The abbreviations **LXE** and **LXT** may be used in place of **LEXSEE** and **LEXSTAT**.

**LXE 93 ga. app. 230**

**LXT ca civ 43.6**

The services may also be accessed by typing the citation and then pressing the **[LEXSEE]** or **[LEXSTAT]** keys.

Another way to access the two services is through the **Select Service** menu, which is accessed with the **[SELECT SERV]** key or by transmitting *.ss.*

Use **LEXSEE** to view **93 ga. app. 230.**

## 2. Leaving LEXSEE and LEXSTAT

To leave **LEXSEE** or **LEXSTAT** and return to your research, transmit **resume lexis.** You may also transmit **resume sh** or **resume ac** if you were in either of the two services when you accessed **LEXSEE** or **LEXSTAT.**

If you have been in **LEXSEE** and execute a **LEXSTAT** command, you may return to **LEXSEE** by transmitting **resume lexsee.** Similarly, if you are in **LEXSTAT** and execute a **LEXSEE** command, you can return to **LEXSTAT** by transmitting **resume lexstat.**

## O. Performing Segment Searches

As we demonstrated when we viewed the OPINIONBY segment in our search results, LEXIS documents contain segments that are similar to fields within a relational database. In creating a search within a LEXIS file, you may specify a segment in which to search. For example, you may have a case to be heard before a specific judge. You can view the published cases on your subject in which the judge has written an opinion by typing your search and using the **AND** connector to search within the **WRITTENBY** segment for that judge's name.

Different types of documents contain different types of Segments. After you have selected a Library and File, pressing the **[SEGMTS]** key, or transmitting **.se**, will display a list of the Segments available for that File.

Many of the common segments, and their usage, are explained below.

## 1. The Name Segment (NAME)

The Name segment contains the name of the case. When you search for a case name, it is unlikely that you will know the exact name of the case. Therefore, it is best to search for a case name using one or more of the party's names.

**NAME (Yancey)**

**NAME (Yancey AND Munda)**

The first search, using one name, may not be specific enough. There could be several cases within the Georgia State Cases database that contain the name "Yancey" within the name of the case. The second search would be the correct one to use. It would only find those cases in which both names were found within the name of the case.

## 2. The Judge Segments (WRITTENBY, OPINIONBY, DISSENTBY, CONCURBY)

The Judge segments contain the last names of the judges responsible for case opinions. There are four Judge segments:

**WRITTENBY**

**OPINIONBY**

**DISSENTBY**

**CONCURBY**

The WRITTENBY segment contains the OPINIONBY, DISSENTBY, and CONCURBY segments. It, therefore, will contain the name of any judge who wrote an opinion in the case.

The OPINIONBY segment contains the name of the judge who authored the majority opinion in the case.

The DISSENTBY segment contains the names of any judges who wrote dissenting opinions in the case.

The CONCURBY segment contains the names of any judges who wrote concurring opinions in the case.

In the California Library, CASES File, a search can be conducted to locate opinions rendered by Justice Rose Bird with any of the following searches.

**WRITTENBY (BIRD)**

**OPINIONBY (BIRD)**

**DISSENTBY (BIRD)**

**CONCURBY (BIRD)**

If you are not at the Library Screen, press the **[CHG LIBRARY]** key or transmit **.cl**. From the Library Screen, type **CAL** to select the California Library. Type **CASES** to select the File of

Supreme and Appellate Court cases. Then, use any of the Judge segments above to draft a search for opinions authored by Justice Bird.

## 3. The Counsel Segment (COUNSEL)

The **Counsel** segment may be searched to find the published cases in which a particular attorney or firm has represented one of the parties.

For example, if you worked for the fictitious firm of Filo, Gibb, Stevens and Martin, in Texas, you could conduct the following search within the Texas Library, CASES File, to see all of the published cases in which your firm has represented one of the parties.

### COUNSEL (Filo AND Gibb)

There is no need to include the entire firm name. The names "Filo" and "Gibb" are so unique that using only their names should be sufficient for this search.

## 4. The Docket Number Segment (NUMBER)

Some decisions in LEXIS contain the docket number of the case. For these cases, the Docket Number segment may be searched. The following are examples of the Docket Number search.

### NUMBER (89-3454)

### NUMBER (C-87345)

## 5. The Court Segment (COURT)

The Court segment can be used to view cases within your results that were decided by a particular court. With most of the individual State Libraries, the desired court file may be selected before you begin a search. With larger files containing multiple state or federal courts, however, this segment search can be useful.

For example, in a Federal Court case file, the following searches could be used to limit the cases to only those decided within a particular State District Court, or to the number of the District Court.

### COURT (GEORGIA)

### COURT (SECOND)

### COURT (SECOND OR GEORGIA)

## 6. The Date Segment (DATE)

The Date segment allows you to restrict the dates of the documents that are retrieved by a search. The Date segment search *is not followed by conditions enclosed within parentheses.* It must be connected to search conditions or another segment search with the AND connector. There are three date segment formats:

**DATE IS**        or **DATE = or DATE EQU**

**DATE BEF**        or **DATE <**

**DATE AFT**        or **DATE >**

If we wanted to run our Level 1 search, but only wished to have cases that were decided after 1980 within our results, we could use the following search:

**DATE AFT 1980 AND (parent guardian w/10 liab! w/50 minor w/50 operat! w/50 vehicle or auto!)**

A list of some of the other acceptable date restrictions are shown below:

| | |
|---|---|
| **DATE BEF 1980** | **DATE AFT 1980** |
| **DATE BEF JAN 25, 1980** | **DATE AFT JAN 25, 1980** |
| **DATE < JAN 1980** | **DATE > JAN 1980** |
| **DATE IS 1980** | **DATE IS JANUARY 1980** |
| **DATE IS 1-25-80** | **DATE IS 1-80** |
| **DATE IS 1/25/80** | **DATE IS 1/80** |

**DATE AFT 1980 AND DATE BEF 1985**

**DATE > 1/25/80 AND DATE < 1/31/80**

When only the last two numbers of a year appear, LEXIS assumes that a 19 precedes it. If you want the year 1880, you will need to type out the whole year.


## 7. Expanding Segment Searches

Segment searches may be expanded by placing search conditions before or after the segment search terms. For example, we could locate all California State Cases involving the death penalty where Rose Bird was the judge authoring the majority opinion with the following search in the California CASES File:

**OPINIONBY (bird) AND "death penalty"**

Similarly, we could locate all of the cases regarding embezzlement where Justice Bird authored an opinion with the following search:

**WRITTENBY (bird) AND embezzl!**

The key here is using the AND connector after the segment search to connect with the search conditions.

## P. PRINTING AND DOWNLOADING

### 1. Printing a Screen

You may print the contents of a screen you are viewing in LEXIS by pressing the [**PRINT SCREEN**] key. Press this key now if you have a printer attached to your computer.

### 2. Printing a Document

You may print a document from LEXIS, or download a document to a magnetic disk, by pressing the [**PRINT DOC**] key or by transmitting **.pr** while viewing the document. The Document Delivery Screen will appear allowing you to select a document delivery option as shown in Figure 6.26.

```
            Choosing a Document Delivery Option

    Enter the number of a delivery option:

        1.    Printed on the printer attached to this terminal or
              computer, after you sign off.
                              OR
              Copied to a disk, after you sign off (if this option
              is available to you).

        2.    Printed on the stand-alone printer assigned to
              your personal identification number.

    Press TRANSMIT to accept selection.
------------------------------------------------------------------------
To cancel your document delivery request, press N and then the TRANSMIT key.
For further explanation, press the H key (for HELP) and then the TRANSMIT key.
Press Alt-H for Help or Alt-Q to Quit.
```

**Figure 6.26** The Document Delivery Screen

Option **1** will print to a printer attached to your computer or to a magnetic disk. Option **2** will print to the LEXIS printer in your computer room, or in another location. Selecting **1** will bring up another screen asking you to confirm your print order. Press **Y** to confirm the order. Press **[Enter]** to return to your research.

## Q. COMPLETING YOUR RESEARCH

When you have completed your research, you can begin a new search (**.ns**), change the File (**.cf**), change the Library and File (**.cl**) or begin research for another client (**c**). You may also sign off from LEXIS (**.so**).

If you sign off from LEXIS, a screen appears displaying your last search request as shown in Figure 6.27. From this screen you may save your research to resume later in the day, or transmit **N** to leave LEXIS. If you have selected documents to print, you will be asked if you wish the documents to print at this time or the next time you enter LEXIS.

```
      DATE:  JANUARY 15, 1993
    CLIENT:  BATTAILE BOOK
   LIBRARY:  GA
      FILE:  CASES

Your search request is:
 (PARENT OR GUARDIAN W/10 LIAB! W/50 MINOR W/50 OPERAT! W/50 VEHICLE OR AUTO!)
 OR "FAMILY PURPOSE DOCTRINE"
 AND "NOT LIABLE"

Number of CASES found with your search request through:
    LEVEL   1...      7  LEVEL   2...     125  LEVEL   3...      33

If you want to save and resume your research on this problem later today (until
2:00 A.M. Eastern Time), press the Y key (for YES) and then the TRANSMIT key.
If you do not, press the N key (for NO) and then the TRANSMIT key.

After you exercise one of the above options, the time used in this research
session will be displayed.

If you do not want to end this research session, press the SIGN OFF key again.

For further explanation, press the H key (for HELP) and then the TRANSMIT key.
 Press Alt-H for Help or Alt-Q to Quit.
```

**Figure 6.27** This screen is displayed when you sign off from LEXIS.

# *Summary*

LEXIS is a computer assisted legal research database. The database is stored on mainframe computers, and accessed by the legal professional through the telephone lines from a computer or terminal. The LEXIS database contains materials found in law libraries, periodicals, government agencies, and many other sources.

After entering LEXIS, you are prompted for your Personal Identification Number and a Research Identifier. The Personal Identification Number is supplied by LEXIS. The Research Identifier identifies the client and matter to whom the research is to be billed.

Performing research in LEXIS requires that you choose a Library and File in which to search. A Library contains Files of related materials. The Files contain the materials to be searched. You perform your research within the Files.

To develop a search you need to define the issue to be researched, select the appropriate Library and File, and select key words, alternatives, universal characters, and connectors to be used in the search. After selecting a Library and File, you are prompted to enter the search. If your search does not locate cases that are relevant to your issue, or if too many or too few cases are found, you will need to modify the search. LEXIS allows you to perform your searches in levels. If the Level 1 search does not yield the desired results, the search may be expanded or narrowed in subsequent levels.

If you know the citation of materials you wish to view, you may use the LEXSEE and LEXSTAT services. LEXSEE will locate cases; LEXSTAT will locate statutes.

Searches may also be performed within segments of LEXIS documents. After selecting a Library and File, the Segments command will display the segments available for the documents within the chosen file. The segments may be searched by typing the segment name followed by search conditions in parentheses.

Materials from LEXIS may be printed using the [PRINT SCREEN] key or the [PRINT DOC] key.

When you have completed a research session, you may begin research for a new client by changing the Research Identifier, or end your LEXIS session by signing off.

# LEXIS Keys and Commands

## MOVING WITHIN DOCUMENTS

[FIRST PAGE] .fp

[NEXT PAGE] .np

[PREV PAGE] .pp

[FIRST DOC] .fd

[NEXT DOC] .nd

[PREV DOC] .pd

## ON-LINE INFORMATION

h    Help

t    Displays the elapsed time of the research session.

r    Displays the current search request.

p    Displays the number of LEXIS pages in the current document (with the current display format).

## CHECKING CITATIONS

sh   Shepard's Citations

ac   Auto-Cite

## PRINTING

[PRINT SCRN]        Prints the current screen.

[PRINT DOC] .pd     Accesses the print menu.

## RETRIEVING A DOCUMENT

LEXSEE     Retrieves a case or ruling by its citation.

LEXSTAT    Retrieves a statute or code section by its citation.

## DISPLAY OPTIONS

| | |
|---|---|
| [KWIC] .kw | Search terms surrounded by 25 words. |
| [VAR KWIC] .vk | Search terms surrounded by 50 words. |
| [FULL] .fu | Full document. |
| [CITE] .ci | List of citations. |
| [SEGMTS] .se | Displays selected segments of the documents. |
| [DIF LEVEL] .dl | Displays the results of a different level of the search. |

## CHANGING A SEARCH

| | |
|---|---|
| m | Modifies a search. |
| [NEW SEARCH] .ns | Begins a new search in the same Library and File. |
| [CHG FILE] .cf | Returns you to the screen displaying the Files for the current Library. |
| [CHG LIB] .cl | Returns you to the Library Screen. |
| [FOCUS] .fo | Allows you to search within the search results. |
| [EXIT FOCUS] .ef | Exits Focus. |

## LEAVING LEXIS

| | |
|---|---|
| [SIGN OFF] .so | Sign off |

# LEXIS Universal Characters and Connectors

## UNIVERSAL CHARACTERS

**!**
The "root expander." Used to locate all words with a common root. Example: **auto!** will locate "auto," "automobile," "automotive," "automatic," etc.

**\***
Used to replace a single character within a word. Example: **dr\*nk** will locate "drink," "drank," and "drunk."

## CONNECTORS

**or**
Retrieves documents containing *either* the word before *or* the word after the connector.

**and**
Retrieves documents containing *both* the word before *and* word after the connector.

**and not**
Excludes documents from the search results which contain the word or phrase found after the connector.

**pre/n**
Retrieves documents in which the word before the connector *precedes* the word after the connector by **n** number of words.

**w/n**
Retrieves documents in which the word before the connector is *within* **n** words of the word after the connector.

**not w/n**
Retrieves documents in which the word before the connector is included within the document. It excludes documents in which the word before the connector is *within* **n** words of the word after the connector.

**w/seg**
Retrieves documents in which the word before the connector is found *within the same segment* as the word after the connector. Segments are parts of documents. For example, cases have segments, among others, for the majority and dissenting opinions.

**not w/seg**
Retrieves documents in which the word before the connector is included within the document. However, it *excludes documents* in which the word before the connector is found *within the same segment* as the word after the connector.

**" "**
Retrieves documents in which a word or phrase is present in the exact pattern in which it appears within the quotation marks.

## CONNECTOR PRIORITY

or    w/n, pre/n, not w/n    w/seg    not w/seg    and    and not

# *Exercise*

For the examples set out below, write out the issue involved, and develop a search for LEXIS using key words, alternatives, universal characters, and connectors. If you have the opportunity, try your search in a LEXIS Library and File. Remember to begin with a broad search. You can write a broad search for Level 1 and then specify the modifications you would use in subsequent levels.

1. A woman leaving a supermarket slips and falls on an icy sidewalk outside the front doors of the supermarket. Is the supermarket liable for the woman's injuries?

2. An employee of a corporation steals some corporate checks, writes many to himself, and cashes them at the corporation's bank. He is fired for embezzlement. The signatures on the checks were obviously forged. Is the bank responsible for any of the amount embezzled?

3. Your firm has just received some responses to discovery from the Defendant and you realize that you have another cause of action. What are the state statutes and court rules regarding the amendment of complaints after an answer has been filed?

# Chapter Index

# CHAPTER 7

# WESTLAW®

# Chapter Preface

This chapter, along with Chapter 6 of the workbook, explains how to use the computer assisted legal research databases, LEXIS and WESTLAW. Both databases house a vast library of materials from Federal and State statutes and cases, to legal digests, texts and periodicals, and to specialty publications and materials for different areas of law such as tax, medical malpractice, patent and trademarks, etc.

This chapter will cover how to access the WESTLAW database and search for documents to aid in your legal research. Remember that when using legal research databases, time is money. Therefore, use the databases to locate the citations relevant to your research. Then, read the material after leaving the database. If the citation is to material that is readily available to you, read it in the bound volume. If the material is not available, download a copy of the material onto a magnetic disk or to a printer.

## A. WESTLAW

WESTLAW is the legal research database available through West Publishing Company ("West"). The service is accessed with a modem through the telephone lines with your own computer, or a computer or terminal supplied by West. If you are using your own computer to access WESTLAW, West supplies a software program which directs the communications between your computer and WESTLAW.

## B. ENTERING WESTLAW

You will enter WESTLAW by highlighting a menu option, or by typing a command. The WESTLAW software connects to WESTLAW through your computer's modem and the telephone lines. When the connection is completed to WESTLAW, the WESTLAW Logo Screen appears and prompts for your password as shown in Figure 7.1.

```
===============================================================================
   **            **  ******        ****  ******** **             *   **          **
  **    *     **  **                **        **    **          ***  **   *     **
   ** *** **     *****              **        **    **       ** **  **  **  *** **
    *** ***       **            **           **    **      **     **   *** ***
      *    *     ****** *****              **     ****** **         **  *    *
```

A COMPUTER-ASSISTED LEGAL RESEARCH SERVICE OF WEST PUBLISHING COMPANY

COPYRIGHT (C) 1992 BY WEST PUBLISHING COMPANY. COPYRIGHT IS NOT CLAIMED AS TO ANY PART OF THE ORIGINAL WORK PREPARED BY A U. S. GOVERNMENT OFFICER OR EMPLOYEE AS PART OF THAT PERSON'S OFFICIAL DUTIES. ALL RIGHTS RESERVED. NO PART OF A WESTLAW TRANSMISSION MAY BE COPIED, DOWNLOADED, STORED IN A RETRIEVAL SYSTEM, FURTHER TRANSMITTED OR OTHERWISE REPRODUCED, STORED, DISSEMINATED, TRANSFERRED OR USED, IN ANY FORM OR BY ANY MEANS, WITHOUT WEST'S PRIOR WRITTEN AGREEMENT. EACH REPRODUCTION OF ANY PART OF A WESTLAW TRANSMISSION MUST CONTAIN NOTICE OF WEST'S COPYRIGHT AS FOLLOWS: "COPR. (C) WEST 1992 NO CLAIM TO ORIG. U.S. GOVT. WORKS". WESTLAW AND WESTNET ARE REGISTERED SERVICE MARKS OF WEST PUBLISHING CO. REG. U.S. PAT. AND TM. OFF.

AVAILABLE 24 HOURS MONDAY THROUGH SATURDAY
AND SUNDAY FROM 8 AM, CST
PLEASE TYPE YOUR PASSWORD AND PRESS ENTER:   (PASSWORD MAY NOT BE DISPLAYED)

**Figure 7.1** The WESTLAW Logo Screen

## 1. Password

The password requested at the WESTLAW Logo Screen is supplied to subscribers by West. After entering your password, you are greeted by the WESTLAW Bulletin Board, which displays recent developments important to legal professionals (see Figure 7.2). These recent developments include new court decisions, news items, legislative action, and information on expanded databases in the system.

```
                      WELCOME TO WESTLAW
           **********************************
           * IMPORTANT NEW WESTLAW FEATURES *
           **********************************
   * JUMP LINKS from case headnotes to the related text in the opinion
   * KEY NUMBER SERVICE providing a complete outline of the Digest system
   * ALL STOP WORDS except "the" are now searchable in Terms and Connectors
     queries when they begin or end a phrase such as "take over" or at-will
   * EXPANDED TOPIC FIELD including complete hierarchy of concepts used to
     classify the points of law
   * MOST CURRENT Key Number classifications

FAMILY AND MEDICAL LEAVE ACT OF 1993 is now on WESTLAW.   Type FI PL 103-3.

JURY VERDICT and SETTLEMENT SUMMARIES (LRP-JV) has been added to WESTLAW!
DATABASE ANNOUNCEMENTS (For more information, enter NEW from the Directory.)
EDR-DOCKET EDR Civil Enforcement    PH-JGMT     PH - Civil & Small Claims
            Docket                               Judgments
PH-BKR      PH - Bankruptcy Filings  PH-CADFLT   CA Notice of Default Data
PH-TXLIEN   PH - Tax Lien Filings    WGL-TXACCT  Taxation for Accountants

Identify this research session. Type your CLIENT billing information and press
ENTER
```

**Figure 7.2** The WESTLAW Bulletin Board

## 2. The Research Identifier

At the Bulletin Board screen, WESTLAW prompts for the entry of a research identifier. A research identifier identifies the client or matter for which the research is being performed. When your office receives a billing statement from WESTLAW, the time attributable to each research identifier is noted on the bill.

You may change the research identifier at any time while in WESTLAW by typing **client** and pressing the **[Enter]** key. WESTLAW will prompt for a new research identifier and return you to the WESTLAW Directory to begin a new research session.

## C. LEAVING WESTLAW

You may leave WESTLAW at any time by pressing the **[Sign Off]** key or typing **off**.

## D. THE WESTLAW DIRECTORY

The WESTLAW Directory is the main screen, which displays the types of materials available in the WESTLAW database (see Figure 7.3). These materials are grouped under the headings:

**General Material**

**Text and Periodical**

**Citators**

**Special Services**

**Topical Material**

**Specialized Material**

```
_____ WELCOME TO THE WESTLAW DIRECTORY _____P1_____

GENERAL MATERIAL     TEXT & PERIODICAL        CITATORS         SPECIAL SERVICES
Federal      P2      Law Reviews,   P399   Insta-Cite,  P441  Dictionaries  P451
State        P7        Texts & CLEs        Shepard's,         EZ ACCESS     P500
DIALOG       P184    Restatements   P440   Shepard's PreView  Other Services P499
News & Info. P232      & Unif. Laws         & QuickCite       Customer Info. P501
------------------------------------- TOPICAL MATERIAL ------------------------------
Antitrust    P242    Family Law     P291   Labor        P335  Taxation       P383
Bankruptcy   P245    Finance/Bank.  P294   Legal Ser.   P342  Tort Law       P392
Business     P249    First Amend.   P300   Malpractice  P347  Transport.     P394
Civil Rights P260    Gov't Benefit  P302   Maritime Law P350  Worker Comp.   P396
Commercial   P264    Gov't Cont.    P305   Military Law P352   SPECIALIZED MAT'L
Commun. Law  P268    Health Law     P311   Pension      P354  BNA            P445
Crim. Just.  P270    Immigration    P317   Product Liab P357  Directories    P452
Education    P274    Insurance      P319   Real Prop.   P360  Gateways       P457
Energy       P278    Intell. Prop.  P323   Sci. & Tech. P363   (e.g. Dow Jones)
Environment  P283    International  P328   Securities   P369  Highlights     P497
                                           Soc. Science P379  Other Pubs.    P475

If you wish to:
    View another Directory page, type P followed by its NUMBER and press ENTER
    Select a known database, type its IDENTIFIER and press ENTER
    Obtain further information, type HELP and press ENTER
```

**Figure 7.3** The WESTLAW Directory

## 1. General Material

General Material includes all federal and state case law, statutes, administrative law, and regulations. It also includes the DIALOG database, which contains a large selection of business, medical, science, technology, and news databases.

## 2. Text and Periodical

Text and Periodical includes law reviews, legal texts, continuing legal education materials, and bar journals.

## 3. Citators

Citators include Shepard's® Citations, Insta-Cite, Shepard's PreView®, and QuickCite.

## 4. Special Services

Special Services includes customer information, dictionaries, and other services provided by WESTLAW.

## 5. Topical Material

Topical Material includes legal materials on a variety of specialized topics. For example, the Family Law topic includes databases on the subjects of adoption, guardianship, divorce, marriage, and other family law topics.

## 6. Specialized Material

Specialized Material includes information and databases supplied by other publishers.

## E. SELECTING A DATABASE

Each of the databases within WESTLAW may be searched to find materials relevant to the issue you are researching. To select a database from the WESTLAW Directory Screen, type **db** followed by the **Database Identifier**.

$$\textbf{db} \underline{\quad\quad}$$

The Database Identifier is an abbreviation of the full database name. West provides a bound Database List which contains the Database Identifiers for all materials found in WESTLAW.

The Database Identifier for the New York Cases database is abbreviated **NY-CS**. To immediately proceed to that database from the WESTLAW Directory, you would type:

**db NY-CS**

If you do not know the Database Identifier of the database you wish to search, you may move through the WESTLAW Directory a page at a time by pressing the **[Enter]** key, or select a particular page to view. To select a particular page, type **p** followed by a page number. For example, further information about the **State** topic, under the **General Material** heading, can be seen by typing the page number to the right of the topic: **p7**.

```
_____WESTLAW DIRECTORY WELCOME SCREEN_____P1_____
_____GENERAL STATE DATABASES                                             P7_____

--------------------------- STATE DATABASES: DOCUMENT INDEX ---------------------
Multistate ....... Next Page    Court Orders .... P17    Reg. Tracking ..P9
Admin. Law/Code .. P9           Court Rules ..... P18    Statutes-Anno. .P23
At. Gen. Op. ..... P11          Indices ......... P19    Statutes-Unanno.P24
Bill Tracking .... P12          Legis. Service .. P20    Uniform Laws ...P440
Case Law ......... P16          Regional Rptrs .. P22
-------------- STATE AND TERRITORY DATABASES: DIRECTORY LOCATIONS -----------
AL..P25   DC..P50   IA..P72   MN..P96    NM..P120   PA..P142   VT..P165
AK..P28   FL..P53   KS..P75   MS..P99    NY..P123   PR..P146   VI..P168
AZ..P31   GA..P56   KY..P78   MO..P102   NC..P126   RI..P147   VA. P169
AR..P34   GU..P59   LA..P81   MT..P105   ND..P129   SC..P150   WA. P172
CA..P37   HI..P60   ME..P84   NE..P108   MP..P132   SD..P153   WV. P175
CO..P41   ID..P63   MD..P87   NV..P111   OH..P133   TN..P156   WI. P178
CT..P44   IL..P66   MA..P90   NH..P114   OK..P136   TX..P159   WY. P181
DE..P47   IN..P69   MI..P93   NJ..P117   OR..P139   UT..P162
----------------------------------------------------------------------------
If you wish to:
  Select a database, type its IDENTIFIER, e.g., ALLSTATES and press ENTER
  View information about a database, type SCOPE followed by its IDENTIFIER
     and press ENTER
```

**Figure 7.4** Page 7 of the WESTLAW Directory

From the screen shown in Figure 7.4, any of the State Databases can be selected by typing the Database Identifier. Since the Database Identifier is listed on the current screen, it is not necessary to precede the Database Identifier with the **db** command. You can access databases not listed on this screen by preceding their Database Identifier with the **db** command.

Further information about the other databases shown in Figure 7.4 can be seen by selecting the page number to the right of the Database Identifier.

In this chapter, we will be doing research in Georgia state case law. To see the materials available in the Georgia database, the page number to the right of the Georgia Database Identifier is typed **p56**. Figure 7.5 shows the contents of the Georgia Database.

```
_____WESTLAW DIRECTORY WELCOME SCREEN_____P1_____
_____GENERAL STATE DATABASES:   GEORGIA                                        P56_____
              GENERAL CASE LAW                         GENERAL STATUTES
   GA-CS         Georgia Courts        GA-ST-ANN    Annotated Statutes
                                       GA-ST        Unannotated Statutes
         GENERAL ADMINISTRATIVE LAW    GA-ST-IDX    General Index
   GA-AG       Attorney General Opinions GA-LEGIS   Legislative Service
   GA-REGTRK   Regulation Tracking      GA-BILLTRK  Bill Tracking
                                                 HISTORICAL STATUTES
    TOPICAL/SPECIALIZED DATABASES INDEX  Annotated Statutes 1988-91
   Public Records Databases ... Next Page e.g., GA-STANN88
   Specialized Databases ...... Next Page Legislative Service 1990-92
   Topical Admin. Law ......... Next Page e.g., GA-LEGIS90
   Topical Case Law .......... Enter P58
                                                    COURT RULES
                                       GA-RULES     Court Rules
   If you wish to:                     GA-ORDERS    Court Orders
       Select a database, type its IDENTIFIER, e.g., GA-AG and press ENTER
       View information about a database, type SCOPE followed by its IDENTIFIER
         and press ENTER
       View the INDEX to State Databases, type P7 and press ENTER
```

**Figure 7.5**  The Georgia Database

Figure 7.5 shows that the Database Identifier for Georgia Case Law is **GA-CS**. All state databases in WESTLAW are identified by their two-character postal abbreviation. From this screen, you may access this database by typing **GA-CS**.

Had you known the Database Identifier for Georgia State Cases when you first entered WESTLAW, you could have immediately selected this database at the WESTLAW Directory Screen by typing **db GA-CS**.

After the database has been selected, you are prompted to enter a query at a screen similar to the one shown in Figure 7.6.

```
Please enter your query.
Your database is GA-CS
Your search method uses TERMS AND CONNECTORS




If you wish to:
   Enter your query, type it as desired and press ENTER
   Enter a Natural Language description, type NAT and press ENTER
   View a list of available fields, type F and press ENTER
   View detailed information about this database, type SCOPE and press ENTER
COPR. (C) WEST 1993 NO CLAIM TO ORIG. U.S. GOVT. WORKS
```

**Figure 7.6**  The Query Entry Screen

*WESTLAW*

## F. DEVELOPING A QUERY

A query is a search within a database. The most important task in automated legal research is developing the query. A good query yields results that are relevant to the issue being researched. A poorly designed query may find too many, too few, or irrelevant cases.

It is important to design your query *before* you access WESTLAW. A good query takes some time to think through, and time is money when you are in WESTLAW.

There are three steps in developing a query:

**1) Identify the issue to research.**

**2) Choose the appropriate database.**

**3) Draft the query.**

### 1. Identifying the Issue to Research

The issue to be researched is the point for which you are seeking support, rebuttal, or an answer. An example of an issue is:

**In Georgia, is a parent liable for a minor's negligent operation of the parent's vehicle, when the minor has not been given permission to operate the vehicle?**

### 2. Choosing the Appropriate Database

Choosing the appropriate database is the selection of the type of materials needed to support, rebut, or answer the issue. We have chosen the Georgia State Cases database (GA-CS) to search for cases that answer the question posed in this issue.

### 3. Drafting the Query

In drafting a query for a full-text database such as WESTLAW, key words, alternatives, expanders, and connectors are used.

### a. Key Words (Search Terms)

Key words, or Search Terms, are words that will most likely be found in materials that address the issue. Some key words for our issue are shown below.

> **Key Words**:  **parent**
> **liable**
> **minor**
> **operation**
> **vehicle**

### b. Alternatives

The next step in developing the query is to think of alternatives for the key words. Alternatives are other words that may have been used in the materials in place of the key words. For example, an alternative for *parent* is *guardian*. An alternative for *liable* is *liability*. The key words, and some possible alternatives, are shown below.

> **Alternatives**:  parent  **guardian**
> liable  **liability**
> minor
> operation  **operate, operating**
> vehicle  **automobile**

### c. The Expander and Wildcard Characters

When the key words and alternatives have common spellings, such as *liable* and *liability*, WESTLAW's root expander (!) or the wildcard character (*) may be used to simplify the search.

The root expander, !, is used for words with a common root. For example, *liable* and *liability* have the common root *liab*. Using the root expander following this root, *liab!*, will locate all words with this root no matter how long the word.

The wildcard character, *, is used to replace a *single character* any place in a word. For example, *dr*nk* will locate *drink*, *drunk*, and *drank*.

Our query will utilize the root expander to cover some of the key words and their alternatives.

> **Expanders**:  parent  **guardian**
> liab!
> minor
> operat!
> vehicle  **auto!**

WESTLAW automatically searches for the plurals of words. When searching for acronyms, such as "N.A.S.A.," the use of periods and no spaces will pick up other forms such as "NASA" and "NASA." For words that may be hyphenated, such as WILD-CARD, using the hyphenated version will pick up WILD CARD and WILDCARD.

d. *Connectors*

To finish developing the search, the key words and alternatives must be connected. For example, if you are searching for cases that contain the words *parent* and *liability*, you will connect the two words with the **&** connector:

**parent & liab!**

If you are searching for the word *parent* or *guardian* within the same document as *liability*, you will connect *parent* and *guardian* with the **OR** connector, and connect these two words to *liability* with the **&** connector. Parentheses may be used to make sure that WESTLAW processes the search as you have planned. The **OR** connector may be represented by a **space** in WESTLAW.

**(parent guardian) & liab!**

# THE WESTLAW CONNECTORS

**or**      Retrieves documents containing *either* the word before *or* the word after the connector. **Or** may also be indicated by a space between the words.

**&**      Meaning "and." Retrieves documents containing both the word before *and* word after the connector.

**%**      Meaning "but not." Retrieves documents which do not contain the word following the %.

**/p**      Retrieves documents in which the words on either side of the connector are found in the *same paragraph.*

**/s**      Retrieves documents in which the words on either side of the connector are found in the *same sentence.* This is a more limiting search than /p. Note that all of the materials located with /s will also be located with /p, because if the words are within the same sentence, they will naturally be located within the same paragraph.

**+s**      Retrieves documents in which the words before the connector *precede* the words after the connector.

**+n**    Retrieves documents in which the words before the connector *precede* the words after the connector by n number of words.

**/n**    Retrieves documents in which the words before the connector are *within* n words of the words after the connector.

**" "**    Retrieves documents in which a word or phrase is present in the exact pattern in which it appears within the quotation marks.

The **OR** connector will be used in our example between the key words and their alternatives. We will use the "same sentence" (/s) and "same paragraph" (/p) connectors between the other search terms. The /s connector will be used between *parent, guardian* and *liab!.* These terms are likely to be found within the same sentence. The /p connector will be used for the remaining search terms. West recommends that you write out your issue, key words, alternatives, final search terms, connectors, and the actual search on a piece of paper, as shown in Figure 7.7, prior to entering WESTLAW.

The actual search will be:


**parent guardian /s liab! /p minor /p operat! vehicle auto!**


## CONNECTOR PRIORITY


WESTLAW uses the following connector priority in processing the query.


**space (or),  +n,  /n,  +s,  /s,  /p,  &,  %**


WESTLAW will begin our search of the Georgia State Cases database by locating all decisions in which the key words *or* their alternatives are found. It will then take that group of cases and keep only those in which *parent* or *guardian* is found within the *same sentence* as *liab!.* Finally, WESTLAW will take the remaining cases and limit them further to only those that contain the conditions set forth with the /p connector.

The query is entered in the Query screen of the Georgia State Cases database as shown in Figure 7.8. Pressing the **[Enter]** key processes the query.

In Georgia, is a parent liable for a minor's negligent operation of the parent's vehicle, when the minor has not been given permission to operate the vehicle?

parent      guardian                 liab!
liable       liability
minor
operation    operate, operating     operat!
vehicle      automobile           auto!

parent       guardian
liab!
minor
operat!
vehicle       auto!

parent guardian /s liab! /p minor /p operat! /p vehicle auto!

**Figure 7.7** The Query Development

```
PARENT GUARDIAN /S LIAB! /P MINOR /P OPERAT! /P VEHICLE AUTO!


Please enter your query.
Your database is GA-CS
Your search method uses TERMS AND CONNECTORS




If you wish to:
    Enter your query, type it as desired and press ENTER
    Enter a Natural Language description, type NAT and press ENTER
    View a list of available fields, type F and press ENTER
    View detailed information about this database, type SCOPE and press ENTER
COPR. (C) WEST 1993 NO CLAIM TO ORIG. U.S. GOVT. WORKS
```

**Figure 7.8** The query is entered at the Query screen


# G. THE QUERY RESULTS


After processing the query, WESTLAW displays the first case which meets the search conditions of the query as shown in Figure 7.9. The printed search results display the search terms in capital letters. On the WESTLAW screen, the search terms are highlighted.

```
                    COPR. (C) WEST 1993 NO CLAIM TO ORIG. U.S. GOVT. WORKS
Citation            Rank(R)           Page(P)            Database        Mode
354 S.E.2d 162      R 1 OF 18         P 1 OF 13          GA-CS           T
  181 Ga.App. 816
(CITE AS: 354 S.E.2D 162)
                              CABRAL
                                v.
                          WHITE, et al.
                           No. 73043.
                    Court of Appeals of Georgia.
                          Jan. 23, 1987.
                    Rehearing Denied Feb. 18, 1987.
  AUTOMOBILE owner brought action against MINOR child and his parents to recover
damages resulting from child's wrecking of AUTOMOBILE.  The Superior Court,
Gwinnett County, Stark, J., directed verdict for parents and child, and
AUTOMOBILE owner appealed.  The Court of Appeals, Beasley, J., held that:  (1)
jury question existed as to whether child committed willful or malicious act
which would bring into effect civil and limited LIABILITY of his PARENTS
precluded directed verdict in PARENTS' favor, and (2) family purpose doctrine
did not preclude AUTOMOBILE owner from seeking damages from child who received
permission for owner's son to OPERATE VEHICLE.
  Reversed.
```

**Figure 7.9** The first eighteen cases found in the search


*WESTLAW*

The headings at the top of each WESTLAW screen in the search results are explained below.

| | |
|---|---|
| **Citation** | The citation of the case. |
| **Rank** | The number of the case in the group of cases found by the query. |
| **Page** | The current page number, and total number of WESTLAW pages, of the case. The page number from the case reporter can be seen under the case citation. |
| **Database** | The database being searched. |
| **Mode** | The current mode. The mode can be T for term or P for page. Typing **T** or **P** and pressing **[Enter]** will change to the desired mode. |

**Term Mode:** When WESTLAW is in the Term Mode, pressing the **[Enter]** key will move to the next instance within the case where the search conditions are met, or move to the next case. The + or – keys, or the **[Next Page]** and **[Prev Page]** keys, will also move between pages of search terms.

**Page Mode:** When WESTLAW is in the Page Mode, pressing the **[Enter]** key moves one page at a time through the case. The + and – keys, or the **[Next Page]** and **[Prev Page]** keys, will also move forward or backward through the pages. You may also specify a page to move to by typing **p** followed by the page number (e.g., **p3**).

Also displayed on the first screen for a case is a synopsis prepared by West's editors. Pressing the **[Enter]** key from this screen (when in the Term Mode) will move you to the first instance within the case where your search conditions have been met as shown in Figure 7.10.

Pressing **[Enter]** again will move to another instance within the case where the search conditions have been met, or move on to the next case.

Typing **r**, and pressing the **[Enter]** key, will take you immediately to the next case as shown in Figure 7.11.

```
                              COPR. (C) WEST 1993 NO CLAIM TO ORIG. U.S. GOVT. WORKS
354 S.E.2d 162                R 1 OF 18          P 10 OF 13            GA-CS             T
(CITE AS: 354 S.E.2D 162, *163)
 exhibition of speed or acceleration" is also a misdemeanor.  OCGA s 40-6-186(b)
 and (c).  The General Assembly has expressly stated in the "points" statute
 that:  "The State of Georgia considers dangerous, negligent, and imcompetent
 drivers to be a direct and immediate threat to the welfare and safety of the
 general public,...."  OCGA s 40-5-57(a).
  Juvenile traffic offenses are given special treatment in OCGA s 15-11-49.
 They may be considered acts of delinquency if transferred to the delinquency
 calendar at the discretion of the court.  OCGA s 15-11-49(b) and (g).  Racing
 on highways and streets, i.e., a violation of OCGA s 40-6-186, is expressly
 excluded from being treated as a juvenile traffic offense.
 > [1] Considering the evidence and the applicable law, we are compelled to
 conclude that the jury could find that Chris White committed a "willful or
 malicious act" which would bring into effect the civil and limited liability of
 his parents under OCGA s 51-2-3.  > Arrington v. Trammell, 83 Ga.App. 107, 62
 S.E.2d 451 (1950);  > Mercer v. Woodard, 166 Ga.App. 119, 127(13), > 303
 S.E.2d 475 (1983).
 > [2] 2. The "family purpose car doctrine" was inapplicable to the legal
 relationship between the car owners and MINOR driver who was not a member of
 the family.  That doctrine involves LIABILITY of a PARENT or head of household
 to third persons based on permitting a family member to use a VEHICLE for a
 family purpose.  See e.g., Hubert v. Harpe, 181 Ga. 168, 173, 182 S.E. 167
```

**Figure 7.10** The next screen containing the search terms

```
                              COPR. (C) WEST 1993 NO CLAIM TO ORIG. U.S. GOVT. WORKS
Citation                     Rank(R)            Page(P)             Database          Mode
284 S.E.2d 416               R 2 OF 18          P 1 OF 12           GA-CS             T
 248 Ga. 600
(CITE AS: 284 S.E.2D 416)
                                   Billy James REEVES
                                           v.
                                  Billy Thomas BRIDGES.
                                  Billy Thomas BRIDGES
                                           v.
                                   Billy James REEVES.
                                   Nos. 37742, 37743.
                                Supreme Court of Georgia.
                                     Nov. 19, 1981.
                              Rehearing Denied Dec. 15, 1981.
 Parent brought action against liquor store owner for violation of statute
providing cause of action for parent of minor child against person who sells or
furnishes spiritous liquors to minor.  The Spalding Superior Court, Andrew J.
Whalen, Jr., J., entered order denying cross motions for summary judgment, and
appeals were taken.  The Supreme Court, Clarke, J., held that:  (1) statute
providing cause of action for parent of minor child against person who sells or
furnishes spiritous liquors to the minor was constitutional, and (2) intent to
sell to a minor was essential element for recovery under the statute, and thus
parent was required to show that defendant either knew or should have known
```

**Figure 7.11** The second case in the search results

## H. VIEWING THE SEARCH RESULTS

The following are commands commonly used when viewing your search results. When you type a command, it appears in the upper left-hand corner of the screen.

### 1. Go Back (gb)

The [Go Back] key or typing **gb** will take you back one step in your research session.

### 2. List of Citations (L)

After you have performed a query, you may see a list of the documents found by the search by typing **L**. Figure 7.12 shows the first page of the list of citations found by our initial query.

```
                    COPR. (C) WEST 1993 NO CLAIM TO ORIG. U.S. GOVT. WORKS
CITATIONS LIST (Page 1)            Search Result Documents: 18
Database: GA-CS

    1.  Cabral v. White, 181 Ga.App. 816, 354 S.E.2d 162 (Ga.App., Jan 23, 1987)
        (NO. 73043)

    2.  Reeves v. Bridges, 248 Ga. 600, 284 S.E.2d 416 (Ga., Nov 19, 1981)
        (NO. 37742, 37743)

    3.  Stewart v. Stephens, 225 Ga. 185, 166 S.E.2d 890 (Ga., Mar 20, 1969)
        (NO. 25065)

    4.  Calhoun v. Eaves, 114 Ga.App. 756, 152 S.E.2d 805
        (Ga.App., Nov 08, 1966) (NO. 42317)

    5.  Stansell v. Fowler, 113 Ga.App. 377, 147 S.E.2d 793
        (Ga.App., Mar 01, 1966) (NO. 41732)

    6.  Strickland v. Moore, 113 Ga.App. 209, 147 S.E.2d 682
        (Ga.App., Feb 25, 1966) (NO. 41781)

    7.  Barlow v. Lord, 112 Ga.App. 352, 145 S.E.2d 272 (Ga.App., Sep 09, 1965)
        (NO. 41404)
```

**Figure 7.12** A list of the citations found by the query is accessed by typing L

You may view any case in this list by typing its corresponding number. For example, typing **4** will display the fourth case. Pressing the [Next Doc] key will return you to your research.

### 3. Viewing Documents in Sequence (d)

The **d** command allows you to view documents which precede or follow the document you are viewing, even if the documents have not been retrieved by the query. This command is not available in case law databases. It is most helpful when you are searching statutes. When a statute has been found that meets your search request, you may look at the statutes which are found before or after the statute using the **d** command. The **d** commands are shown below.

| | |
|---|---|
| **d** | **next document** |
| **d–** | **preceding document** |
| **d+n** | **ahead n number of documents** |
| **d–n** | **back n number of documents** |

Typing **xd** will cancel the **d** command and return you to your query results.

## 4. Star Paging (st)

So that you may cite to a specific page in the bound volume of a publication, WESTLAW indicates the pages of the publication with a star (*) followed by the page number. WESTLAW calls this Star Paging (see Figure 7.13).

```
                       COPR. (C) WEST 1993 NO CLAIM TO ORIG. U.S. GOVT. WORKS
284 S.E.2d 416         R 2 OF 18          P 11 OF 12          GA-CS          P
(CITE AS: 284 S.E.2D 416, *418)
furnishes liquor to a minor child would not be unconstitutional, we do not find
that the legislature intended to impose strict liability in enacting Code
Ann. s 105-1205.  We have no general rule of strict liability in Georgia.
> Ford Motor Co. v. Carter, 239 Ga. 657, 238 S.E.2d 361 (1977).  Our statutes
which have attributes of strict liability are strictly construed, and we will
not read strict liability into a statute when the intent of the legislature is
not perfectly clear.  Also compelling is the fact that the statute which is
under consideration here dates back to 1863, *419 long before the advent of
any strict liability in Georgia.
> [4] Code Ann. s 105-1205 has been found to be an action for indirect
injury to the person and analogized to actions for such torts as abducting or
harboring the wife of another, alienation of affection, adultery or criminal
conversation, seduction of a daughter, or gaming with the minor son of
another.  Hosford v. Hosford, 58 Ga.App. 188, 198 S.E. 289 (1938);
Edwards v. Monroe, 54 Ga.App. 791, 189 S.E. 419 (1936).  Under the statute,
selling or furnishing liquor to the minor child of another is an intentional
tort.  It is almost redundant to state that an essential element of an
intentional tort is intent to commit the act.  Restatement, Second, Torts s 8A
(1965), defines intent as the actor's desire to cause the consequences of his
act or as his belief that the consequences are substantially certain to result
from it.  In this case, the prohibited act is furnishing or selling liquor to
```

**Figure 7.13** The pages upon which the text appears in the bound volumes are indicated by a star (*) followed by the page number

If Star Paging is not displayed, type **st**. To view a specific page of the material you are currently viewing, type **st**, followed by the page number. For example, to see page 417 of this case, you would type:

**st 417**

To remove Star Paging from the material you are currently viewing, type **xst**. Typing **st** will restore the star paging.

## 5. The Time Command (time)

Typing **time** will display the elapsed time of the current research session from anywhere within WESTLAW. Pressing **[Enter]** will return you to your research.

## 6. The Map Command (map)

The **map** command provides you with a list of the steps you have taken while moving through WESTLAW. This command is used as an alternative to issuing several go back (**gb**) commands. An example of a map is shown in Figure 7.14.

```
                         COPR. (C) WEST 1993 NO CLAIM TO ORIG. U.S. GOVT. WORKS
                                                          Page 1 of 1
Service or Database              Request

1. WESTLAW Directory             ...
2. GA-CS                         PARENT GUARDIAN /S LIAB! /P MINOR /




       NOTE:  If you go back to one of the above saved results,
              all requests with a larger number will be discarded.

  If you wish to:
       Go back to one of the above services, type its NUMBER and press ENTER
       Return to the last substantive screen, press ENTER
       Receive further information on Map, type HELP and press ENTER
```

**Figure 7.14** A map of the route taken through WESTLAW may be seen by typing map

You may step back to any of the steps listed by typing the number of the step. The search results of the most recent search remain stored by the program. Press **[Enter]** to return to your research.

## 7. Black's Law Dictionary (di)

If, while you are reviewing your search results, you come across a word for which you do not know the meaning, you may look it up in Black's Law Dictionary. Black's Law Dictionary is accessed with the dictionary command, **di**. For example, the meaning of habeas corpus can be found by typing:

**di habeas corpus**

The results of the command are shown in Figure 7.15.

```
BLACK'S LAW DICTIONARY   6TH EDITION                          P   1 OF   2

HABEAS CORPUS

     Lat. (You have the body.)  The name given to a variety of writs (of which
these were anciently the emphatic words), having for their object to bring a
party before a court or judge.  In common usage, and whenever these words are
used alone, they are usually understood to mean the habeas corpus ad
subjiciendum (see infra).  U. S. v. Tod, 263 U.S. 149, 44 S.Ct. 54, 57, 68
L.Ed. 221.  The primary function of the writ is to release from unlawful
imprisonment.  People ex rel. Luciano v. Murphy, 160 Misc. 573, 290 N.Y.S.
1011.  The office of the writ is not to determine prisoner's guilt or
innocence, and only issue which it presents is whether prisoner is restrained
of his liberty by due process.  Ex parte Presnell, 58 Okl.Cr. 50, 49 P.2d 232.
     A form of collateral attack.  An independent proceeding instituted to
determine whether a defendant is being unlawfully deprived of his or her
liberty.  It is not an appropriate proceeding for appeal-like review of
discretionary decisions of a lower court.  Sheriff, Clark County v. Hatch, 100
Nev. 664, 691 P.2d 449, 450.  For federal habeas corpus procedures, see 28
U.S.C.A. s 2241 et seq.

To leave the Dictionary system. . . . . . . . . . Enter GOBACK or GB
COPR. (C) WEST 1993 NO CLAIM TO ORIG. U.S. GOVT. WORKS
```

**Figure 7.15** The definition of habeas corpus can be found by typing di habeas corpus

To leave the dictionary, press the **[Go Back]** key or type **gb**.

## I. CHECKING CITATIONS

In reviewing the results of our query, the twelfth case, *Yancey v. Munda*, contains a headnote that comes very close to responding to the question contained within our issue (see Figure 7.16).

The validity of this case may be checked using Insta-Cite, Shepard's Citations, Shepard's PreView and/or QuickCite.

```
                              COPR. (C) WEST 1993 NO CLAIM TO ORIG. U.S. GOVT. WORKS
91 S.E.2d 204                 R 12 OF 18          P 5 OF 9          GA-CS              P
(CITE AS: 91 S.E.2D 204)
YANCEY v. MUNDA
> [4]
> 48A      AUTOMOBILES
> 48AV       Injuries from OPERATION, or Use of Highway
> 48AV(A)      Nature and Grounds of Liability
> 48Ak187        Government;  Immunity and Waiver Thereof
> 48Ak195          Owner's Liability for Acts of Member of Family

> 48Ak195(5)  k. VEHICLE kept for use of family.
Ga.App. 1956
To hold PARENT LIABLE under the family-purpose doctrine for negligence of a
MINOR child in OPERATING a motor VEHICLE owned by PARENT, it must be made to
appear that PARENT kept VEHICLE for comfort and pleasure of family and
expressly or impliedly made it available to the MINOR child for such purpose.
```

**Figure 7.16** A headnote from the ninth case, *Yancey v. Munda*

### 1. Insta-Cite (ic)

Insta-Cite provides a direct history of a particular case, and a list of the cases which negatively affect the precedential value of the case. A direct history provides a list of cases involving the same parties and facts. Cases which negatively affect the precedential value of a case are those cases which criticize or overrule the case.

### 2. Shepard's® Citations (sh)

Shepard's Citations provides, for a particular case, a list of all parallel cases (the citations for the case in different reporters), and all cases which cite the particular case in their opinions.

### 3. Shepard's PreView® (sp)

Shepard's PreView provides an update to a case's current Shepard's Citations. This update includes citations appearing in the advance sheets of the National Reporter System.

### 4. QuickCite (qc)

QuickCite provides an update to Shepard's PreView. QuickCite runs an actual search through the WESTLAW database to find any new citations to a particular case which have not yet made it into Shepard's PreView.

> *QuickCite runs a new query within your database. Running this new query discards your previous search results. Do not use QuickCite unless you are ready to leave your query results.*

## 5. Accessing the Citation Services

There are three ways to access the citation services:

a. *While Viewing a Case*

While viewing a case on the screen, you may access a citation service for that case by typing the service's two-letter identification.

| | |
|---|---|
| **ic** | **Insta-Cite** |
| **sh** | **Shepard's Citations** |
| **sp** | **Shepard's PreView** |
| **qc** | **QuickCite** |

b. *From Any WESTLAW Screen*

From any WESTLAW screen, you may access a citation service for a particular case by typing the two-letter identifier for the service followed by the case citation.

**ic 91 S.E.2d 204**

**sh 91 S.E.2d 204**

**sp 91 S.E.2d 204**

**qc 91 S.E.2d 204**

The four services do not always use the same abbreviations for the case reporters. To see a list of the publication abbreviations in any of these services, type **pubs**.

c. *From the WESTLAW Directory*

From the WESTLAW Directory, any of the four services may be accessed by typing its two-letter identifier. WESTLAW will then prompt you to enter a case citation.

From within Insta-Cite, Shepard's Citations, or Shepard's PreView, you may access any other citing service, including QuickCite, by typing the service's two-letter identifier.

While viewing the *Yancey v. Munda* case on the screen, we may access Insta-Cite by typing **ic** (see Figure 7.17).

```
                        INSTA-CITE                          Only Page
CITATION: 91 S.E.2d 204
=>   1   YANCEY V. MUNDA, 93 Ga.App. 230, 91 S.E.2d 204 (Ga.App., Jan 20, 1956)
          (NO. 35999)

Note: This result is for the highlighted citation.  To view history for another
      case in this display, type IC and its NUMBER and press ENTER.  For
      indirect history prior to 1972 use Shepard's.  See SCOPE for more info.
(C) Copyright West Publishing Company 1993
```

**Figure 7.17** Insta-Cite for *Yancey v. Munda*

From Insta-Cite, we may access Shepard's Citations by typing **sh** (see Figure 7.18).

```
                      SHEPARD'S  (Rank 1 of 3)            Only Page
CITATIONS TO: 91 S.E.2d 204
CITATOR: SOUTHEASTERN REPORTER CITATIONS
DIVISION: Southeastern Reporter 2nd
COVERAGE: First Shepard's volume through Dec. 1992 Supplement
Retrieval                                        Headnote
   No.      --Analysis--- -----Citation------      No.
             Same Text ( 93 Ga.App. 230)
                         126 S.E.2d at 457          1
    1        147 S.E.2d 793, 795                     4
    2        160 S.E.2d 274, 277                     1

NOTE:  Check Shepard's PreView (SP), Insta-Cite (IC), and QuickCite (QC).
Copyright (C) 1993 McGraw-Hill, Inc.; Copyright (C) 1993 West Publishing Co.
```

**Figure 7.18** Shepard's Citations for *Yancey v. Munda*

Any of the cases listed in the citing services may be viewed by typing the number next to the case.

The go back command (**gb**) will return you to your search results from the citation services.

## J. Finding Materials When You Know the Citation

When you are browsing through your search results, you will often find a reference to a case or code section that is not included within the search results. To view the case, code section, or other material, you may use the **Find Command (fi)** followed by the material's citation. The Find Command can be used from any WESTLAW screen, including the WESTLAW Directory Screen.

To find a case, use **fi** followed by the case citation.

**fi 406 S.E.2d 266**

To return to your research, press the **[Go Back]** key or type **gb**.

To find a statute, use **fi** followed by the **state abbreviation**, the **chapter**, **statute**, or **code title**, and then the **statute number**. For example, to find California Code of Civil Procedure Section 377, you would type:

**fi ca civ pro 377**

The go back command will return you to your research.

A complete list of publication abbreviations and formats can be seen by typing **fi pubs**. The go back command will return you to your research.

You may perform a number of steps while working within Find, including browsing through the found material and checking its citations. WESTLAW remembers where you were when you began the Find Command. When you are through with Find, the go back command (**gb**) will return you to the screen where you originally executed the Find Command.

## K. Changing or Editing a Query Search

The following commands are used to change an existing query, create a new query, or run a query in a different database. The last command discussed, **Locate**, will allow you to run a query within your search results.

### 1. Editing a Query (q)

When a query has found too many, too few, or irrelevant cases, you will need to edit your query. To edit a query, type **q** and press **[Enter]**.

This command will return you to the query entry screen and allow you to change the query. Pressing the **[Enter]** key after editing the query will perform the processing and give you new search results.

## 2.  The Same Query in a Different Database (sdb)

The same query may be performed on a different database by typing **sdb**, followed by the database identifier of the new database. For example, we could run our Georgia query in the California State Cases database by typing:

**sdb CA-CS**

## 3.  Editing the Existing Query in a Different Database (qdb)

The existing query may be edited for searching within a new database by typing **qdb**, followed by the database identifier for the new database. For example, our initial query in the Georgia State Cases database could be edited and run in the California State Cases database by typing:

**qdb CA-CS**

## 4.  A New Query in the Same Database (s)

A new query may be initiated within the same database by typing **s**. This command returns you to the query entry screen to type in a new query.

In reviewing the results of our first query, the term "family purpose doctrine" is used throughout the search result cases. Therefore, it would be prudent to run a new query, in the Georgia State Cases database, searching for all cases containing the phrase "Family Purpose Doctrine." We will run the new query in the same database, by typing **s**.

The query entry screen returns, and prompts for a new query. We will enter our new query by typing **"family purpose doctrine"** (see Figure 7.19). This phrase is enclosed in quotation marks so that WESTLAW will search for the phrase exactly as it appears in the quotation marks. Without the quotation marks, WESTLAW would search for all cases containing the words *family* or *purpose* or *doctrine*. Queries may be entered in lowercase or uppercase letters, without affecting the query results.

Pressing the **[Enter]** key processes the query. This new query finds 125 cases. The first case found is shown in Figure 7.20 below.

```
"FAMILY PURPOSE DOCTRINE"


Please enter your query.
Your database is GA-CS
Your search method uses TERMS AND CONNECTORS




If you wish to:
    Enter your query, type it as desired and press ENTER
    Enter a Natural Language description, type NAT and press ENTER
    View a list of available fields, type F and press ENTER
    View detailed information about this database, type SCOPE and press ENTER
```

**Figure 7.19** A new query searching for the phrase "Family Purpose Doctrine"


```
Citation                Rank(R)              Page(P)           Database      Mode
422 S.E.2d 570          R 1 OF 125           P 1 OF 17         GA-CS         T
  205 Ga.App. 551
(CITE AS: 422 S.E.2D 570)
                                  LEE
                                   v.
                          BARTUSEK et al.
                            No. A92A1736.
                      Court of Appeals of Georgia.
                          Sept. 23, 1992.
  Driver brought actions for damages arising out of collision which occurred
when traffic light malfunctioned.  The State Court, Fulton, Adams, J., entered
judgment for defendant driver, and plaintiff appealed.  The Court of Appeals,
McMurray, J., held that instructions and evidentiary rulings were proper.
  Affirmed.
```

**Figure 7.20** The first of 125 cases found with the new query

## 5. Locating Terms Within Your Retrieved Documents (loc)

Occasionally, after executing a query and observing your search results, you will want to run an additional query within the search results. The Locate command (**loc**) allows you to locate terms, which need not have been in your original query, within the search results.

Within the 125 cases found with the query "family purpose doctrine," we can locate the cases in which the phrase "not liable" is present in the opinion. Remember, our issue is questioning whether a parent is liable for the negligence of a minor when the minor did not have permission to operate the vehicle. In particular, we are looking for cases in which the parent has been held not liable for the negligence of the minor.

To locate the phrase "not liable" within the search results, the following command is typed:

**loc "not liable"**

Again, we have enclosed the term in quotation marks, because we are searching for the exact phrase. This search can be entered at any of the screens displaying your search results. If your locate search is going to be longer than 23 characters, type **loc** and press **[Enter]**. WESTLAW will display a screen which will allow you to enter a longer Locate query.

After executing the locate command, the WESTLAW Mode changes to **T LOCATE**. Pressing the **[Enter]** key will move you through the cases, within the initial search results, which contain the terms of the locate command. In reviewing the located cases, the case of *Kurtz v. Williams* is found. To see a list of the cases found with the locate command, type **lloc**. In our example, the *Kurtz* case is number 65. Pressing the **[Enter]** key displays the first instance within *Kurtz v. Williams* where the Locate search conditions are met as shown in Figure 7.21.

```
222 S.E.2d 145        R 65 OF 125        P 3 OF 5        GA-CS        T LOCATE
(CITE AS: 222 S.E.2D 145)
Kurtz v. Williams
 > [2]
 > 48A       AUTOMOBILES
 > 48AV         Injuries from Operation, or Use of Highway
 > 48AV(A)        Nature and Grounds of Liability
 > 48Ak187          Government;  Immunity and Waiver Thereof
 > 48Ak195            Owner's Liability for Acts of Member of Family
 > 48Ak195(5)           Vehicle Kept for Use of Family

 > 48Ak195(6)   k. Acts by permission or direction of member of family.
Ga.App. 1975.
Owner of automobile was NOT LIABLE for accident caused by son's negligent
driving of vehicle where son had only learner's driving permit and where
accident occurred when son had no permission to drive vehicle without his
father and mother present therein and after son had taken vehicle's keys and
driven it away without knowledge or consent of any family member.
```

**Figure 7.21** Pressing the **[Enter]** key moves to the first instance within the case
where the search conditions of the Locate command are met

This case will be valuable in support of our issue. Its citation should be checked using Insta-Cite, Shepard's Citations, and Shepard's PreView to insure that it is good law, and to locate other cases which support this issue. A case should not be read while in WESTLAW, because of the cost of the time on the system, so the citation of the case should be noted and found in the bound volume. If your office does not have the bound volumes of the reporter, the case may be printed on your printer, or downloaded to a magnetic disk.

The locate command is canceled by typing **xloc**. This command returns you to where you were in your search results when you first executed the Locate command.

## 6. A New Query in a Different Database (db)

A new query may be initiated in a different database by typing **db** followed by the database identifier for the new database. This command will take you to the query entry screen for that database and prompt for a new query. For example, to run a new query in the Texas State Cases database, you would type:

**db TX-CS**

## L. DATE RESTRICTIONS

The **date** command allows you to restrict the dates of the documents which are retrieved by a search. For example, if we want to run our query, but only wish to have cases which were decided after 1980 within our results, we could use the following search:

**date(after 1980) & parent guardian /s liab! /p minor /p operat! /p vehicle auto!**

It is important that you use the **&** connector here to connect the date search with your other search conditions. A list of some of the other acceptable date restrictions are shown below:

| | |
|---|---|
| **date(before 1980)** | **date(after 1980)** |
| **date(bef jan 25 1980)** | **date(aft jan 25 1980)** |
| **date(<jan 1980)** | **date(>jan 1980)** |
| **date(1980)** | **date(january 1980)** |
| **date(1-25-80)** | **date(1-80)** |
| **date(1/25/80)** | **date(1/80)** |
| **date(after 1980 & before 1985)** | |
| **date(>1/25/80 & <1/31/80)** | |

When only the last two numbers of a year appear, WESTLAW assumes that a 19 precedes it. If you want the year 1880, you will need to type out the whole year.

## M. SEARCHING FIELDS

WESTLAW also includes fields within its databases. Different types of materials (cases, statutes, periodicals) contain different types of fields. At the query screen for a database, you may see a list of the available fields by typing **f**. The list of fields available in the **Georgia State Cases** database is shown in Figure 7.22.

```
                              FIELDS

   .TI   TITLE       CO   COURT      TO   TOPIC       DI   DIGEST
    CI   CITATION    JU   JUDGE      HE   HEADNOTE
    SY   SYNOPSIS    AT   ATTORNEY   OP   OPINION

If you wish to:
    Limit your search to a specific field or fields, use a field restriction
       in your query, e.g., TI(MIRANDA & ARIZONA)
    Limit your search by date, add a date restriction to your query with the
       & connector, e.g., DA(3/91) & your query
    Return to the Enter Query screen, press ENTER
```

**Figure 7.22** The available Fields within a database can be seen by typing f

Some of the more common WESTLAW Fields are explained below.

### 1. The Title Field (ti)

The Title field contains the title of the case. When you search for a case title, it is unlikely that you will know the exact title of the case. For example, the good case, which we found with our query of the Georgia cases, was titled:

### D. T. KURTZ by n/f, et al. v. K. L. WILLIAMS et al.

It is unlikely that we would remember this exact case title. You can search for this case using one or more of the parties' names as shown below:

### ti(Kurtz)

### ti(Kurtz & Williams)

The first search would not be specific enough. There are probably many cases within the Georgia State Cases database that contain the name "Kurtz" within the title of the case. The second search would be the correct one to use. It would only find those cases in which both names were found within the title.

## 2. The Judge Field (ju)

The Judge field contains the last name of judges who authored the majority opinions in cases. If we were in the California State Cases database searching for all of the majority opinions authored by Judge Rose Bird, the search would be conducted as follows:

**ju(bird)**

## 3. The Opinion Field (op)

The Opinion field contains the text of the opinion of a case, the court, the names of counsel, the names of the judges, and the concurring and/or dissenting opinions. This field could be searched to see the cases that your firm, or an opposing firm, has had published in the case reporters. For example, if you worked for the fictitious firm of Filo, Gibb, Stevens, and Martin, in Texas, you could conduct the following search within the Texas State Cases database to see all of the published cases in which your firm has represented one of the parties.

**op(filo & gibb)**

There is no need to include the entire firm name. The names "Filo" and "Gibb" are so unique that using only their names should be sufficient for this search.

## 4. The Citation Field (ci)

The Citation field contains the citation of the case. Normally, you will search for a citation using the Find (**fi**) command. However, the Find command is not available with some publications. With these publications, you will need to access the database and use a search of the citation field.

To search the citation field, you use the command **ci** followed by the citation in parentheses. The connector **+5** is used with these searches in place of the publication abbreviation. For example, a search within the California State Cases database for:

**44 Cal.3d 208**

could be conducted with the following command:

**ci(44 +5 208)**

If we were to use the command **ci(44 Cal.3d 208)**, WESTLAW would interpret the spaces within the case citation as the **or** connector. WESTLAW would search for **44** or **Cal.3d** or **208** within the citation field of all materials within the database. Quotation marks within the parentheses would be acceptable, **ci("44 Cal.3d 208")**, as long as the publication abbreviation is correct. The best way to perform a search of the citation field is to use the **+5** connector in place of the publication abbreviation.

## 5. The Synopsis Field (sy)

The Synopsis field contains a summary, prepared by West's editors, of the issues of the case, the case's holding, and the case's history. The Synopsis is the paragraph summary contained on the first WESTLAW page of each case as shown in Figure 7.23.

```
                    COPR. (C) WEST 1993 NO CLAIM TO ORIG. U.S. GOVT. WORKS
Citation            Rank(R)          Page(P)         Database        Mode
387 S.E.2d 403      R 1 OF 9         P 1 OF 10       GA-CS           T
 193 Ga.App. 172
(CITE AS: 387 S.E.2D 403)
                              HARVEY et al.
                                   v.
                              TAYLOR et al.
                              No. A89A1214.
                        Court of Appeals of Georgia.
                             Oct. 12, 1989.
 Plaintiffs injured when car in which they were riding was forced off the road
by another vehicle sued owner and driver of other car.  The State Court, Fulton
County, Baxter, J., entered summary judgment for owner and driver and
plaintiffs appealed.  The Court of Appeals, Sognier, J., held that:  (1)
material issues of fact, precluding summary judgment, existed as to whether
son-in-law of owner of vehicle had been involved in accident;  (2) owner of
vehicle and principal driver were NOT LIABLE as a matter of law;  and (3) owner
was NOT LIABLE under FAMILY PURPOSE DOCTRINE.
 Affirmed in part, reversed in part.
```

**Figure 7.23** The Synopsis Field contains a summary
of the case prepared by West's editors

Within the parentheses of the Synopsis field command you can search for terms that would be found in the Synopsis of the desired cases.

For example, to search for the terms "family purpose doctrine" and "not liable" within the Synopsis field of the Georgia State Cases database, you would first access this database, and then type the following command:

**sy("family purpose doctrine" & "not liable")**

Remember, when you are searching for a multiple word phrase such as family purpose doctrine, you must enclose that phrase within quotation marks to avoid WESTLAW interpreting the space between the words as the **or** connector.

## 6. The Topic Field (to)

The Topic field contains the West topic number, topic name, key number, and key description. Topics and Key Numbers are used within WESTLAW and West publications.

WESTLAW is the only computer assisted legal research database which uses these classifications.

West classifies the cases received for publishing in their digests into many topics. Each topic also contains several subsections, called key numbers. The headnote from *Kurtz v. Williams*, which was relevant to our issue, is shown again in Figure 7.24.

```
                     COPR. (C) WEST 1993 NO CLAIM TO ORIG. U.S. GOVT. WORKS
222 S.E.2d 145          R 65 OF 125        P 3 OF 5          GA-CS        P
(CITE AS: 222 S.E.2D 145)
Kurtz v. Williams
 > [2]
 > 48A      AUTOMOBILES
 > 48AV        Injuries from Operation, or Use of Highway
 > 48AV(A)        Nature and Grounds of Liability
 > 48Ak187          Government;  Immunity and Waiver Thereof
 > 48Ak195            Owner's Liability for Acts of Member of Family
 > 48Ak195(5)           Vehicle Kept for Use of Family

 > 48Ak195(6)  k. Acts by permission or direction of member of family.
Ga.App. 1975.
Owner of automobile was not liable for accident caused by son's negligent
driving of vehicle where son had only learner's driving permit and where
accident occurred when son had no permission to drive vehicle without his
father and mother present therein and after son had taken vehicle's keys and
driven it away without knowledge or consent of any family member.
```

**Figure 7.24**  A WESTLAW Headnote

You may find cases dealing with the same issue as one you have found by simply searching for other cases that contain headnotes with the same Topic and Key Number.

The Topic field for the headnote in Figure 7.24 contains the following:

| | |
|---|---|
| **Topic Number** | **48A** |
| **Topic Name** | **AUTOMOBILES** |
| **Key Number** | **k195(6)** |
| **Key Description** | **Acts by permission or direction of member of family.** |

You can search for a particular Topic Number by typing **to**, followed by the Topic Number in parentheses.

**to(48A)**

You could search for Topic Number 48A, or an additional Topic Number, 197, with the following search:

**to(48A 197)**

The space between the two Topic Numbers is interpreted as the **or** connector.

*WESTLAW*

You may search for a word or phrase contained in the Topic Name or Key Description by enclosing the word or phrase within parentheses.

**to(automobile)**

Remember, the singular form of a word will also pick up plurals.

To search for a full Topic and Key Number, **48Ak195(6)**, you are not required to specify the Topic Field in your search. The order of the numbers and letters in a Topic and Key Number are so unique that they are unlikely to be found anywhere in a case but within the Topic Field. A query for the Topic and Key Number in our example would look as follows:

**48Ak195(6)**

## 7. The Headnote Field (he)

The Headnote field contains all of the headnotes of the cases within a database. A search for the phrases "family purpose doctrine" and "not liable" within a headnote could be formulated as follows:

**he("family purpose doctrine" /p "not liable")**

## 8. The Digest Field (di)

The Digest field is a combination of the Citation, Topic, Court, Headnote and Title fields. When you search within this field, you use the **/p** connector. All of the items within the Digest field are considered to be within the same paragraph. A search of the Digest field for *automobile*, *permission* and "family purpose doctrine" could be conducted as follows:

**di(auto! /p permi! /p "family purpose doctrine")**

## 9. Expanding Field Searches

Field searches may be expanded by adding search conditions after the field search terms. The key is to use the **&** connector to connect the Field search with the other search conditions. For example, we could locate all California State Cases which include the phrase "death penalty," where Rose Bird was the judge authoring the majority opinion, with the following search in the **CA-CS** database:

**ju(bird) & "death penalty"**

Similarly, we could locate all of the cases regarding embezzlement, where Justice Bird authored the majority opinion, with the following search:

**ju(bird) & embezzl!**

### 10. Combining Field Searches

Field searches may be combined within a single query. Two fields may be searched for the same term by listing the two fields and separating them with a comma. For example, the phrase "death penalty" could be searched for in the **Synopsis** and **Digest** fields simultaneously with the following search:

**sy,di("death penalty")**

You may also combine two field searches using the **&** connector. For example, a search looking for cases containing **Topic Number 48A** (Automobiles), where Justice Bird authored the majority opinion, would look as follows:

**to(48A) & ju(bird)**

### 11. The Locate Command and Field Searches

Field searches can also be used with the Locate command to search within query results. For example, after we had run the "family purpose doctrine" search within the Georgia State Cases database, we could have run a Locate search looking for the cases on this subject in which the majority opinion had been authored by one of the appellate court justices who was to hear our client's case. To locate the cases within our search results where Justice Bird had authored the majority opinion, we would use the following Locate command:

**loc ju(bird)**

After reviewing the documents found with the Locate search, and/or viewing a list of these cases with **lloc**, the locate command is canceled by typing **xloc**.

## N. PRINTING AND DOWNLOADING

### 1. Printing a Screen

You may print the contents of a screen you are viewing in WESTLAW by pressing the **[PRINT SCREEN]** key.

## 2. Printing a Document

You may print a document from WESTLAW, or download a document to a magnetic disk, by pressing the **[Offline Print]** key or by typing **pr**. The **Offline Printing and Downloading Menu** will appear as shown in Figure 7.25.

```
Select one of the following COMMANDS to store information for later offline
printing or downloading:

CURRENT DOCUMENT                           SELECTED DOCUMENTS
   T    All Term mode pages                   T#   All Term mode pages
   D    All pages                             D#   All pages
   P    Last displayed page                   F#   First page including West
   P#   Selected pages                             synopsis (if available)
                                              L#   List of citations

ALL DOCUMENTS
   AT   All Term mode pages
   AD   All pages
   F    First page including West synopsis (if available)
   L    List of all citations

          NOTE:   # represents a range or selection of pages or documents.
                  EXAMPLE:  P1-4 = Pages 1 through 4; P1,4 = Pages 1 and 4




If you wish to:
   Store information, type a COMMAND and press ENTER
   Cancel this request and resume your research, press ENTER
```

**Figure 7.25** The Offline Printing and Downloading Menu

The options available from this menu will differ depending upon your location in WESTLAW. The options available allow you to print or download from the current document, selected documents, or all documents in your search results.

### a. *Current Document*

The current document is the document that you are viewing when you access this menu. The options under current document allow you to save for printing or downloading.

**T**   All of the pages which contain the search terms, or Locate terms.

**D**   All of the pages of the current document.

**P**   The page of the current document which was on the screen when the menu was accessed.

**P#**   A selected page, or pages, of the current document (e.g., P4 or P1-5 or P1,3,4,6-8).

b. *Selected Documents*

Selected Documents are documents from your search results which you designate by their rank number. For example, all of the pages of documents 1 through 5 could be designated by typing **D1-5**. All of the pages of documents 3, 10, and 21 could be designated by typing **D3,10,21**. The options under Selected Documents are shown below.

**T#** All pages which contain the search terms, or Locate terms, for the specified documents.

**D#** All of the pages of the specified documents.

**F#** The first page, including the West Synopsis, of the specified documents.

**L#** A list of the citations of the specified documents.

c. *All Documents*

The options available under this heading are performed upon all the documents within the search results.

**AT** All pages within the search results containing the search terms, or Locate terms.

**AD** All pages of all of the documents in the search results.

**F** The first page, including the West Synopsis, of every document in the search results.

**L** A list of the citations of all the documents in the search results.

An additional command, **LLOC**, will print a list of the citations of the documents within the search results that contain the Locate terms.

After one of the options from this menu has been selected, a screen summarizing your offline printing or downloading request is displayed as shown in Figure 7.26.

You may assign or change the destination of your request by typing one of the commands shown at the bottom of the screen.

Pressing the **[Enter]** key will return you to your research in WESTLAW.

```
Your request to store information has been completed and approximately 30 lines
have been stored.

    SUMMARY OF YOUR REQUEST
    Client Identifier:   BATTAILE
    Database:            GA-CS
    Lines:               30
    Command:             P
    Destination:         ???

    NOTE:  All requests, excluding "Print it Now on STP", will be sent to the
           specified destination after you sign off.




If you wish to:
    Continue your research, press ENTER
    Assign a destination, type the COMMAND and press ENTER
      FAX  Fax Machine             DLD  Download to Disk        SAV  Save
      ATP  Attached Printer        WMO  WESTPRINT Mail-out      DIS  Discard
    Sign off WESTLAW, type OFF and press ENTER
```

**Figure 7.26** After an offline printing or downloading option is selected, the destination of the materials must be specified

## O. COMPLETING A RESEARCH SESSION

When you have completed a research session, you may begin a new search, begin research for a new client, or sign off from WESTLAW.

**db**       Returns you to the WESTLAW Directory Screen to begin a new search.

**client**   Lets you change the research identifier so that you may begin research for another client or matter. After you enter the new identifier, you will be sent to the WESTLAW Directory Screen.

**off**      This command signs you off of WESTLAW. You will be asked if you would like to save the results of your last search (saves until the end of the day). After you have responded, a screen will appear displaying the time spent on WESTLAW.

## P. Natural Language Searching

WESTLAW has added a Natural Language Searching technique to its database called WESTLAW is Natural™ (WIN™). This technique allows you to use natural language in your query instead of using terms and connectors. To perform a Natural Language search, access a database and type **nat**. This will change the search technique from terms and connectors to Natural Language. If you wish to return to terms and connectors, you will type **tc**.

To enter the Natural Language query you will look at your issue and type a query into the Query screen using normal language. For example, a Natural Language search for our issue in the Georgia State Cases database could be written as:

> **is a parent (guardian) liable for a minor's operation of the parent's (guardian's) vehicle (automobile) when permission has not been given**

Alternative terms are entered in parentheses. Pressing the **[Enter]** key will display your search description and process the search.

In the search results, WESTLAW will provide a preset number of cases that most closely match the search description. The default number of cases is set at 20. This number may be changed to any number from 1 to 100 in the Options Directory by typing **opt**.

You may browse within your search results in the same manner as you do with a terms and conditions search. The Term Mode will display the five portions of each document which most accurately match your search description. Typing **best** will display the portion of the document which most closely matches the search description.

Restrictions as to date or court may be added to the search by typing **res** at the Query screen. You will need to erase any existing search description and then press **[Enter]**. A Restrictions screen will be displayed where you can enter the restrictions. Pressing **[Enter]** will return you to the Query screen and redisplay your search description. Pressing **[Enter]** again will process the query.

## *Summary*

WESTLAW is a computer assisted legal research database. The database is stored on mainframe computers, and accessed by the legal professional through the telephone lines from a computer or terminal. The WESTLAW database contains materials found in law libraries, periodicals, government agencies, and many other sources.

After entering WESTLAW, you are prompted for your Password and a Research Identifier. The Password is supplied by WESTLAW. The Research Identifier identifies the client and matter to whom the research is to be billed.

Performing research in WESTLAW requires that you select a database in which to search. The databases within WESTLAW contain a variety of materials to aid in your research. After selecting a database, you are prompted to enter a query. A query is a search.

To develop a search you need to define the issue to be researched, select the appropriate database, and select key words, alternatives, root expanders, universal characters and connectors to be used in the search. If your search does not locate cases that are relevant to your issue, or if too many or too few cases are found, you may edit your query. If you are using a Natural Language search, you may type your search description in a normal sentence.

If you know the citation of materials you wish to view, you may use the Find command to locate these materials.

Searches may also be performed within fields contained in the WESTLAW documents. After selecting a database, typing **f** will display the fields available for the documents within the chosen database. The fields may be searched by typing the field name in parentheses followed by search conditions.

Materials from WESTLAW may be printed using the **[PRINT SCREEN]** key, or by accessing the Offline Printing and Downloading Menu with the **[Offline Print]** key or by typing **pr**.

When you have completed a research session, you may begin research for the same client by typing **db**, begin research for a new client by changing the research identifier, or sign off from WESTLAW.

# WESTLAW Keys and Commands

## MOVING WITHIN DOCUMENTS

**[Enter]**    Moves to the next page in a document or the next instance of the search terms depending upon the current mode.

**r**    Moves to the next case in the rank.

**r#**    Moves to a specified case identified by its rank number.

**d**    Moves to the next document in sequence.

**d-**    Moves to the previous document in sequence.

**d+n**    Moves ahead n number of documents in sequence.

**d-n**    Moves back n number of documents in sequence.

**xd**    Cancels the **d** command.

**gb**    Moves back one step in your research.

**map**    Provides a map of the steps taken in the current research session.

## CHECKING CITATIONS

**sh**    Shepard's Citations

**sp**    Shepard's PreView

**ic**    Insta-Cite

**qc**    QuickCite

## PRINTING

**[PRINT SCRN]**    Prints the current screen.

**[Offline Print] pr**    Accesses the print menu.

## MISCELLANEOUS COMMANDS

**l**    List of citations.

## MISCELLANEOUS COMMANDS (cont.)

**st**    Activates star paging.

**xst**    Cancels star paging.

**time**    Displays the elapsed time of the current research session.

**date**    Restricts search results to specific dates.

**di**    Dictionary.

## CHANGING A SEARCH

**db**    Begins a new query in a new database.

**q**    Allows you to edit the existing query.

**qdb**    Allows you to edit the existing query in a different database.

**s**    Allows you to begin a new query in the same database.

**sdb**    Allows you to run the same query in a different database.

**loc**    Locates terms within your search results.

**xloc**    Cancels the Locate command.

**client**    Allows you to change the Research Identifier.

**nat**    Changes from a terms and connectors search to a Natural Language search.

**tc**    Changes from a Natural Language search to a terms and connectors search.

## RETRIEVING A DOCUMENT

**fi**    Retrieves a case or statute by its citation.

## LEAVING WESTLAW

**off**    Signs you off from WESTLAW.

# Exercise

For the examples set out below, write out the issue involved, and develop a search for WESTLAW using key words, alternatives, universal characters and connectors. If you have the opportunity, try your search in a WESTLAW database.

1. A woman leaving a supermarket slips and falls on an icy sidewalk outside the front doors of the supermarket. Is the supermarket liable for the woman's injuries?

2. An employee of a corporation steals some corporate checks, writes many to himself, and cashes them at the corporation's bank. He is fired for embezzlement. The signatures on the checks were obviously forged. Is the bank responsible for any of the amount embezzled?

3. Your firm has just received some responses to discovery from the Defendant and you realize that you have another cause of action. What are the state statutes and court rules regarding the amendment of complaints after an answer has been filed?

# *Chapter Index*